T0332738

Formal and Adaptive Methods for Automation of Parallel Programs Construction:

Emerging Research and Opportunities

Anatoliy Doroshenko
Institute of Software Systems, Ukraine

Olena Yatsenko
Institute of Software Systems, Ukraine

A volume in the Advances in
Systems Analysis, Software
Engineering, and High Performance
Computing (ASASEHPC) Book Series

Published in the United States of America by
    IGI Global
    Engineering Science Reference (an imprint of IGI Global)
    701 E. Chocolate Avenue
    Hershey PA, USA 17033
    Tel: 717-533-8845
    Fax: 717-533-8661
    E-mail: cust@igi-global.com
    Web site: http://www.igi-global.com

Library of Congress Cataloging-in-Publication Data

Names: Doroshenko, Anatoliy, 1948- author. | Yatsenko, Olena, 1978- author.
Title: Formal and adaptive methods for automation of parallel programs
  construction : emerging research and opportunities / by Anatoliy
  Doroshenko and Olena Yatsenko.
Description: Hershey, PA : Engineering Science Reference, [2021] | Includes
  bibliographical references and index.
Identifiers: LCCN 2019000519| ISBN 9781522593843 (h/c) | ISBN 9781522593867
  (eISBN) | ISBN 9781522593850 (s/c)
Subjects: LCSH: Parallel programming (Computer science) | Automatic
  programming (Computer science)
Classification: LCC QA76.642 .D67 2019 | DDC 005.2/75--dc23 LC record available at https://
lccn.loc.gov/2019000519

This book is published in the IGI Global book series Advances in Systems Analysis, Software Engineering, and High Performance Computing (ASASEHPC) (ISSN: 2327-3453; eISSN: 2327-3461)

British Cataloguing in Publication Data
A Cataloguing in Publication record for this book is available from the British Library.

For electronic access to this publication, please contact: eresources@igi-global.com.

Advances in Systems Analysis, Software Engineering, and High Performance Computing (ASASEHPC) Book Series

ISSN:2327-3453
EISSN:2327-3461

Editor-in-Chief: Vijayan Sugumaran Oakland University, USA

MISSION

The theory and practice of computing applications and distributed systems has emerged as one of the key areas of research driving innovations in business, engineering, and science. The fields of software engineering, systems analysis, and high performance computing offer a wide range of applications and solutions in solving computational problems for any modern organization.

The **Advances in Systems Analysis, Software Engineering, and High Performance Computing (ASASEHPC) Book Series** brings together research in the areas of distributed computing, systems and software engineering, high performance computing, and service science. This collection of publications is useful for academics, researchers, and practitioners seeking the latest practices and knowledge in this field.

COVERAGE

- Computer System Analysis
- Storage Systems
- Metadata and Semantic Web
- Computer Networking
- Enterprise Information Systems
- Software Engineering
- Engineering Environments
- Parallel Architectures
- Human-Computer Interaction
- Virtual Data Systems

IGI Global is currently accepting manuscripts for publication within this series. To submit a proposal for a volume in this series, please contact our Acquisition Editors at Acquisitions@igi-global.com or visit: http://www.igi-global.com/publish/.

Titles in this Series

For a list of additional titles in this series, please visit:
http://www.igi-global.com/book-series/advances-systems-analysis-software-engineering/73689

Balancing Agile and Disciplined Engineering and Management Approaches for IT Services and Software Products
Manuel Mora (Universidad Autónoma de Aguascalientes, Mexico) Jorge Marx Gómez (University of Oldenburg, Germany) Rory V. O'Connor (Dublin City University, Ireland) and Alena Buchalcevová (University of Economics, Prague, Czech Republic)
Engineering Science Reference • © 2021 • 354pp • H/C (ISBN: 9781799841654) • US $225.00

Urban Spatial Data Handling and Computing
Mainak Bandyopadhyay (DIT University-Dehradun, India) and Varun Singh (MNNIT-Allahabad, India)
Engineering Science Reference • © 2020 • 300pp • H/C (ISBN: 9781799801221) • US $245.00

FPGA Algorithms and Applications for the Internet of Things
Preeti Sharma (Bansal College of Engineering, Mandideep, India) and Rajit Nair (Jagran Lakecity University, Bhopal, India)
Engineering Science Reference • © 2020 • 257pp • H/C (ISBN: 9781522598060) • US $215.00

Advancements in Instrumentation and Control in Applied System Applications
Srijan Bhattacharya (RCC Institute of Information Technology, India)
Engineering Science Reference • © 2020 • 298pp • H/C (ISBN: 9781799825845) • US $225.00

Cloud Computing Applications and Techniques for E-Commerce
Saikat Gochhait (Symbiosis Institute of Digital and Telecom Management, Symbiosis International University, India) David Tawei Shou (University of Taipei, Taiwan) and Sabiha Fazalbhoy (Symbiosis Centre for Management Studies, Symbiosis International University, India)

For an entire list of titles in this series, please visit:
http://www.igi-global.com/book-series/advances-systems-analysis-software-engineering/73689

701 East Chocolate Avenue, Hershey, PA 17033, USA
Tel: 717-533-8845 x100 • Fax: 717-533-8661
E-Mail: cust@igi-global.com • www.igi-global.com

Table of Contents

Preface.. vii

Acknowledgment xvii

Chapter 1
Algebras of Algorithms, Parallel Computing, and Software Auto-Tuning............1

Chapter 2
Formalized Algorithm Design and Auto-Tuning of Programs 36

Chapter 3
Term Rewriting-Based Programming 76

Chapter 4
Algebra-Dynamic Models for CPU- and GPU-Parallel Program Design and
the Model of Auto-Tuning 112

Chapter 5
Software Tools for Automated Program Design, Synthesis, and Auto-Tuning .143

Chapter 6
Practical Examples of Automated Development of Efficient Parallel Programs180

Chapter 7
Software Design Based on Using Ontologies and Algorithm Algebra..............217

Conclusion 256

Appendix.. 259

Related Readings..261

About the Authors..276

Index...277

Preface

Current and emerging scientific and industrial applications require significant computing power provided by parallel platforms such as multicore, clusters, grids, cloud computing and GPGPU (General-Purpose computing on Graphics Processing Units). Modern software development tools for such platforms are quite complex and require the use of new programming models as well as knowledge of software and hardware details. Thus, the problem of developing the tools for automated design of parallel programs and their adaptation to computing platform is very relevant. One of the promising areas in modern parallel programming is the development of abstract models, formal and adaptive methods of design, analysis and implementation of algorithms and programs. Such models and methods are constructed, particularly, in the framework of algebraic programming and algorithmics.

The algebraic programming (Doroshenko & Shevchenko, 2006; Kapitonova & Letichevsky, 1990, 1993) is based on term rewriting theory and provides the description of processes of program design, algebraic transformations, proving mathematical theorems and development of intelligent agents by means of mathematical facilities based on a concept of a transition system. These facilities allow defining the behavior of systems and their equivalence. Transition systems can be components, programs and their specifications, objects interacting with each other and with an environment where they exist (Letichevsky & Gilbert, 2000). The evolution of such system is described by means of a history of system functioning. Algebraic programming integrates procedural, functional and logic programming and uses special data structures — term graphs, which allows using various means of representation of data and subject domain knowledge in the form of expressions in a many-sorted algebra of data. In algebraic programming, terms represent data, and term rewriting systems, which are expressed by means of systems of equalities, represent computing algorithms. The term rewriting technique is both a powerful formal tool for transformation of formal systems and a practical tool for programming allowing to implement transformations of complex objects. This technique enables to represent and automate transformations of program models in a high-level declarative style. Symbolic computation systems which allow working with mathematical objects of complex hierarchical structure are the most relevant. Algebraic programming theory provides the construction of mathematical information environment with universal constructs, computing mechanisms adapted to features of programming systems development and functioning. The applications of rewriting rules are being actively considered, particularly in papers (Garrido & Meseguer, 2006; Hemel, Kats, Groenewegen, & Visser, 2008; Meseguer, Olveczky, Stehr, & Talcott, 2002; Visser, 2007). Algebraic programming is the basis of insertion programming (A. Letichevsky, O. Letychevskyi, & Peschanenko, 2012; A. Letichevsky, O. Letichevskyi, Peschanenko, Blinov, & Klionov, 2011) which provides programming of systems based on models of agent behavior, transition systems and bisimulation equivalence. The examples of rewriting rules systems include Maude (Meseguer et al., 2002), Stratego (Bravenboer, Kalleberg, Vermaas, & Visser, 2008), ASF+SDF (van den Brand, Heering, Klint, & Olivier, 2000), TXL (Cordy, 2006), Jess (Friedman-Hill, 2003), APS (Letichevsky, Kapitonova, & Konozenko, 1993), TermWare (Doroshenko & Shevchenko, 2006). The main directions of application of such systems are program analysis (detecting errors and inconsistencies with programming standards), transformation of source code (in particular, refactoring, optimization, raising the security of a program, support of legacy code), creation of new (domain-specific) languages or extension of general-purpose languages, modeling (development and processing of high-level program models, transition from high-level models to a source code). One of the advantages of formal program models (in particular, based on the algebraic approach) is that they can be used for proving the correctness of program transformations.

The algorithmics (which is also called the algebra of algorithmics) is the direction of computer science being developed within the Ukrainian algebraic-cybernetic school (Doroshenko, Tseytlin, Yatsenko, & Zachariya, 2006; Andon, Doroshenko, Tseytlin, & Yatsenko, 2007; Andon, Doroshenko, Zhereb, Shevchenko, & Yatsenko, 2017). It dates back to fundamental works of Academician V. M. Glushkov (1965, 1966, 1968) aimed to solve the problems of design automation of computer logic structure and programming. As a result, the system of algorithm algebra (SAA) (later called the Glushkov's algebra (GA)) have been constructed and examined and structural schematology and a method of multilevel structural program design have been developed

(Glushkov, Tseytlin, & Yushchenko, 1978, 1980, 1989). SAA is focused on solving the problems of formalization, design and improvement of sequential and parallel algorithms by some criteria (e.g., memory usage, execution time). The objects of research in algorithmics are models of algorithms and programs represented in the form of high-level specifications — schemes. The method of algorithmics is based on computer algebra and logic and is used for constructing algorithms in various subject domains. It also unifies the use of various discrete models (logic, automaton theoretical, grammatical and algorithmic) to describe programming paradigms. Algorithmics uses three interdependent forms of algorithmic knowledge representation: analytical (in the form of an algebraic formula called a regular scheme of an algorithm), natural linguistic (the text in the conventional language of human communication) and visual (flowgraphs). These forms give a comprehensive understanding of specifications and facilitate the achievement of demanded program quality. Algebra-algorithmic models are closely linked to methods (metarules) of designing algorithms and programs: descending (involution), ascending (convolution) and combined (reorientation). It is necessary to mention also the transformation metarule allowing to transform algorithms with the purpose of their improvement. The algebra-algorithmic approach is supported by developed software tools providing automated design and synthesis of programs. The process of program development is based on using SAA and fixation of basic notions (predicates and operators) associated with a specific subject domain. One of the areas of development of the algebra of algorithms consists in using algebra-dynamic models. Such models combine a representation of a program in algebra-algorithmic form and modeling a process of execution using a transition systems theory. Thus, the possibility of formal transformations of algebraic program representation is preserved and also new facilities for modeling specific states of parallel program execution appear. The algebra of algorithmics is close to the area of intentional programming (Czarnecki & Eisenecker, 2000), the purpose of which consists in creating various subject domains and their integration with the use of abstractions, biology and ecology of programming. The abstraction is the analytical representation of knowledge related to a chosen subject domain (for example, algebraic formulas). The biology of programming consists in the availability of connections between close subject domains. The biological component of algorithmics is reflected in a theory of clones (meta-algebras or families of algebras) (Doroshenko et al., 2006) which formalizes basic programming paradigms (structural, non-structural, object-oriented). The ecology represents tools of automated construction of different subject domains and their integration. However, in contrast to intentional programming, algorithmics uses three interdependent forms of algorithmic knowledge representation mentioned above. One of the essential problems of algorithmics is to increase the adaptability of programs to specific conditions of their use, e.g. optimizing application code for a given parallel platform. In particular, the problem can be solved by usage of parameter-driven generation of algorithm specifications by means of higher-level specifications (Yatsenko, 2012).

Programming of efficient algorithms, especially parallel ones, has always been a challenging task. The performance growth of a parallel program is limited by Amdahl's law, so efficient programs should minimize the fraction of sequential computation as well as synchronization and communication overhead. Such optimizations are usually hardware platform-dependent, and the program that is optimized for one platform is likely not optimal on another platform. Therefore, there is a need for tools that can perform such adaptation to a specific platform in automated mode. One traditional solution of this problem is provided by parallelizing compilers (e.g., Intel parallel compilers, OpenUH, Omni OpenMP, Oracle Solaris Studio). The quality of automated parallelization has increased recently; still, such tools are only applicable to programs with simple computing structure. The reasons include the complexity of static analysis of large codebases, increasing complexity of parallel architectures, as well as their diversity. An alternative to parallelizing compilers is provided by auto-tuning (Naono, Teranishi, Cavazos, & Suda, 2010; Durillo & Fahringer, 2014), a method that has already proven its efficiency and versatility. It can automate the search for an optimal program version out of a set of provided possibilities, by running each candidate and measuring its performance on a given parallel architecture. Its main benefit is a high level of abstraction — a program is optimized without explicit knowledge of hardware implementation details, such as a number of cores, cache size or memory access speed. Instead, parallel programs use subject domain concepts such as a number and a size of independent tasks, or algorithm details such as data traversal methods. The drawbacks of auto-tuning approach include significant one-time costs of optimization process itself: if the number of program versions is large enough, the optimization process may run for many hours and even days. Also, there is an additional development overhead — creation of auto-tuner application. Well-known examples of auto-tuners are specialized libraries like ATLAS (Whaley, Petitet, & Dongarra, 2001) and FFTW (Frigo & Johnson, 1998), stand-alone software applications Atune-IL (Schaefer, Pankratius, & Tichy, 2009), ActiveHarmony (Tapus, Chung, &

Hollingsworth, 2002), POET (Yi, Seymour, You, Vuduc, & Quinlan, 2007), FIBER (Katagiri, Kise, Honda, & Yuba, 2003).

This book proposes formal and adaptive methods and tools for constructing parallel programs, based on the algebra of algorithms, term rewriting and auto-tuning paradigm. One of the main application domains of the developed tools is a weather forecasting problem. Forecasting systems are getting more complex every year as underlying mathematical models evolve and the amount of computed data grows swiftly. Taking into account a large demand on meteorological prognoses in different fields of human activity, designing and development of programs for solving this problem are extraordinarily actual. In addition, reliability and efficiency of meteorological forecasts are of large and sometimes critical importance, which puts high demands on the accuracy of the results and response time of forecasting programs. A large amount of computation over huge data arrays demands the use of parallel computing.

ORGANIZATION OF THE BOOK

The book is organized into seven chapters. In the opening chapters, a theoretical basis of algorithmics and term rewriting, and also the development of formal and adaptive models and methods for program constructing and auto-tuning are considered.

In the first chapter, an overview of programming methods (algebraic, parallel, adaptive and other) related to the approach of program design proposed in the book is given. Several algorithm algebras are considered (Dijkstra's algebra, algebra of flowgraphs, Glushkov's SAA and algebra of algorithmics), intended for formalized description of algorithms in the form of high-level specifications (schemes). The main notions related to software auto-tuning are given.

The second chapter deals with formalized construction and auto-tuning of algorithms and programs. The metarules of designing algorithm schemes and algorithmic language SAA/1 intended for multilevel structured designing and documenting of sequential and parallel algorithms in a natural linguistic form are considered. Metarules are used for transition between various algorithms (transformation) and generation of new algorithmic knowledge. The method of parameter-driven generation of algorithm specifications by means of higher-level algorithms (hyperschemes) is proposed. Hyperscheme is a parameterized algorithm for solving a certain class of problems; setting specific values of parameters and subsequent interpretation of a hyperscheme allows obtaining algorithms adapted to specific conditions of their use. The parallel computation model of auto-tuning based on a well-known abstract parallel machine with random memory access (PRAM) is described. The examples of designing parallel algorithms in SAA are given.

The third chapter presents the basic notions and examples related to algebraic programming based on rewriting rules. An overview of existing software implementations of rewriting rules systems is given. The main directions of application of rewriting rules technique for working with program code are considered.

The fourth chapter deals with the development of algebra-dynamic models of parallel programs, which are based on concepts of transition systems theory, algebra of algorithms and rewriting rules technique. High-level models of sequential and multithreaded programs are developed for central processing units (CPU) and graphics processing units (GPU). The method of automated transformation of a sequential program to a parallel one, which is based on usage of rewriting rules, is proposed. An evolutionary model of an auto-tuner as an extension of a transition system concept is described. Some properties of multithreaded programs (deadlock-freeness, absence of conflicts, equivalence) are also considered.

The fifth chapter is devoted to developed software tools, which are based on algebra-algorithmic models and formal methods of constructing algorithms and programs. The integrated toolkit for design and synthesis of programs (IDS), the rewriting rules system TermWare and the auto-tuning framework TuningGenie are considered.

The sixth chapter presents the examples of application of the developed software tools for design, generation, transformation and auto-tuning of programs for multicore processors and graphics processing units. In particular, the developed algebra dynamic models and the rewriting rules toolkit are used for parallelization and optimization of programs for NVIDIA GPUs supporting the CUDA technology. TuningGenie framework is applied for tuning of sorting and meteorological forecasting programs to a target platform. The parallelization of Fortran programs using rewriting rules technique on sample problems in the field of quantum chemistry is also considered.

In the seventh chapter, the approach to development of parallel programs using ontologies and algebra-algorithmic tools is described. The process of program design is based on combined usage of program design ontology, SAA and the toolkit for design and synthesis of programs. The ontology includes the concepts from different subject domains (sorting, physics) and, if necessary, can be extended with concepts from new domains. For constructing the ontology, the Web Ontology Language (OWL) and Protégé system are applied. The method for automatic generation of an initial (skeleton) scheme of an algorithm based on its description in the program design ontology is proposed and implemented in IDS toolkit. The application of the proposed approach is illustrated by examples of developing parallel sorting, meteorological forecasting and N-body simulation programs.

REFERENCES

Andon, P. I., Doroshenko, A. Yu., Tseytlin, G. O., & Yatsenko, O. A. (2007). *Algebra-algorithmic models and methods of parallel programming.* Kyiv: Academperiodyka. (in Russian)

Andon, P. I., Doroshenko, A. Yu., Zhereb, K. A., Shevchenko, R. S., & Yatsenko, O. A. (2017). *Methods of algebraic programming: Formal methods of parallel program development.* Kyiv: Naukova dumka. (in Russian)

Bravenboer, M., Kalleberg, K. T., Vermaas, R., & Visser, E. (2008). Stratego/ XT 0.17. A language and toolset for program transformation. *Science of Computer Programming, 72*(1–2), 52-70.

Cordy, J. R. (2006). The TXL source transformation language. *Science of Computer Programming, 61*(3), 190–210. doi:10.1016/j.scico.2006.04.002

Czarnecki, K., & Eisenecker, U. (2000). *Generative programming: Methods, tools, and applications.* Boston: Addison-Wesley.

Doroshenko, A., & Shevchenko, R. (2006). A rewriting framework for rule-based programming dynamic applications. *Fundamenta Informaticae, 72*(1-3), 95–108.

Doroshenko, A., Tseytlin, G., Yatsenko, O., & Zachariya, L. (2006). A theory of clones and formalized design of programs. In *Proceedings of the 15th International Workshop "Concurrency, Specification and Programming" (CS&P'2006)* (pp. 328-339). Berlin: Humboldt University Press.

Durillo, J., & Fahringer, T. (2014). From single- to multi-objective auto-tuning of programs: Advantages and implications. *Scientific Programming – Automatic Application Tuning for HPC Architectures, 22*(4), 285-297.

Friedman-Hill, E. (2003). *Jess in action.* Greenwich: Manning Publications Co.

Frigo, M., & Johnson, S. (1998). FFTW: An adaptive software architecture for the FF. *Acoustics. Speech and Signal Processing, 3,* 1381–1384.

Garrido, A., & Meseguer, J. (2006). Formal specification and verification of Java refactorings. In *Proceedings of 6th IEEE International Workshop on Source Code Analysis and Manipulation (SCAM'06)* (pp. 165-174). Washington: IEEE Computer Society. 10.1109/SCAM.2006.16

Glushkov, V. M. (1965). Automata theory and structural design problems of digital machines. *Cybernetics, 1*(1), 3–9. doi:10.1007/BF01071436

Glushkov, V. M. (1966). Minimization of microprograms and algorithm schemes. *Cybernetics, 2*(5), 1–2. doi:10.1007/BF01073662

Glushkov, V. M. (1968). Simple algorithms for the analysis and synthesis of pushdown automata. *Cybernetics, 4*(5), 1–7. doi:10.1007/BF01073662

Glushkov, V. M., Tseytlin, G. O., & Yushchenko, K. L. (1978). Certain problems of the theory of structured program schemes. *Inform. Proc. Lect, 7*(6), 253–260.

Glushkov, V. M., Tseytlin, G. O., & Yushchenko, K. L. (1980). *Methods of symbolic multiprocessing.* Kyiv: Naukova dumka. (in Russian)

Glushkov, V. M., Tseytlin, G. O., & Yushchenko, K. L. (1989). *Algebra. Languages. Programming* (3rd ed.). Kyiv: Naukova dumka. (in Russian)

Hemel, Z., Kats, L. C. L., Groenewegen, D. M., & Visser, E. (2008). Code generation by model transformation: A case study in transformation modularity. *Software & Systems Modeling, 9*(3), 375–402. doi:10.100710270-009-0136-1

Kapitonova, Yu. V., & Letichevsky, A. A. (1993). Algebraic programming: Methods and tools. *Cybernetics and Systems Analysis, 29*(3), 307–312. doi:10.1007/BF01125535

Katagiri, T., Kise, K., Honda, H., & Yuba, T. (2003). FIBER: A generalized framework for auto-tuning software. In *Proceedings of the International Symposium on High Performance Computing 2003 (ISHPC 2003) (LNCS)* (Vol. 2858, pp. 146-159). Berlin: Springer. 10.1007/978-3-540-39707-6_11

Letichevsky, A., Letichevskyi, O., Peschanenko, V., Blinov, I., & Klionov, D. (2011). Insertion modeling system and constraint programming. In *Proceedings of the 7th International Conference "ICT in Education, Research and Industrial Applications. Integration, Harmonization and Knowledge Transfer" (ICTERI 2011)* (pp. 51-64). Berlin: Springer.

Letichevsky, A. A., & Gilbert, D. R. (2000). A model for interaction of agents and environments. In *Proceedings of the 14th International Workshop on Algebraic Development Techniques (WADT 1999) (LNCS)* (Vol. 1827, pp. 311-328). 10.1007/978-3-540-44616-3_18

Letichevsky, A. A., & Kapitonova, Yu. V. (1990) Algebraic programming in APS system. In *Proceedings of the International Symposium on Symbolic and Algebraic Computation (ISSAC'90)* (pp. 68-75). New York: ACM Press. 10.1145/96877.96896

Letichevsky, A. A., Kapitonova, Yu. V., & Konozenko, S. V. (1993). Computations in APS. *Theoretical Computer Science, 119*(1), 145–171. doi:10.1016/0304-3975(93)90343-R

Letichevsky, A. A., Letychevskyi, O. A., & Peschanenko, V. S. (2012). Insertion modeling system. In *Proceedings of the 8th International Conference on Perspectives of System Informatics (PSI'11)* (pp. 262-273). Berlin: Springer.

Meseguer, J., Olveczky, P. C., Stehr, M.-O., & Talcott, C. (2002). Maude as a wide-spectrum framework for formal modeling and analysis of active networks. In *Proceedings of the DARPA Active Networks Conference and Exposition (DANCE'02)* (pp. 494-510). Washington: IEEE Computer Society. 10.1109/DANCE.2002.1003516

Naono, K., Teranishi, K., Cavazos, J., & Suda, R. (2010). *Software automatic tuning: From concepts to state-of-the-art results*. Berlin: Springer. doi:10.1007/978-1-4419-6935-4

Schaefer, C. A., Pankratius, V., & Tichy, W. F. (2009). Atune-IL: An instrumentation language for auto-tuning parallel applications. In *Proceedings of the 15th International Euro-Par Conference (Euro-Par'2009) (LNCS)* (Vol. 5704, pp. 9-20). Berlin: Springer. 10.1007/978-3-642-03869-3_5

Tapus, C., Chung, I.-H., & Hollingsworth, J. K. (2002). Active Harmony: Towards automated performance tuning. In *Proceedings of the 2002 ACM/IEEE conference on Supercomputing (SC'02)* (pp. 1-11). Los Alamitos, CA: IEEE Computer Society.

van den Brand, M., Heering, J., Klint, P., & Olivier, P. (2000). Compiling language definitions: The ASF+SDF compiler. *ACM Transactions on Programming Languages and Systems*, *24*(4), 334–368. doi:10.1145/567097.567099

Visser, E. (2007). WebDSL: A case study in domain-specific language engineering. In *Proceedings of the International Summer School on Generative and Transformational Techniques in Software Engineering (GTTSE 2007) (LNCS)* (Vol. 5235, pp. 291-373). Berlin: Springer.

Whaley, R., Petitet, A., & Dongarra, J. J. (2001). Automated empirical optimizations of software and the ATLAS Project. *Parallel Computing*, *27*(1-2), 3–35. doi:10.1016/S0167-8191(00)00087-9

Yatsenko, O. (2012). On parameter-driven generation of algorithm schemes. In *Proceedings of the 21st International Workshop "Concurrency, Specification and Programming" (CS&P'2012)* (pp. 428-438). Berlin: Humboldt University Press.

Yi, Q., Seymour, K., You, H., Vuduc, R., & Quinlan, D. (2007). POET: Parameterized optimizations for empirical tuning. In *Proceedings of the Parallel and Distributed Processing Symposium 2007 (IPDPS 2007)* (pp. 447). Piscataway, NJ: IEEE Computer Society.

Acknowledgment

This book is the result of the authors' cooperation in the field of developing a theory, methodology and software tools for automated constructing of efficient parallel programs based on algebra-algorithmic approach and rewriting rules technique. However, it could not be born without the help and support of our colleagues from the Computing Theory Department of Institute of Software Systems of National Academy of Sciences of Ukraine.

The authors are grateful to all of them.

Chapter 1

Algebras of Algorithms, Parallel Computing, and Software Auto-Tuning

ABSTRACT

This chapter gives an overview of programming methods (algebraic, parallel, adaptive, and other) related to the approach of the program design proposed in the book. Algorithm algebras intended for formalized description of algorithms in the form of high-level schemes are considered: Dijkstra's algebra associated with technology of structured programming; Kaluzhnin's algebra for graphical description of non-structured schemes of algorithms; Glushkov's algebra for description of structured schemes, including the facilities for computation process prediction and design of parallel algorithms; the algebra of algorithmics, which is based on the mentioned algebras. The signature of each algebra consists of predicate and operator constructs conforming to a specific method of algorithm design, that is, structured, non-structured, and other. Basic notions related to software auto-tuning are considered, and the classification of auto-tuners is given.

INTRODUCTION

In the following subsections, the programming methods (formal, algebraic, functional, logic, parallel and adaptive) associated with the methodology of software design being proposed in the book are considered.

DOI: 10.4018/978-1-5225-9384-3.ch001

Algebraic programming is a special form of programming activity in which programs are constructed in terms of algebraic objects and their transformations. Objects of a subject domain and reasoning about these objects are represented by algebraic expressions (e.g., terms, predicate formulas, algorithm schemes) in many-sorted algebra (Sannella & Tarlecki, 2012). The transformation of expressions is provided by application of equalities or rewriting rules. A number of systems are known, which support various forms of algebraic programming, such as Casl (Mossakowski, Haxthausen, Sanella, & Tarlecki, 2008), Maude (Meseguer, Olveczky, Stehr, & Talcott, 2002), APS (Letichevsky, Kapitonova, & Konozenko, 1993).

Functional and logic programming (Harrison, 1997; Kowalski, 2014; Kowalski & Hogger, 1992; Paulson & Smith, 1991) belong to the declarative programming paradigm, under which a program describes what result must be received instead of a description of a sequence of its obtaining. A functional program defines a system of rewriting rules that can evaluate the desired function. A logic program defines a search space of problem reductions that can solve all instances of the desired goal.

The development of modern software is characterized by dynamic expansion in construction and usage of parallel computing models, which became ubiquitous and permeate the most aspects of architecture and programming tools of computer systems. Network technologies and Internet facilities, operating systems and application software in present circumstances more or less are based on concepts of parallel and distributed computing. Solving complex scientific and technological tasks requires significant computing resources; sustainable use of these resources has always been one of the main problems in software development. Programming efficient algorithms has become more complicated after the transition to multicore processor architecture. For achieving the maximum program performance, it is necessary to adapt a program to a computing environment in which it will be executed. The modern methodology of software auto-tuning (Durillo & Fahringer, 2014; Naono, Teranishi, Cavazos, & Suda, 2010) allows automating this process. The idea of auto-tuning consists in empirical evaluation of several versions of a program and selection of the best one. Traditionally, the selection is made by a separate tuner program which generates various program modifications. In this chapter, an overview of the main concepts and tools related to software auto-tuning is given.

PROGRAMMING MODELS AND METHODS

Formal Methods

Formal methods are mathematically rigorous techniques and tools for the specification, design and verification of software and hardware systems (Butler, 2001). The specifications used in formal methods are well-formed statements in mathematical logic and the formal verifications are rigorous deductions in that logic, i.e. each step follows from a rule of inference and hence can be checked by a mechanical process. Formal design can be seen as a three-step process including formal specification, verification and implementation.

The need for formal specification systems has been noted for years. In (Backus, 1960), a formal notation for describing programming language syntax was presented later named Backus-Naur form (BNF) (Knuth, 1964). During the formal specification phase, the engineer rigorously defines a system using a modeling language. Modeling languages are fixed grammars that allow users to model complex structures out of predefined types. This process of formal specification is similar to the process of converting a word problem into algebraic notation.

Once a formal specification has been developed, the specification may be used as the basis for proving properties of the specification. The proof can be either human-directed or automated. Automated techniques fall into three general categories ("Formal methods", 2019):

· **automated theorem proving:** a system attempts to produce a formal proof from scratch, given a description of the system, a set of logical axioms, and a set of inference rules;
· **model checking**: a system verifies certain properties by means of an exhaustive search of all possible states that a system could enter during its execution;
· **abstract interpretation**: a system verifies an over-approximation of a behavioural property of the program, using a fixpoint computation over a (possibly complete) lattice representing it.

After the model has been specified and verified, it is implemented by converting the specification into code. As the difference between software and hardware design grows narrower, formal methods for developing embedded systems have been developed (Collins, 1998). LARCH, for example, has a

VHDL implementation. Similarly, hardware systems such as the VIPER and AAMP5 processors have been developed using formal approaches.

An alternative to this approach is the lightweight approach to a formal design. In a lightweight design, formal methods are applied sparingly to a system. This approach offers the benefits of formal specification, but also avoids some of the difficulties.

Formal methods are applied in different areas of hardware and software, including routers, Ethernet switches, routing protocols, security applications. In software development, formal methods are mathematical approaches to solving software and hardware problems at the requirements, specification, and design levels ("Formal methods", 2019). Formal methods are most likely to be applied to safety-critical or security-critical software and systems, such as avionics software. Software safety assurance standards, such as DO-178C allows the usage of formal methods through supplementation, and Common Criteria mandates formal methods at the highest levels of categorization.

For sequential software, examples of formal methods include the B-Method, the specification languages used in automated theorem proving, RAISE, and the Z notation.

In functional programming, property-based testing has allowed the mathematical specification and testing of the expected behaviour of individual functions.

The Object Constraint Language (and specializations such as Java Modeling Language) has allowed object-oriented systems to be formally specified.

For concurrent software and systems, Petri nets, process algebra, and finite state machines allow executable software specification and can be used to build up and validate application behavior.

Another approach to formal methods in software development is to write a specification in some form of logic — usually a variation of first-order logic — and then to directly execute the logic as though it were a program. The example is OWL language based on Description Logic (DL). There is also work on mapping some version of English (or another natural language) automatically to and from logic, and executing the logic directly. Examples are Attempto Controlled English, and Internet Business Logic, which do not seek to control the vocabulary or syntax. A feature of systems that support bidirectional English-logic mapping and direct execution of the logic is that they can be made to explain their results, in English, at the business or scientific level.

Algebraic, Insertion and Algebra-Algorithmic Programming

Algebraic programming is based on term rewriting theory (Kapitonova & Letichevsky, 1993). The terms represent data and systems of rewriting rules (expressed as systems of equalities) represent computation algorithms. The elementary step of computation includes pattern matching, verification of terms and substitution. Order of selection of rewriting rules and subterms of a given term for matching with left parts of equalities is defined by a rewriting strategy (Doroshenko & Shevchenko, 2006). Strictly speaking, the strategy determines the result of the computation, a term. Rewriting strategy can be described in a lower-level programming paradigm, for example, procedural or functional, which results in the necessity of integration of the paradigms. The idea of integration of paradigms (procedural, functional, algebraic and logical) found the embodiment in the Algebraic Programming System (APS) (Letichevsky et al., 1993), which uses specialized data structures, the graph terms, for the representation of data and knowledge about subject domains.

The concepts of algebraic programming underlie the insertion programming (A. A. Letichevsky, O. A. Letychevskyi, & Peschanenko, 2012) based on agent behavior models, transition systems and bisimulation equivalence notion (Letichevsky & Gilbert, 2000). The insertion programming considers a program as an algebraically defined transformation of a set of states of an information environment, where an active information environment, which has an observed behavior, is considered instead of the passive environment (the memory). The basis of the insertion programming is the model of the behavior of agents in environments based on concepts of a transition system (a basic standard in the behavioral theory of interactive processes) and a relation of bisimulation equivalence of agents with respect to an environment (the state of an agent is identical with its behavior). Unlike agent-oriented programming, which pays more attention to the problems of intellectualization of agents, insertion programming embraces the behavioral aspects of agents.

The algebra of algorithmics (*AA*) (Andon et al., 2007; Doroshenko, Tseytlin, Yatsenko, & Zachariya, 2006) is a direction within the Ukrainian algebraic-cybernetic school rising from the fundamental works of Academician V. M. Glushkov (Glushkov, 1965; Glushkov, Tseytlin, & Yushchenko, 1980, 1989) associated with development of the system of algorithmic algebras and the toolkit for automated program synthesis called MULTIPROCESSIST (Yushchenko, Tseytlin, Hrytsay, & Terzyan, 1989). The specific feature of

AA is a formalization of processes of design and synthesis of algorithms and programs. These objects are designed in terms of regular schemes, which are representations in the system of algorithmic algebra (SAA). The development of facilities of equivalent transformations provided the possibility of improvement of objects being designed according to selected criteria (for example, used memory, execution time). The theory of clones (Andon et al., 2007; Doroshenko et al., 2006), which formalizes basic programming paradigms and aspects of forming different subject domains, was proposed. The tools for automatization of programming were also developed (Doroshenko, Ivanenko, Ovdii, & Yatsenko, 2016; Doroshenko, Zhereb, & Yatsenko, 2013).

The algebra of algorithmics is close to the directions of algebraic algorithmics (Naudin & Quitte, 1992) and intentional programming (Czarnecki & Eisenecker, 2000). The algebraic algorithmics (AlgA) belongs to methods of top-down programming, whereas intentional programming belongs to bottom-up programming. AlgA is the formalized approach to the description of methods of processing mathematical (algebraic) objects. It combines different algebras and data processing algorithms, which are applied for proving basic theorems in corresponding algebras. The purpose of intentional programming consists in creating various subject domains and their integration with the use of abstractions, biology and ecology of programming. The abstraction is an analytical representation of knowledge related to a chosen subject domain (for example, formulas in corresponding algebras). The biology of programming consists in the availability of "genetic" connections between close subject domains. The ecology represents the means of automation of construction of different subject domains and their integration.

In contrast to AlgA and intentional programming, *AA* uses three interdependent forms of algorithmic knowledge representation:

· **analytical:** in the form of an algebraic formula, which is called a regular scheme;
· **natural linguistic**: the text in the conventional language of human communication;
· **visual:** flowgraphs.
Example 1. For illustration of the above-mentioned representation forms, consider the fragment of the bubble sorting algorithm (Andon et al., 2007). The analytical form of this fragment is specified as the following regular scheme:

$$ALT = ([l > r \mid Y_1] \; Transp(l,r \mid Y_1) * R(Y_1), \; R(Y_1)).$$

The main compound operator of the given scheme is called *ALT* and is a ternary operation of branching of the form "if-then-else", which is denoted as ($[u]A,B$). The logical variable u of this operation is replaced by the predicate $l>r|Y_1$ and the operator variables *A* and *B* are substituted by the operators *Transp*$(l, r| Y_1) * R(Y_1)$ and $R(Y_1)$, respectively. The mentioned predicate and operators are defined on the marked array *M* of data being processed:

$$M: H \; Y_1 \; a_1 \; ... \; a_n \; K,$$

where *H, K* are markers fixing the beginning and the end of the array *M*, respectively; Y_1 is a pointer, which can move over the array with the help of the shift operator; *l* and *r* are the elements directly to the left and to the right of the pointer Y_1, accordingly; *Transp*$(l, r| Y_1)$ is the operator of a transposition of elements *l* and *r*; $R(Y_1)$ is the operator shifting the pointer Y_1 over the array *M* by one element to the right.

The visual form of this fragment is given as a flowgraph in Figure 1.

The corresponding textual representation of the above fragment is the following:

```
ALT =
=== IF 'l > r at Y(1) in (M)'
    THEN
        "Transpose l, r at Y(1) in (M)"
        THEN
        "Shift Y(1) by (1) in (M) to the right"
    ELSE "Shift Y(1) by (1) in (M) to the right"
    END IF
```

Algorithm schemes can be modified by using the metarules of schemes design: a convolution (abstracting), an involution (detailed elaboration), a reorientation (a combination of convolution and involution) and a transformation (a conversion of a scheme by means of application of equalities).

Facilities of the algebra of algorithmics were applied for designing programs in subject domains of symbolic processing (sorting, search, language processing) (Doroshenko et al., 2006; Doroshenko et al., 2013), meteorological forecasting (Doroshenko et al., 2016) and other (Andon et al., 2007; Doroshenko et al., 2013).

Figure 1. The flowgraph of the compound operator ALT

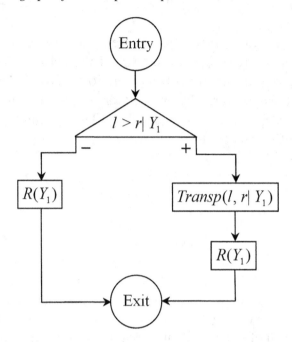

Functional and Logic Programming

The *functional programming* (Harrison, 1997; Paulson & Smith, 1991) is the paradigm where the execution of a program is the calculation of some expression that describes application of functions (in a mathematical sense) to input data. Unlike the traditional programming approach (imperative programming), where execution of a program is considered as a sequential transition of states in computer memory (i.e., change of variables values), there is no concept of a variable and an assignment in functional programming, a function does not have the obvious internal state, but operates only on data. As a result, side effects are absent, a program becomes simpler to debug, and it also implies more natural parallelization for multicore processors. In addition, higher-order functions allow using functional abstraction to a greater extent, and automatic inference of types makes program text substantially more compact.

Basic features of functional languages are the following: conciseness and simplicity, strict typing, modularity, functions are values, cleanness (absence of side effects), call-by-need ("lazy") evaluation.

Functional languages are classified as follows:

· pure, that use only a functional paradigm (for example, Haskell);
· hybrid, that have characteristics of both functional and imperative languages. Prime examples are Scala and Nemerle, which unite features of object-oriented and functional languages;
· non-strict, that support lazy evaluation, i.e. the arguments of a function are calculated only when they are really necessary at the calculation of a function. The examples of non-strict languages are Haskell, F#, Gofer, Miranda;
· strict, that does not support lazy calculations (for example, Standard ML).

Some functional languages (Scala, Clojure, F#, Nemerle, SML.NET) are implemented above virtual machines (JVM, .NET), i.e. applications written in these languages can work in the runtime environment (JRE, CLR) and use built-in classes.

Below, a brief description of some functional programming languages is given.

LISP ("LISt Processor") is considered to be the first functional programming language, untyped. Linked lists are one of Lisp's major data structures, and Lisp source code is made of lists. Thus, Lisp programs can manipulate source code as a data structure, giving rise to the macro systems that allow programmers to create new syntax or new domain-specific languages embedded in Lisp. Lisp has changed since its early days, and many dialects have existed over its history. Today, the best-known general-purpose Lisp dialects are Clojure, Common Lisp, and Scheme.

ML ("Meta Language") is a general-purpose functional programming language which has roots in Lisp, and has been characterized as "Lisp with types". Features of ML include a call-by-value evaluation strategy, first-class functions, automatic memory management through garbage collection, parametric polymorphism, static typing, type inference, algebraic data types, pattern matching, and exception handling. Its types and pattern matching make it well-suited and commonly used to operate on other formal languages, such as in compiler writing, automated theorem proving, and formal verification. Today there are several languages in the ML family; the three most prominent are Standard ML (SML), OCaml and F#.

Miranda is a purely functional programming language with lazy evaluation, polymorphic strong typing, and a powerful module system. It had a strong influence on the subsequent development of the field, influencing, in particular, the design of Haskell, to which it has many similarities.

Haskell is one of the most widespread non-strict languages. It has a strong, static type system. The simplified dialect of Haskell is Gofer (GOod For Equational Reasoning), intended for learning functional programming.

In *logic programming*, a program consists of a theory and a proposition to be proved (Kowalski, 2014; Kowalski & Hogger, 1992). A theory is defined by means of axioms and inference rules (implications). A proposition statement that needs to be proved is entered into the program as a goal. The execution of a program consists in searching for proof of the proposition in the knowledge base which is a set of facts and rules. While in the functional programming functions are one-directed, i.e. they get arguments and return a result, in the logical programming a difference between input and output is conditional. It is possible to specify a desirable output and get an input that it will provide. Another important difference is the nondeterminism of logical languages. A result is not necessarily determined explicitly. Thus, as an arbitrary proposition can be proved variously, a system implementing logic programming language (for example, Prolog) consistently suggests to renew an attempt to prove a goal in a different way. For proving propositions, unification (an algorithmic process of solving equations between symbolic expressions) and a resolution technique are used. In logic programming, as well as in functional, the low-level details of methods of calculations and sequences of elementary executions are unknown for a programmer. The greater part of the responsibility for their efficiency depends upon the translator of the used programming language. At present, there are several implementations of Prolog. Generally, a code generated by a translator of this language can be compared in terms of efficiency with the code of a corresponding program in an imperative language.

The first logic programming language was Planner, which had a possibility to automatically infer a result from data and a set of rules for searching variants called a plan. Planner was used in order to bring down requirements to hardware resources (by means of backtracking method) and provide the possibility to infer facts without active use of a stack. Further, Prolog was developed, that did not require variants searching plan, and was a simplification of Planner in this sense. The logic programming languages originating from Planner are QA-4, Popler, Conniver, QLISP. Planner was a basis for several alternative logic programming languages that do not use the backtracking method, for example, Ether. Derivatives from Prolog are Mercury, Visual Prolog, Oz, and Fril languages.

Parallelism and Parallel Computing Models

The parallel computing system (PCS) provides simultaneous (parallel) execution of operations of one or several programs. The main ideas for parallelizing operations in computer systems are the notion of pipelining of data flow computation and the concept of true parallelism, i.e. independent and simultaneous execution of operations on different devices of a computer.

The main characteristics of PCS include the following:

· **the number and quality of processors:** systems with the number of processors $p>100$ are called *massively parallel*. The parallel systems which consist of identical processors, are called *homogeneous* and the others are called *heterogeneous*;
· **memory type:** describes the access of the processors to main memory: *shared memory* is global to the entire PCS and is equally accessible to all processors, distributed memory is split into private regions (according to the number of processors), the access to any one of which has only one processor, thus such memory is *local*;
· **the system of communication between the processors:** characterizes the topology of communication of processors, such as static topology (linear, ring, star, matrix), dynamic topology (with switch connections), commutators, etc.;
· **control method:** *synchronous* (centralized), if commands in all processors of PCS are executed in accordance with a single signal from the central control unit, and an *asynchronous* (distributed), if the execution of commands in processors is not synchronized.

There are several classifications of PCS architectures in concordance with the above-mentioned characteristics. The most famous among them is the taxonomy proposed by M. J. Flynn (Flynn, 1972; "Flynn's taxonomy", 2018). The four categories of architectures defined by Flynn are based upon the number of concurrent instruction (or control) streams and data streams available in the architecture:

· **SISD (Single Instruction Single Data):** A sequential computer which exploits no parallelism in either the instruction or data streams. The single control unit fetches a single instruction stream from memory. Examples of SISD architecture are traditional uniprocessor machines like older personal computers and mainframe computers;

· **SIMD (Single Instruction Multiple Data):** A computer which exploits multiple data streams against a single stream to perform operations which may be naturally parallelized. For example, an array processor or a graphics processing unit (GPU);

· **MISD (Multiple Instruction Single Data):** Multiple instructions operate on one data stream. Uncommon architecture which is generally used for fault tolerance. Heterogeneous systems operate on the same data stream and must agree on the result;

· **MIMD (Multiple Instruction Multiple Data).** Multiple autonomous processors simultaneously executing different instructions on different data. MIMD architectures include multicore superscalar processors, and distributed systems, using either one shared memory space or a distributed memory space.

As of 2006, the entire top 10 and most of the TOP500 supercomputers are based on MIMD architecture ("Flynn's taxonomy", 2018). Flynn's classification is useful, but not complete. In ("Flynn's taxonomy", 2018), it is supplemented, in particular, by Single Instruction, Multiple Threads (SIMT) category, an execution model where single instruction, multiple data (SIMD) is combined with multithreading.

The important models used in developing parallel applications (Buyya, 1999) are:

· shared-memory model (multithreading);
· distributed-memory model (message passing model);
· hybrid model.

The *shared-memory model* allows multiple threads to exist within the context of one process. These threads share the process resources but are able to execute independently. Various mechanisms such as locks/semaphores are used to control access to the shared memory, resolve contentions and to prevent race conditions and deadlocks. From a programming perspective, threads implementations commonly comprise a library of subroutines that are called from within parallel source code and a set of compiler directives embedded in either sequential or parallel source code. The examples of implementation of this model are POSIX Threads ("Multi-Threaded Programming with POSIX Threads", n.d.), OpenMP ("OpenMP Application Programming Interface", 2015), CUDA ("NVIDIA CUDA technology", n.d.).

The *distributed-memory model* means that a set of tasks use their own local memory during computation. Multiple tasks can reside on the same physical machine and/or across an arbitrary number of machines. Tasks exchange data through communications by sending and receiving messages. Data transfer usually requires cooperative operations to be performed by each process. For example, a send operation must have a matching receive operation. From a programming perspective, message passing implementations usually comprise a library of subroutines. Calls to these subroutines are embedded in source code. MPI ("MPI: A Message-Passing Interface Standard", 2012) is the "de facto" industry standard for message passing. The standard defines syntax and semantics of a core of library routines useful to a wide range of users writing portable message-passing programs in C, C++, and Fortran.

The *hybrid model* combines the shared-memory and distributed-memory programming models. Currently, a common example of a hybrid model is the combination of the message passing model (MPI) with the threads model (OpenMP). Another similar and increasingly popular example of a hybrid model is using MPI with CPU-GPU (Graphics Processing Unit) programming.

The process of parallel program design includes four main stages: decomposition, communication, synchronization and mapping (Buyya, 1999). The *decomposition* is the process of partitioning of the applied task and the data on which it operates into smaller subtasks. The *communication* focuses on the flow of information and coordination among the tasks that are created during the decomposition stage. The specific features of the applied problem and the decomposition method determine the communication pattern among these cooperative tasks. The four popular communication patterns commonly used in parallel programs are local/global, structured/unstructured, static/dynamic, and synchronous/asynchronous. The *synchronization* is the coordination of parallel tasks in real time, which is generally associated with communications. It is often implemented by establishing a synchronization point within a program where a task may not proceed further until another task or tasks reach the same or logically equivalent point. The most common means of synchronization are critical sections, semaphores, barriers, mutexes, etc. *Mapping* is assigning each task to a processor such that it maximizes the utilization of system resources (such as CPU) while minimizing the communication costs. Mapping decisions can be taken statically (at compile-time/before program execution) or dynamically at runtime by load-balancing methods.

Formal models of parallel computing (Bird, 1993; Dijkstra, 1976; Doroshenko, 2000; Kordic, 2008) represent a convenient tool for solving the problems of formalized design, analysis and transformation of parallel algorithms and programs. In particular, algebra-algorithmic models (Andon et al., 2007) are based on functions over data structures and regular programs represented in the algebra of algorithms, the basic operators and conditions of which are defined based on these functions. The models of parallel macro pipeline computations have been further developed within the framework of the *algebra-dynamic* approach to construction of parallel programs. The set of algebra-dynamic models developed in (Doroshenko, 2000) reflects the system of aspects of parallelism models for multiprocessor systems: algorithmic, programmatic and coordination. The algebra-dynamic approach allows to integrate the information analysis of program operators into the operational semantics of parallel programming language and implement the idea of asynchronousity of computations at intracomponental level or to display the obtained information in the coordination part of the model and implement the potential asynchronousity of computations at the level of intercomponental interactions. In (Andon, Doroshenko, & Zhereb, 2011; Doroshenko, Zhereb, & Yatsenko, 2010), the algebra-dynamic approach was applied for formal design and automated transformation of parallel programs for graphics processing units.

The Main Algorithm Algebras

In this subsection, the algebras of algorithms intended for the analytical description of algorithms are considered.

The basis of an algebraic formalism being considered in this subsection is the concept of the abstract automaton model of a computer (Glushkov et al., 1980), which is the interaction of a control automaton Ψ and an operational automaton Φ. The automatons Ψ and Φ are also called control and operational structures, respectively. The control structure Ψ is a system of control terminals $\Psi=\{\Psi_q|q\in I\}$. The operational structure Φ is the composition $R(\Phi)=\{\Phi_q|q\in I\}$ of nonintersecting substructures Φ_q associated with corresponding control terminals Ψ_q. The set of states $IS=\{m_i|i\in I\}$ of the automaton Φ is called an *information set*. On the set IS, the set of operators $OP=\{A_j|j\in I\}$ and the set of logic conditions $P_r=\{u_k|k\in I\}$ are defined. The interaction of automatons Ψ and Φ is carried out according to a feedback principle (Figure 2). The input of the automaton Ψ is a set of logic conditions u_k, which characterize the current state of the operational automaton Φ. According to the mentioned set, the control automaton produces an operator A_j, which transforms the current state of the automaton Φ. The considered cycle is repeated until the automaton Ψ transits to a final state. The composition of the control and operational automatons is also called a *discrete transducer*.

Figure 2. The abstract automaton model of a computer

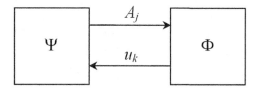

Algorithms of functioning of the discrete transducer in the given concept of an abstract automaton model are represented by schemes in corresponding algebras of algorithms.

Dijkstra's Algebra

In 1968, E. Dijkstra proposed the idea of construction and research of the algebra of programs, which is based on well-known programmer constructs: composition, branching and loop. *Dijkstra's algebra* (Andon et al., 2007; Doroshenko et al., 2006; Tseytlin, 1998) is a two-sorted algebraic system

$$DA = <\{Pr,Op\}; \Omega_{DA}>,$$

which consists of a set of conditions (predicates) *Pr* and a set of operators *Op*, both defined on information set *IS*. Set *IS* is a set of all data (input, output and intermediate) being processed by algorithms. The signature Ω_{DA} includes Boolean operations taking values in *Pr* and generating compound conditions, and also operations taking values in *Op* and generating compound operators. Predicates from the set *Pr* are functions which map elements of the set *IS* to elements of the set $E_2=\{0,1\}$, where 0 is for false, 1 is for true. Operators from set *Op* map information set *IS* to itself.

Compound predicates from the set *Pr* are constructed from basic ones by using the following Boolean operations:

· disjunction $u \vee u'$, where $u \in Pr$, $u' \in Pr$ are logic variables;
· conjunction $u \wedge u'$;

· negation $\bar{u}$.

Compound operators from the set *Op* are built from elementary ones by means of the following operations:

· composition $A*B$ which is the sequential execution of operators $A \in Op$ and $B \in Op$;
· alternative (branching) ([u]A,B) which executes operator A, if the condition u is true, and applies operator B otherwise;
· loop operation {[u]A} which executes the operator A repeatedly until the condition u is true.

Operator variables $A=\{A_1,A_2,...,A_n\}$ and logic variables $U=\{u_1,u_2,...,u_m\}$ are used as elementary (basic) operators and logic conditions, accordingly.

Example 2. As an illustration, consider the process of designing the bubble sorting algorithm using the operations of Dijkstra's algebra. The algorithm processes the input numerical array M, which is initially marked in the following way:

$$M : H \ Y_1 \ a_1 \ a_2 \ ... \ a_n \ K.$$

Here H and K are markers fixing the beginning and the end of the array M; a_i is the element of the array, $i=1,...,n$; Y_1 is the pointer moving over M in the direction from left to right.

On array M, the following basic predicates and operators are defined:

· the predicate *Sorted*(M) which takes true value, if the array M is sorted and false otherwise;
· the predicate $d(Y_1,K)$ which takes true value, if Y_1 reached the marker K and false otherwise;
· the predicate $l>r|Y_1$ which takes true value, if the specified relation holds for the elements located directly to the left and to the right of the pointer Y_1;
· the operator *Transp*($l,r|Y_1$) which swaps the elements adjacent to the pointer Y_1;
· the identity operator E which does not change a state of the array;
· the operator $R(Y_1)$ shifting the pointer Y_1 over the array M one symbol to the right;

· the operator $SET(Y_1, H)$ placing the pointer Y_1 in a position directly to the right of the marker H.

By superposition of the main operations of Dijkstra's algebra (loop, alternative, branching) and the above-listed basic elements, the following scheme of the sorting algorithm is obtained:

$Bubble = \{[Sorted(M)]\ \{[d(Y_1, K)]\ ([l > r \mid Y_1]\ Transp(l, r \mid Y_1), E) * R(Y_1)\} * SET(Y_1, H)\}.$

The essence of the given scheme consists in cyclic scanning of the pointer Y_1 over the array M in the direction from left to right until the condition $d(Y_1, K)$ is true, after which Y_1 returns to the marker H. This cyclic process continues until the condition $Sorted(M)$ is true. During such scanning, the operator $Transp(l, r \mid Y_1)$ or the operator E is executed depending on the value of the condition $l > r \mid Y_1$.

Algebra of Flowgraphs

In this subsection, the basic definitions concerning flowgraphs of algorithms are given, and the algebra flowgraphs (Kaluzhnin's algebra) (Andon et al., 2007) is considered.

Two sets of variables $\tilde{U} = \{U_j \mid j = 1, 2, ..., m\}$ and $\tilde{A} = \{A_i \mid i = 1, 2, ..., n\}$ are fixed, where U_j are logic variables; A_i are operator variables. Let G be a directed graph having the set of vertices (nodes) $V = \tilde{U} \cup \tilde{A}$ with the binary relation R defined on V and associated with the set of edges of the graph G. Each vertex of the graph is marked by some variable $v \in V$. The node marked with a logic variable $U_j \in \tilde{U}$ is called a *recognizer* (or a *u*-node) and the node marked with the operator variable $A_i \in \tilde{A}$ is called an *operator* (or an *A*-node). Besides the vertices, G contains edges of two types: ordinary and logic. Logic edges are supplied by plus and minus marks. Each operator has only one outgoing edge, whereas recognizer has two outgoing edges, one of which is signed with a plus and another with a minus. Is should be noticed that different *A*-nodes (*u*-nodes) can be marked with the same operator variable (accordingly, logic variable).

The graph G also contains two additional nodes with labels "Entry" and "Exit". "Entry" node has no incoming edges, and "Exit" node has no outcoming edges. Other nodes can be marked by labels of two types: operator labels contained in rectangles and predicate labels contained in triangles. The transition to "Exit" node completes the work of an algorithm.

The considered connected graph G is called a *flowgraph* of an algorithm.

Let G be some flowgraph with nodes marked with logic variables $U_j \in \tilde{U}$ and operator variables $A_i \in \tilde{A}$. Let IS be information set on which the set of operators Op and the set of predicates Pr is defined. Operators are functions taking values from IS, and predicates are logic functions taking values from the set of logic values $E_2 = \{0,1\}$, where 0 is false value, 1 is true value. The basic predicate $u \in Pr$ is assigned to each logic variable $U_j \in \tilde{U}$ in the flowgraph G; the basic operator $B \in Op$ is assigned to each operator variable $A_i \in \tilde{A}$. This assignment is called the *interpretation of the flowgraph G*. Flowgraph G is called *interpreted* and is designated as $G/\overset{\frown}{F}$, where $\overset{\frown}{F} \subseteq Pr \cup Op$.

Consider the process of moving along the nodes of the interpreted flowgraph $G/\overset{\frown}{F}$ during processing of input data. Let $m \in IS$ be the element arriving at the entry node of the interpreted flowgraph $G/\overset{\frown}{F}$. At passing the nodes of this flowgraph, according to a direction of edges, the element m is changed under the influence of operators corresponding to A-nodes. Let on some step the element m is transformed to $m' \in IS$. Consider the following two cases.

· The element m arrives at the input of A-node assigned with operator $A \in \overset{\frown}{F}$ accordingly to the given interpretation. Then the element $m'' = A(m')$ continues to move along one edge outcoming from the given A-node, $m'' \in IS$.

· The element m arrives at the input of a recognizer assigned with predicate $u \in \overset{\frown}{F}$ according to selected interpretation. In this case, m moves without changes along one of the edges. If $u(m') = 1$, it moves along the plus edge, if $u(m') = 0$, along the minus edge.

If during functioning of flowgraph $G/\overset{\frown}{F}$, an element $m \in IS$ which arrived at the entry node, was transformed to $\tilde{m} \in IS$ and reached the exit node, then $\tilde{m}$ is regarded as the result of application of the algorithm represented by interpreted flowgraph $G/\overset{\frown}{F}$. This fact is denoted as $\tilde{m} = G/\overset{\frown}{F}(m)$.

Let flowgraphs G and G' be defined on the same set of predicate and operator variables $V = \tilde{U} \cup \tilde{A}$. All the occurrences of the operator $A_j \in \tilde{A}$ in flowgraph G are substituted with flowgraph G'. As a result, the new flowgraph $G'' = G(A_j \Rightarrow G')$ which is the *superposition* of flowgraphs G and G' is obtained. In (Tseytlin, 1998) the concept of a generalized flowgraph was introduced and the algebra of such flowgraphs with signature consisting of superposition operation was constructed.

Kaluzhnin's algebra is the two-sorted algebra

$$KA = <\{Pr,Op\}; \Omega_{KA}>,$$

where *Pr* is the set of logic conditions represented in graph form; *Op* is the set of operator flowgraphs; Ω_{KA} is the signature which includes the following operations: Boolean functions, operation of sequential execution of operators, unary operation of flowgraph restructuring (which consists in switching of some edges, outcoming from an operator node or a recognizer, to some other node of the flowgraph with subsequent elimination of nodes unreachable from a root). The operation of flowgraph restructuring corresponds to "go to" operation included in the signature of Yanov's algebra (Tseytlin, 1998) focused on the analytic representation of non-structured algorithm schemes.

Example 3. Figure 3 shows the flowgraph of the bubble sort algorithm which corresponds to the scheme considered in Example 2.

Glushkov's System of Algorithmic Algebras and Parallel Computing

The inclusion of a prediction operation into the signature of the considered above Dijkstra's algebra leads to Glushkov's algorithmic algebras (Andon et al., 2007). Like algebraic specifications in general, Glushkov's SAA is focused on the analytical form of representation of algorithms and formalized transformation of these representations, in particular, for the purpose of optimization of algorithms by given criteria. Glushkov's SAA (or Glushkov's algebra, GA) is the two-sorted algebra

$$GA = <\{Pr,Op\}; \Omega_{GA}>,$$

where sorts *Pr* and *Op* are sets of operators and logic conditions, accordingly, defined on information set *IS*; Ω_{GA} is the signature of operations. Operators represent mappings (probably, partial) of the information set to themselves, logic conditions are predicates, which are defined on set *IS* and take values of three-valued logic $E_3=\{0,1,\mu\}$, where 0 is for false, 1 is for true and μ is for unknown. The signature $\Omega_{GA} = \Omega_1 \cup \Omega_2$ consists of the system Ω_1 of logic operations taking values in the set *Pr*, and the system Ω_2 of operations taking values in the set of operators *Op*. In SAA, the system of generators representing a finite functionally complete set of logic conditions and operators is fixed. By means of this set and superpositions of operations included in Ω_{GA}, any operators and logic conditions from sets *Pr* and *Op* are generated.

Figure 3. The flowgraph of the bubble sorting algorithm

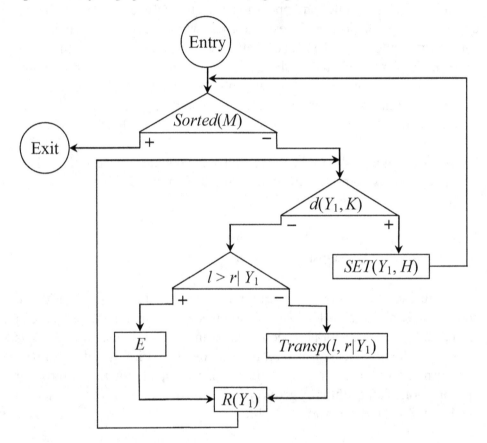

The list of main operations included in the signature of SAA and their modifications (SAA-M, focused on parallel computation) is given in Table 1, where $u \in Pr$, $u' \in Pr$ are logic and $A \in Op$, $B \in Op$ are operator variables; $E \in Op$ is identity operator; $W \in Op$ is the uncertain operator. The operations are shown in analytic and natural language forms. It should be noticed that the operations can also be represented in the flowgraph form based on the considered earlier algebra of flowgraphs.

Table 1. The main operations of SAA and SAA-M

Type	Operation name	Representation form	
		Analytic	**Natural linguistic**
Logic	Disjunction	$u \vee u'$ $u + u'$	u OR u'
	Conjunction	$u \wedge u'$ $u \cdot u'$	u AND u'
	Negation	$\overline{u}$	NOT(u)
	Prediction	$A \cdot u$	AFTER A CONDITION u
Operator	Composition	$A*B$	A THEN B $A;B$
	Alternative (branching)	$([u]A,B)$	IF u THEN A ELSE B END IF
	Loop	$\{[u]A\}$	WHILE NOT u LOOP A END OF LOOP
	Asynchronous disjunction	$A//B$	A PARALLEL B
	Control point	$CP(u)$	CP u
	Synchronizer	$S(u)$	WAIT u

Table 2. The truth tables for disjunction $u \vee u'$, conjunction $u \wedge u'$ and negation $\overline{u}$

$\vee$	0	μ	1		$\wedge$	0	μ	1		u	$\overline{u}$
0	0	μ	1		0	0	0	0		0	1
μ	μ	μ	1		μ	0	μ	μ		μ	μ
1	1	1	1		1	0	μ	1		1	0

Logic operations are generalized Boolean operations: disjunction $u \vee u'$, conjunction $u \wedge u'$, negation $\bar{u}$ (defined by the truth tables shown in Table 2), and also the prediction operation $A \cdot u$ (left multiplication of the condition u by the operator A), which consists in checking the value of the predicate u after the execution of the operator A.

Consider the operations included in the signature, which generate operators from the set .

Consider the operations included in the signature $\Omega_2 \subset \Omega_{GA}$, which generate operators from the set Op.

The *composition* $A * B$ is a binary operation defined on the set Op, consisting in sequential application of the operators $A \in Op$, $B \in Op$.

The *alternative* (*branching*) $([u]A,B)$ is a ternary operation, which depends on the condition $u \in Pr$ and the operators $A \in Op$, $B \in Op$. This operation generates the operator $C = ([u]A,B)$, such that

$$C(m) = \begin{cases} A, & \text{if } u(m) = 1, \\ B, & \text{if } u(m) = 0, \\ W, & \text{if } u(m) = \frac{1}{4} \end{cases}$$

for any $m \in IS$.

The *loop* $\{[u]A\}$ is a binary operation, which depends on the condition $u \in Pr$ and the operator $A \in Op$. Its essence consists in cyclic application of the operator A at false value of u until the condition u is true.

Some derivative operations included in the signature $\Omega_2 \subset \Omega_{GA}$ are the following.

The *for loop* operation For (*var, start_expr, end_expr*) $\{A\}$ is applied to iterate over a range of values of the variable *var*; *start_expr* to *end_expr* are numerical expressions, which define initial and final values of the variable *var*. This operation sequentially executes operator $A \in Op$ for all the values of *var* in the interval [*start_expr, end_expr*].

The *switch* operation SELECT($u_1 \rightarrow A_1$, ..., $u_n \rightarrow A_n$) executes one of the operators A_i ($i = 1,..,n$), if the value of the corresponding condition u_i is true, and then breaks computation without checking the values of other conditions.

In SAA, the basis $Z \subset Pr \cup Op$ is fixed.

The superposition of operations included in signature Ω_{GA} and elements of the basis Z, represents the compound operator (algorithm) $F/Z \in Op$ in SAA and is called an interpreted *regular scheme* (RS) F/Z.

The *modified* SAA (SAA-M) (Glushkov et al., 1980) with the extended signature of operations Ω'_{GA} is focused on formalization of parallel computations. Besides the above-considered constructs included in the signature Ω_{GA}, the signature Ω'_{GA} contains the following operations.

The *asynchronous disjunction A//B* is the operation consisting in parallel execution of the operators *A* and *B*. For synchronization of parallel processes, control points and synchronizers are used.

The *control points CP(u)* are fixed positions between operators in an algorithm scheme. Each control point *CP(u)* is associated with the condition *u*, which is false while computation process has not yet reached the point *CP(u)*, true from the moment of achievement of the given point and uncertain in the presence of emergency stops on a path which conducts to the point *CP(u)*. The condition *u* is called a *synchronization condition* associated with the point *CP(u)*.

The delay of computation in schemes of algorithms is implemented by means of *synchronizers*. The synchronizer is defined by means of the loop $S(u)=\{[u] E\}$, where *u* is a logic function which depends on synchronization conditions associated with certain control points of a scheme. The synchronizer located in a certain place of a regular scheme, carries out a delay of computation in the given place of the scheme up to the moment when its synchronization condition *u* is true.

The representation of an algorithm in SAA-M, which specifies asynchronous operator interactions, is called a *parallel regular scheme* (PRS).

Example 4. Consider the parallel algorithm of two-way bubble sorting *PBubble*, obtained as a result of parallelization of the corresponding sequential sorting scheme *Bubble* (see Example 2). Marking of the array to be sorted is the following:

$$M : H \ Y_1 \ a_1 \ a_2 \ \dots \ a_n \ Y_2 \ K,$$

where *H* and *K* are markers fixing the beginning and the end of the array *M*; Y_1 and Y_2 are pointers moving over *M* towards each other. PRS of the algorithm is the following:

$$PBubble = SET(Y_1, H) * SET(Y_2, K) * \{[Sorted(M)] \ INIT\_CP * (Bubble(1) \ // \ Bubble(2))\},$$

23

$$Bubble(1) = \{[d(Y_1, K)] \ TRANSP\_L\} * SET(Y_1, H) * CP(PROC\_FIN(1)) * S(PROC\_FIN(2)),$$

$$Bubble(2) = \{[d(Y_2, H)] \ TRANSP\_R\} * ([d(Y_1, Y_2) = 1] \ S(d(Y_1, Y_2) = 0), E)\} *$$
$$*CP(PROC\_FIN(2)) * S(PROC\_FIN(1)),$$

$$TRANSP\_L = ([l > r \mid Y_1] \ Transp(l, r \mid Y_1), E) * R(Y_1),$$

$$TRANSP\_R = ([l > r \mid Y_2] \ Transp(l, r \mid Y_2), E) * L(Y_2),$$

where *INIT_CP* is the operator initializing the synchronization conditions *PROC_FIN*(1) and *PROC_FIN*(2) with false value; *PROC_FIN*(*i*) (where $i=1,2$) is the predicate which takes true value, if branch *Bubble*(*i*) completed processing, and false otherwise; $L(Y_2)$ is the shift of the pointer Y_2 by one element to the left over the array; $d(Y_1, Y_2)=n$ is the predicate which takes true value, if there are *n* elements between the pointers Y_1 and Y_2.

The essence of *PBubble* scheme consists in conjoint functioning of contradirectional processes *Bubble*(1) and *Bubble*(2) of bubble sorting, which process the array *M* at adverse sides. Compound operators *TRANSP_L* and *TRANSP_R* implement the conditional transposition of adjacent elements of the array and shift of the pointers Y_1 and Y_2 to the right and to the left, respectively. When the pointers reach the critical state (the condition $d(Y_1, Y_2)=1$ is true) the process *Bubble*(2) turns into a waiting state up to the moment when the pointers merge (the condition $d(Y_1, Y_2)=0$ is true), whereas *Bubble*(1) continues to work. Then both processes reach the opposite ends of the array. The described loop repeats until the array is sorted (the condition *Sorted*(*M*) is true).

Other examples of parallel regular schemes are given in Chapter 2.

Algebra of Algorithmics

The algebra of algorithmics (*AA*) (Andon et al., 2007; Tseytlin, 1998) is based on the above considered Dijkstra's, Glushkov's, and Kaluzhnin's algebras, and is focused on solving the problems of formalization, substantiation of correctness and transformation of algorithms in various subject domains.

The *AA* is the two-level system. The theory of clones (Doroshenko et al., 2006) is the basis of the first (top) level. The algorithmic clone is a two-sorted system

$$C_A = <\{L(2), Op\}; SUPER>,$$

where $L(2)$ is a set of all Boolean functions; Op is the operator base consisting of a set of noninterpreted operator schemes; *SUPER* is the signature which contains only the operation of superposition of operations.

The selection of the system of generators of C_A determines the system of algorithmic constructions typical for a method of algorithm and program design. For example, for a structured programming method, such a system consists of constructs included in the signature of operations of Dijkstra's algebra.

Depending on a problem being solved, the chosen method of development of algorithm classes, the technological environment of programming, the construction of necessary algebra of algorithms from the family specified by the corresponding clone is carried out. The signature of the constructed algebra satisfies the theorem of functional completeness for the clone and is the basis of the clone. The constructed algebra of algorithms can be analyzed for the purpose of axiomatization, the development of optimizing transformations, canonization of analytical representations, etc.

At the second (bottom) level of *AA*, the construction of a specific applied algebra of algorithms focused on representation of algorithmic knowledge of the chosen subject domain is carried out. The scheme of development of the applied algebra of algorithms is based on interpretation of elementary operator and predicate variables for the algebra of algorithms constructed at the top level. In turn, the development of sets of interpretations is concerned with construction of many-sorted algebraic systems, associated with abstract data types, classification and inheritance mechanisms.

The algebra of algorithmics is the basis of the algebra-algorithmic models and methods examined in Chapter 2 and also the toolkit for design and synthesis of programs considered in Chapter 5.

Overview of Adaptive Programming Methods

Adaptive programming is designed to allow software to respond to change in its complex environment (Derbyshire & Donovan, 2016; Gouda & Herman,

1991). Often, the motivation for changing program behavior is to satisfy some performance criteria. In this case, adaptivity is a technique for performance optimization in a dynamic environment. One of the paradigms of software application optimization is auto-tuning which allows adapting computations executed by a program to a runtime environment in order to achieve one or a few goals — a reduction of time expenses, energy consumption or a computation cost. Auto-tuning is most common in the area of optimization of high-performance parallel computations but can be applied to any software applications and executing platforms — from mobile devices to supercomputers. Auto-tuning, unlike the automatic parallelization, works with a parallel program and searches in its computations for a compromise between parallelism, synchronization, load balancing, use of different memory levels, etc.

Auto-tuning searches for optimal values of some parameters based on the empiric estimation of some program P in a runtime environment. Each parameter (separately or in connection with other parameters) must have an influence on execution speed and efficiency of the software. The examples of parameters are a number of program threads, a size of the data block in geometric parallelism algorithms, a version of an algorithm from a class of equivalent algorithms (e.g., a class of sorting algorithms), data traversal strategy, etc. Further, a unique set C of parameter values will be called a *configuration*.

Every software variation is uniquely defined by the corresponding configuration, and therefore the task of an auto-tuner is to search for an optimal configuration for a target runtime environment.

The general lifecycle of the auto-tuning process (see Figure 4) consists of the following three steps.

· Apply modification that might affect software performance.
· Estimate actual performance empirically (in a target environment).
· Analyze estimation results. If the efficiency criteria are met, the optimization is finished (exit); otherwise, go to step 1.

Figure 4. Generic tuning workflow

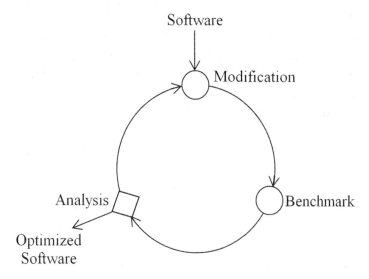

Such lifecycle is the same for all *static* auto-tuners, i.e. the tuners which do not affect runtime execution of software. Optimization is performed via iterative evaluation of software versions until a version with acceptable performance is found, all possible versions are tried or time limit is reached.

Further, various categories of auto-tuner classification are considered.

The classification according to the types of cooperation of a tuner with software being optimized is the following:

· **auto-tuner as a software library:** the object of tuning is a universal set of library functions that are optimized by a tuner-installer. The result of installation in a target environment is a library optimized and generated by a tuner from scratch. The library is used by other software applications. Usually, a tuner and library functions are one unit and obviously tied to a certain subject domain. ATLAS (Whaley, Petitet, & Dongarra, 2001) and FFTW (Frigo & Johnson, 1998) libraries fall into this category;

· **auto-tuner as a stand-alone software application:** in this case, the tuner is created separately from software being optimized. The tuner must have software adaptation mechanisms or be able to generate new variations. The familiar examples of such auto-tuners are Atune-IL (Schaefer, Pankratius, & Tichy, 2009), ActiveHarmony (Tapus, Chung, & Hollingsworth, 2002), POET (Yi, Seymour, You, Vuduc, & Quinlan, 2007) and FIBER (Katagiri, Kise, Honda, & Yuba, 2003). The system for generation of auto-tuners TuningGenie (Ivanenko, Doroshenko, & Zhereb, 2014) described in Chapter 5 also falls into this category;

· **auto-tuner as an operating system extension:** one of the most promising approaches, where universal auto-tuner is a part of operating system and is involved in task scheduling. Unfortunately, because of the architectural complexity of such a solution and a variety of operating systems, an effective software implementation has not been developed yet.

Another important classification of auto-tuners is the classification by an object of optimization:

· **offline auto-tuners** do not launch software being optimized. Instead, some part of a program which includes its main computing functions or a separate small benchmark which can be completely different from the software being optimized is executed. All auto-tuner libraries fall into this category, for example, the library of linear algebra functions for sparse matrices OSKI (Vuduc, Demmel, & Yelick, 2005), the library for optimizing matrix multiplication PHiPAC (Bilmes, Asanovic, Chin, & Demmel, 2014), and already mentioned ATLAS (Whaley et al., 2001) and FFTW (Frigo & Johnson, 1998). Auto-tuning frameworks ActiveHarmony (Tapus et al., 2002) and TuningGenie (Ivanenko et al., 2014) also belong to this category;

· **online auto-tuning:** during tuning iterations, a program being optimized is launched in "real" conditions — the complete computing cycle is executed on input data similar to data with which the program will be executed in the future. The contemporary systems of online auto-tuning include ABCLibScript (Katagiri, 2010), ATune-IL (Schaefer et al., 2009), ActiveHarmony (Tapus et al., 2002), and TuningGenie (Ivanenko et al., 2014) which also allows using results of offline phase in the online phase.

Auto-tuners are also classified by a mechanism of adaptation of software being optimized:

· during the execution of tuning iterations, the **source code transformation** is carried out, as a result of which the new version of a program is obtained. In some auto-tuning systems (Katagiri, 2010; Schaefer et al., 2009), source code of a program is considered as a simple text and transformation is reduced to replacement of a substring or substitution of a template. Some auto-tuners carry out manipulations at another level — the auto-tuner can work with an abstract syntax tree or use higher-level systems, for example, term rewriting system (Doroshenko & Shevchenko, 2006; Ivanenko et al., 2014);

· the alternative approach is **manipulation with program parameters** predefined at the development stage. The new configuration for tuning iteration can be passed to a program being optimized in different ways — as a text file, command line parameters, etc.

CONCLUSION

Algebraic programming and algebras of algorithms considered in this chapter are the basis for formal specification of algorithmic processes with the help of terms and schemes — high-level models of algorithms and programs. The considered Dijkstra's algebra is associated with structured programming technique, Kaluzhnin's algebra is intended for graphical representation of algorithms and Glushkov's algebra is applied for description of sequential and parallel structured schemes. The algebra of algorithmics is based on the mentioned algebras and is intended for formal design of algorithms in different subject domains. Algorithm algebras can be applied for solving theoretical programming problems, such as optimization and verification of algorithms and formalization of semantics of programming languages. The transformation of algorithms is provided by application of equalities and rewriting rules. The auto-tuning paradigm allows optimizing programs to a target computing environment based on experimental evaluation of program performance. It automates the search for the optimal program version out of a set of provided possibilities by running each candidate and measuring its performance on a given multiprocessor architecture. Its main benefit is the high level of abstraction — program is optimized without explicit knowledge of hardware implementation details, such as a number of cores, cache size or memory access speed on various levels. Instead, parallel programs use subject domain concepts such as a number and a size of independent tasks, or algorithm details such as data traversal methods.

REFERENCES

Andon, P. I., Doroshenko, A. Yu., Tseytlin, G. O., & Yatsenko, O. A. (2007). *Algebra-algorithmic models and methods of parallel programming*. Kyiv: Academperiodyka. (in Russian)

Andon, P. I., Doroshenko, A. Yu., & Zhereb, K. A. (2011). Programming high-performance parallel computations: Formal models and graphics processing units. *Cybernetics and Systems Analysis*, *47*(4), 659–668. doi:10.100710559-011-9346-y

Backus, J. W. (1960). The syntax and semantics of the proposed international algebraic language of Zürich ACM-GAMM Conference. *Proceedings of the 1st International Conference on Information Processing*, 125-132.

Bilmes, J., Asanovic, K., Chin, C.-W., & Demmel, J. (2014). Optimizing matrix multiply using PHiPAC: A portable, high-performance, ANSI C coding methodology. In *Proceedings of the 25th ACM International Conference on Supercomputing* (pp. 253-260). New York: ACM. 10.1145/2591635.2667174

Bird, R. S. (1993). Lectures on constructive functional programming. In M. Broy (Ed.), *Constructive Methods in Computer Science. NATO ASI Series F* (Vol. 55, pp. 151–218). Berlin: Springer.

Blelloch, G. E. (1996). Programming parallel algorithms. *Communications of the ACM*, *39*(3), 85–97. doi:10.1145/227234.227246

Butler, R. W. (2001). *What is formal methods?* Retrieved from http://shemesh.larc.nasa.gov/fm/fm-what.html

Buyya, R. (1999). *High performance cluster computing: Programming and applications*. Upper Saddle River, NJ: Prentice Hall.

Collins, M. (1998). *Formal methods*. Retrieved from https://users.ece.cmu.edu/~koopman/des_s99/formal_methods

Czarnecki, K., & Eisenecker, U. (2000). *Generative programming: Methods, tools, and applications*. Boston: Addison-Wesley.

Derbyshire, H., & Donovan, E. (2016). *Adaptive programming in practice: shared lessons from the DFID-funded LASER and SAVI programmes*. Retrieved from https://beamexchange.org/uploads/filer_public/d9/80/d9804a2d-7be5-4614-9ad9-2ec6a536ae20/adaptive_programmine_laser_savi_compressed.pdf

Dijkstra, E. W. (1976). *A discipline of programming*. Prentice Hall.

Doroshenko, A., Ivanenko, P., Ovdii, O., & Yatsenko, O. (2016). Automated program design— An example solving a weather forecasting problem. *Open Physics, 14*(1), 410–419. doi:10.1515/phys-2016-0048

Doroshenko, A., & Shevchenko, R. (2006). A rewriting framework for rule-based programming dynamic applications. *Fundamenta Informaticae, 72*(1-3), 95–108.

Doroshenko, A., Tseytlin, G., Yatsenko, O., & Zachariya, L. (2006). A theory of clones and formalized design of programs. In *Proceedings of the 15th International Workshop "Concurrency, Specification and Programming" (CS&P'2006)* (pp. 328-339). Berlin: Humboldt University Press.

Doroshenko, A., Zhereb, K., & Yatsenko, O. (2010). Formal facilities for designing efficient GPU programs. In *Proceedings of the 19th International Workshop "Concurrency: Specification and Programming" (CS&P'2010)* (pp. 142-153). Berlin: Humboldt University Press.

Doroshenko, A., Zhereb, K., & Yatsenko, O. (2013). Developing and optimizing parallel programs with algebra-algorithmic and term rewriting tools. In *Proceedings of the 9th International Conference "ICT in Education, Research, and Industrial Applications" (ICTERI 2013), Revised Selected Papers (Communications in Computer and Information Science)* (Vol. 412, pp. 70-92). Berlin: Springer. 10.1007/978-3-319-03998-5_5

Doroshenko, A. Yu. (2000). *Mathematical models and methods of organization of highly productive parallel computations: The algebra-dynamic approach*. Kyiv: Naukova dumka. (in Russian)

Durillo, J., & Fahringer, T. (2014). From single- to multi-objective auto-tuning of programs: Advantages and implications. *Scientific Programming — Automatic Application Tuning for HPC Architectures, 22*(4), 285-297.

Flynn, M. J. (1972). Some computer organizations and their effectiveness. *IEEE Transactions on Computers, 21*(9), 948–960. doi:10.1109/TC.1972.5009071

Flynn's Taxonomy. (2018). Retrieved from https://en.wikipedia.org/wiki/Flynn%27s_taxonomy#cite_note-1

Formal Methods. (2019). Retrieved from https://en.wikipedia.org/wiki/Formal_methods#cite_note-10

Frigo, M., & Johnson, S. (1998). FFTW: An adaptive software architecture for the FF. *Acoustics. Speech and Signal Processing*, *3*, 1381–1384.

Glushkov, V. M. (1965). Automata theory and structural design problems of digital machines. *Cybernetics*, *1*(1), 3–9. doi:10.1007/BF01071436

Glushkov, V. M., Tseytlin, G. O., & Yushchenko, K. L. (1980). *Methods of symbolic multiprocessing*. Kyiv: Naukova dumka. (in Russian)

Glushkov, V. M., Tseytlin, G. O., & Yushchenko, K. L. (1989). *Algebra. Languages. Programming* (3rd ed.). Kyiv: Naukova dumka. (in Russian)

Gouda, M., & Herman, T. (1991). Adaptive programming. *IEEE Transactions on Software Engineering*, *17*(9), 911–921. doi:10.1109/32.92911

Harrison, J. (1997). *Introduction to functional programming*. Cambridge: Cambridge university.

Ivanenko, P., Doroshenko, A., & Zhereb, K. (2014). TuningGenie: Auto-tuning framework based on rewriting rules. In *Proceedings of the 10th International Conference "ICT in Education, Research and Industrial Applications. Integration, Harmonization and Knowledge Transfer" (ICTERI 2014) (Communications in Computer and Information Science)* (Vol. 469, pp. 139-158). Cham: Springer. 10.1007/978-3-319-13206-8_7

Kapitonova, Yu. V., & Letichevsky, A. A. (1993). Algebraic programming: Methods and tools. *Cybernetics and Systems Analysis*, *29*(3), 307–312. doi:10.1007/BF01125535

Katagiri, T. (2010). ABCLibScript: A computer language for automatic performance tuning. In K. Naono, K. Teranishi, & J. C. Reiji (Eds.), *Software automatic tuning: From concepts to state-of-the-art results* (pp. 295–313). Berlin: Springer.

Katagiri, T., Kise, K., Honda, H., & Yuba, T. (2003). FIBER: A generalized framework for auto-tuning software. In *Proceedings of the International Symposium on High Performance Computing 2003 (ISHPC 2003) (LNCS)* (Vol. 2858, pp. 146-159). Berlin: Springer. 10.1007/978-3-540-39707-6_11

Knuth, D. E. (1964). Backus Normal Form vs Backus Naur Form. *Communications of the ACM*, *7*(12), 735–736. doi:10.1145/355588.365140

Kordic, V. (2008). *Petri Net: Theory and applications*. Vienna: I-Tech Education and Publishing. doi:10.5772/56

Kowalski, R. (2014). History of logic programming. In D. Gabbay, J. Woods, & J. Siekmann (Eds.), *Computational logic* (pp. 523–569). Elsevier. doi:10.1016/B978-0-444-51624-4.50012-5

Kowalski, R. A., & Hogger, C. J. (1992). Logic programming. In S. C. Shapiro (Ed.), *Encyclopedia of Artificial Intelligence* (2nd ed., pp. 873–891). Hoboken, NJ: John Wiley.

Letichevsky, A. A., & Gilbert, D. R. (2000). A model for interaction of agents and environments. In *Proceedings of the 14th International Workshop on Algebraic Development Techniques (WADT 1999) (LNCS)* (Vol. 1827, pp. 311-328). 10.1007/978-3-540-44616-3_18

Letichevsky, A. A., Kapitonova, Yu. V., & Konozenko, S. V. (1993). Computations in APS. *Theoretical Computer Science, 119*(1), 145–171. doi:10.1016/0304-3975(93)90343-R

Letichevsky, A. A., Letychevskyi, O. A., & Peschanenko, V. S. (2012). Insertion modeling system. In *Proceedings of the 8th International Conference on Perspectives of System Informatics (PSI'11)* (pp. 262-273). Berlin: Springer.

Meseguer, J., Olveczky, P. C., Stehr, M.-O., & Talcott, C. (2002). Maude as a wide-spectrum framework for formal modeling and analysis of active networks. In *Proceedings of the DARPA Active Networks Conference and Exposition (DANCE'02)* (pp. 494-510). Washington: IEEE Computer Society. 10.1109/DANCE.2002.1003516

Mossakowski, T., Haxthausen, A. E., Sanella, D., & Tarlecki, A. (2008). *Casl — the Common Algebraic Specification Language*. Berlin: Springer. doi:10.1007/978-3-540-74107-7_5

MPI: A Message-Passing Interface Standard. (2012). Retrieved from http://mpi-forum.org/docs/mpi-3.0/mpi30-report.pdf

Multi-Threaded Programming with POSIX Threads. (n.d.). Retrieved from http://www.cs.kent.edu/~ruttan/sysprog/lectures/multi-thread/multi-thread.html

Naono, K., Teranishi, K., Cavazos, J., & Suda, R. (2010). *Software automatic tuning: From concepts to state-of-the-art results*. Berlin: Springer. doi:10.1007/978-1-4419-6935-4

Naudin, P., & Quitté, C. (1992). *Algorithmique algébrique avec exercices corrigés*. Paris: Masson. [in French]

NVIDIA CUDA Technology. (n.d.). Retrieved from http://www.nvidia.com/cuda

OpenMP Application Programming Interface Version 4.5. (2015). Retrieved from http://www.openmp.org/wp-content/uploads/openmp-4.5.pdf

Paulson, L. C., & Smith, A. W. (1991). Logic programming, functional programming, and inductive definitions. In *Proceedings of the International Workshop on Extensions of Logic Programming (ELP 1989) (LNCS)* (Vol. 475, pp. 283-309). Berlin: Springer. 10.1007/BFb0038699

Sannella, D., & Tarlecki, A. (2012). *Foundations of algebraic specification and formal software development.* Berlin: Springer. doi:10.1007/978-3-642-17336-3

Schaefer, C. A., Pankratius, V., & Tichy, W. F. (2009). Atune-IL: An instrumentation language for auto-tuning parallel applications. In *Proceedings of the 15th International Euro-Par Conference (Euro-Par'2009) (LNCS)* (Vol. 5704, pp. 9-20). Berlin: Springer. 10.1007/978-3-642-03869-3_5

Skillicorn, D. B. (1991). Models for practical parallel computation. *International Journal of Parallel Programming, 20*(2), 133–158. doi:10.1007/BF01407840

Tapus, C., Chung, I.-H., & Hollingsworth, J. K. (2002). Active Harmony: Towards automated performance tuning. In *Proceedings of the 2002 ACM/IEEE conference on Supercomputing (SC'02)* (pp. 1-11). Los Alamitos, CA: IEEE Computer Society.

Vuduc, R., Demmel, J. W., & Yelick, K. A. (2005). OSKI: A library of automatically tuned sparse matrix kernels. *Journal of Physics: Conference Series, 16*(1), 521–530. doi:10.1088/1742-6596/16/1/071

Whaley, R., Petitet, A., & Dongarra, J. J. (2001). Automated empirical optimizations of software and the ATLAS Project. *Parallel Computing, 27*(1-2), 3–35. doi:10.1016/S0167-8191(00)00087-9

Yi, Q., Seymour, K., You, H., Vuduc, R., & Quinlan, D. (2007). POET: Parameterized optimizations for empirical tuning. In *Proceedings of the Parallel and Distributed Processing Symposium 2007 (IPDPS 2007)* (pp. 447). Piscataway, NJ: IEEE Computer Society.

Yushchenko, K. L., Tseytlin, G. O., Hrytsay, V. P., & Terzyan, T. K. (1989). *Multilevel structured design of programs: Theoretical basis, tools.* Moscow: Finansy i statistika. (in Russian)

KEY TERMS AND DEFINITIONS

Algebra of Algorithmics: A direction within the Ukrainian algebraic-cybernetic school rising from fundamental works of Academician V. M. Glushkov and intended for formalization of processes of design, transformation and synthesis of algorithms and programs in various subject domains.

Algebraic Programming: A special form of programming activity in which programs are constructed in terms of algebraic objects and their transformations. Objects of a subject domain and reasoning about the objects are represented by algebraic expressions.

Auto-Tuning: The paradigm of software application optimization allowing to adapt computations executed by a program to a runtime environment in order to achieve one or a few goals — a reduction of time expenses, energy consumption or a computation cost.

Glushkov's System of Algorithmic Algebras (SAA, Glushkov's Algebra): The two-sorted algebra focused on analytical form of representation of algorithms and formalized transformation of these representations.

Modified System of Algorithmic Algebras (SAA-M): The extension of the Glushkov's system of algorithmic algebras (SAA) intended for formalization of parallel algorithms.

Parallel Regular Scheme (PRS): The representation of asynchronous algorithm in the modified system of algorithmic algebras (SAA-M).

Regular Scheme (RS): A representation of an algorithm in the system of algorithmic algebras (SAA).

Chapter 2
Formalized Algorithm Design and Auto-Tuning of Programs

ABSTRACT

This chapter deals with the process of formalized design of sequential and parallel algorithms based on algorithm algebras. It gives the main concepts associated with metarules of schemes design (convolution, involution, reinterpretation, transformation). The SAA/1 language focused on natural linguistic algorithm representation and based on Glushkov's algebras is described. The algebra-grammatical models for parameter-driven generation of algorithm specifications based on higher-level schemes (hyperschemes) are then constructed. The authors propose the extension of the well-known PRAM model that is the basis of program auto-tuning. The hyperschemes and the auto-tuning are the means of increasing the adaptability of algorithms and programs to specific conditions of their use (for example, target computing platform). Some examples of formalized design of parallel sorting algorithm schemes using operations of Glushkov's algebras are given.

INTRODUCTION

This chapter is devoted to facilities of formalized description and transformation of structured schemes of algorithms (sequential and parallel), represented in analytical and natural linguistic forms. The mentioned facilities are based on V. M. Glushkov's system of algorithmic algebras considered in Chapter 1. The following metarules of schemes design are examined: convolution

DOI: 10.4018/978-1-5225-9384-3.ch002

(abstracting), involution (detailed elaboration), reorientation (combination of convolution and involution) and transformation (modification of a scheme by means of application of equalities). Metarules are applied for transition between algorithms and generation of new algorithmic knowledge. The algorithmic language SAA/1 considered in this chapter is intended for multilevel structured designing and documenting of algorithms and programs in a natural linguistic form.

One of the essential problems of the algebra of algorithmics (Andon, Doroshenko, Tseytlin, & Yatsenko, 2007) is to increase the adaptability of programs to specific conditions of their use (e.g., optimizing application code for a given parallel platform). In particular, the problem can be solved by parameter-driven generation of algorithm specifications based on higher-level algorithms which are called hyperschemes (Yatsenko, 2012; Yushchenko, Tseytlin, & Galushka, 1989). The hyperscheme is a parameterized algorithm for solving a certain class of problems; setting specific values of parameters and subsequent interpretation of a hyperscheme allows obtaining algorithms adapted to specific conditions of their use. Hyperschemes are adjacent to well-known methods of transformational synthesis: term rewriting systems (Baader & Nipkow, 1999; Doroshenko & Shevchenko, 2006), mixed computations (Bulyonkov, 1990) and macrogeneration (Dybvig, 2000). In this chapter, the approach to development of sequential and parallel schemes of algorithms is considered, which is based on the use of algebra-grammatical means of parameter-driven generation of algorithm specifications.

Another approach to program optimization is provided by auto-tuning (Durillo & Fahringer, 2014; Naono, Teranishi, Cavazos, & Suda, 2010; Tichy, 2014), which is the methodology automating the search for the optimal program version out of a set of provided possibilities by running each candidate and measuring its performance on a given computing architecture. In this chapter, the parallel computation model for auto-tuning based on the extension of the well-known abstract parallel machine with random memory access (PRAM) (Eppstein & Galil, 1988) is considered.

The chapter also contains the examples of formalized design of parallel sorting algorithms using the facilities of the modified system of algorithmic algebra SAA (SAA-M) considered in Chapter 1.

Metarules for Designing Algorithm Specifications

The process of algorithm design in algorithmics is associated with application of the following design metarules:

- **involution:** the process of descending design of algorithm schemes;
- **convolution:** the transition to algorithm schemes belonging to a higher level of algorithm description;
- **reinterpretation:** combined design of algorithms, consisting in consecutive application of convolution and involution;
- **transformation:** the process of conversion of algorithms using algebraic equalities.

The involution, convolution and reinterpretation metarules are based on usage of the system of equalities

$$J = \{v_1 = T_1; v_2 = T_2; \ldots; v_r = T_r\},$$

where v_i are predicate and operator variables; T_i are algebraic terms represented in SAA-M, $i=1,2,\ldots,r$.

The regular scheme (RS) of an algorithm which does not contain occurrences of the variables v_i is called an *interpreted scheme*.

The scheme is called *partially interpreted*, if it contains occurrences of the variables v_i and basic predicates and/or operators.

The scheme not containing basic elements is called *non-interpreted*.

Non-interpreted and partially interpreted schemes are called *processing strategies*.

The metarule of *convolution* of the regular scheme F by the system of equalities J consists in finding all the entries of the right parts T_i of the equalities in the scheme F and replacing them with the corresponding left parts (variables) v_i. The result of the convolution of the scheme F by the system J is the processing strategy $s_1 = F \uparrow J$. The convolution is aimed at abstracting the regular scheme.

The metarule of *involution* of the regular scheme F based on the system J, consists in finding all the entries of the variables v_i in the scheme F and replacing them with the corresponding right parts T_i of the equalities. The result of the involution of the scheme F by the system J is the regular scheme

$s_2 = F \downarrow J$. The involution is applied for more detailed elaboration of the regular scheme.

The *reorientation* of the scheme F_1 into the scheme F_2 is a derivative metarule which consists in convolution of F_1 by the system J_1 and involution of the obtained strategy by the system J_2: $F_2 = (F_1 \uparrow J_1) \downarrow J_2$.

The special case of reorientation is the *reinterpretation* of a scheme, which is the replacement of its basic elements (operators and predicates). The reinterpretation defines interrelation between regular schemes which have identical algorithmic structure, but different interpretation in terms of basic concepts of a subject domain.

By means of the metarules, a transition between algorithms is carried out and new algorithmic knowledge in a subject domain is generated.

The metarule of *transformation* is a conversion of schemes as a result of application of equalities

$$t_1(x_1, x_2, ..., x_s) = t_2(x_1, x_2, ..., x_s),$$

where t_1 and t_2 are terms represented in SAA-M, which depend on the variables $x_1, x_2, ..., x_s$.

Example 1. Consider the use of the metarules of convolution and involution for transition from the sorting algorithm *Bubble* to a search algorithm. The sorting algorithm processes the input numerical array M, which is initially marked in the following way:

$$M : H \ Y_1 \ a_1 \ a_2 \ ... \ a_n \ K,$$

where H and K are markers fixing the beginning and the end of the array M; a_i is the element of the array, $i=1,...,n$; Y_1 is the pointer moving over M in direction from left to right.

The regular scheme of the bubble sorting algorithm is the following:

$$Bubble = \{[Sorted(M)]\{[d(Y_1, K)]([l > r \mid Y_1] \ Transp(l, r \mid Y_1), E) * R(Y_1)\} * SET(Y_1, H)\},$$

where $Sorted(M)$ is the predicate taking true value, if the array M is sorted and false otherwise; $d(Y_1, K)$ is the predicate taking true value, if Y_1 reached the marker K and false otherwise; $l>r|Y_1$ is the predicate which takes true value, if the specified relation holds for the elements located directly to the left and to the right of the pointer Y_1; $Transp(l,r|Y_1)$ is the operator which swaps the elements adjacent to the pointer Y_1; E is the identity operator, which does not change a state of the array; $R(Y_1)$ is the operator shifting the pointer Y_1 over the array M one symbol to the right; $SET(Y_1,H)$ is the operator placing the pointer Y_1 in a position directly to the right of the marker H.

For a transition to a search algorithm, the convolution and involution metarules will be applied.

The convolution is used for abstracting the regular scheme and is based on usage of the following system of equalities:

$$J' = \{N_1 = Sorted(M); N_2 = d(Y_1,K); N_3 = l>r\,|\,Y_1;$$
$$O_1 = Transp(l,r\,|\,Y_1); O_2 = SET(Y_1,H)\},$$

where N_i are predicate variables $(i=1,2,3)$; O_j are operator variables $(j=1,2)$.

The convolution of the *Bubble* scheme consists in replacement of predicates and operators of the scheme by corresponding variables N_i and O_j. The result of the convolution of the scheme based on the system J' is the following partially interpreted regular scheme:

$$S_1 = \{[N_1]\,\{[N_2]\,([N_3]\,O_1,E) * R(P_1)\} * O_2\}.$$

Further, the above scheme S_1 will be converted to an algorithm of searching records in a file. The search algorithm will be applied to a file F_0 (a sequence of formatted records)

$$F_0 : H\ Y_1\ a_1\ a_2\ ...\ a_n\ K,$$

where H, K are markers fixing the beginning and the end of file F_0; Y_1 is a pointer moving over file F_0; a_i is a record in the file.

Records in file F_0 are searched according to the array of queries

$$AQ : H\ Y_2\ q_1\ q_2\ ...\ q_s\ K,$$

where each query $q_i: D \rightarrow E_2$ is the predicate defined on the set $D = \{a_1, a_2, \ldots, a_n\}$ of records of the file F_0 and takes values in the set $E_2 = \{0,1\}$ for any $i = 1, \ldots, s$. If $q_i(a) = 1$ for some element $a \in D$, then element a satisfies the query q_i.

For converting the scheme S_1 to the search algorithm, the involution metarule is applied, based on the use of the following system of equalities:

$$J'' = \{N_1 = d(Y_2, K); N_2 = d(Y_1, K); N_3 = SQUERY(r \mid Y_1);$$
$$O_1 = OUTPUT(r \mid Y_1); O_2 = R(Y_2)\},$$

where N_i are predicate variables ($i = 1,2,3$); O_j are operator variables ($j = 1,2$); $d(Y_2, F)$ is the predicate, which takes true value, if the pointer Y_2 reached the end of the array AQ; $d(Y_1, F)$ is the predicate, which takes true value, if the pointer Y_1 reached the end of the file F_0; $SQUERY(r \mid Y_1)$ is the predicate, which takes true value, if the record is found; $OUTPUT(r \mid Y_1)$ is the operator outputting the search result; $R(Y_2)$ is the operator shifting the pointer Y_2 over the array AQ.

The involution consists in replacement of the variables N_i and O_j by corresponding predicates and operators. The result of the involution of scheme S_1 by the system J'' is the following scheme:

$$Search = \{[d(Y_2, K)] \{[d(Y_1, K)] ([SQUERY(r \mid Y_1)] OUTPUT(r \mid Y_1), E) * R(Y_1)\} * R(Y_2)\}.$$

According to the above scheme, the pointer Y_1 scans in direction from left to right over the file F_0. The file F_0 may contain more than one record satisfying the current query which is observed by the pointer Y_2. When such a record is found, operator $OUTPUT(r \mid Y_1)$ is executed and the pointer Y_1 moves by one position to the right. Further, the search is continued until the pointer Y_1 reaches the end of the file. After the pointer Y_1 returns to the beginning of the file, the algorithm proceeds to process the next query.

Example 2. Consider the use of the transformation metarule for modification of the following fragment of *Bubble* scheme:

$$([l > r \mid Y_1] \, Transp(l, r \mid Y_1), E) * R(Y_1).$$

The transformation of the above scheme is based on using the following equality, which is the distributive property of composition and branching operations:

$$R_1: ([u] A, B) * C = ([u] A * C, B * C),$$

where u is a predicate variable; A, B, C are operator variables.

Equality R_1 is applicable under any interpretations of included variables. The following interpretations of variables included in R_1 are introduced:

$$u = l > r \mid Y_1; \ A = Transp(l, r \mid Y_1); \ B = E; \ C = R(Y_1).$$

The given interpretations are substituted as values of variables into equality R_1 and the equality is applied in a direction from right to left. As a result, the following regular scheme is obtained:

$$([l > r \mid Y_1] \ Transp(l, r \mid Y_1) * R(Y_1), \ E * R(Y_1)).$$

The use of the metarules considered in this subsection provides a capability of improvement of algorithms designed in SAA-M by a selected criterion, for example, used memory, computing time and other.

The Algorithmic Language SAA/1

The algorithmic language SAA/1 (Andon et al., 2007) is intended for multilevel structured designing and documenting of sequential and parallel algorithms and programs. The mathematical basis of this language is SAA-M (see Chapter 1). The descriptions of algorithms in SAA/1 language are called SAA schemes and the purpose of this subsection consists in explanation of possibilities of this language.

The basic objects of SAA/1 language are abstractions of operators (converters of data) and conditions (predicates). Identifiers of predicates and operators are subdivided into standard and semantic and can be either basic (elementary) or compound. *Basic* elements are considered in an SAA scheme as a primary, atomic, indivisible abstractions. *Compound* elements are designed from elementary ones by means of the following SAA-M operations represented in a natural language form (see also Chapter 1, subsection "The Main Algorithm Algebras"):

- disjunction: 'condition1' OR 'condition2';
- conjunction: 'condition1' AND 'condition2';
- negation: NOT 'condition';
- sequential execution of operators: "operator1" THEN "operator2"
- (or "operator1"; "operator2");
- branching: IF 'condition' THEN "operator1" ELSE "operator2" END IF;
- cyclic operator execution: WHILE NOT 'condition-of-loop-termination' LOOP "operator" END OF LOOP;
- asynchronous execution of operators: "operator1" PARALLEL "operator2";
- control point: CP 'condition';
- synchronizer: WAIT 'condition'.

Standard identifiers are defined in the alphabet consisting of English letters, numbers and a symbol of underscore. A semantic identifier of a predicate is the sequence of any length of any symbols set into single quotes. A semantic identifier of an operator is set into double quotes. Usage of semantic identifiers essentially facilitates understanding of algorithms represented in SAA/1 language. For example, the following texts can serve as semantic identifiers of an operator and a condition:

"Place the pointer Y(1) at the beginning of the array (M)"

'The array (M) is sorted'

Example 3. As an illustration, consider the following SAA scheme of a bubble sorting algorithm.

```
SCHEME BUBBLE SORT ====
     "Sequential bubble sort"
   END OF COMMENTS

"BUBBLE"
==== "START"
     THEN
     "Place the pointer Y(1) at the beginning of the array (M)"
     THEN
     WHILE NOT 'The array (M) is sorted'
     LOOP
        WHILE NOT 'The pointer Y(1) is at the end of the array
(M)'
        LOOP
```

```
            IF 'The elements l > r at pointer Y(1) in the array
(M)'

            THEN "Transpose the elements l, r at pointer Y(1)
                  in the array (M)"
            ELSE "Empty operator"
            END IF
            THEN
            "Shift the pointer Y(1) by (1) element in the array
(M)
               to the right"
         END OF LOOP
         THEN
         "Place the pointer Y(1) at the beginning of the array
(M)"
      END OF LOOP
      THEN
      "FIN";

"START"
==== "Open the file (F1) for reading"
      THEN
      "Read the data from the file (F1) to the array (M)"
      THEN
      "Close the file (F1)";

"FIN"
==== "Open the file (F2) for writing"
      THEN
      "Write the array (M) into the file (F2)"
      THEN
      "Close the file (F2)";

END OF SCHEME BUBBLE SORT
```

The SAA scheme begins with the SCHEME keyword followed by a name of the scheme and comments to it. The end of the title of the SAA scheme is designated by a keyword sentence END OF COMMENTS. The name of SAA scheme can be character sequence of any length consisting of English alphabet letters, numbers, a point, a comma, minus and slash symbols, and also round, square and angle brackets. The presence of the comment (together with a chain of symbols "=") is optional. Any SAA scheme ends with the END keyword followed by an optional SCHEME keyword and a name of SAA scheme.

It is easy to see the functionality and narrative style of notation of the given algorithm, and also its multilevel structure. The levels of the scheme are marked by the left parts of equalities, and the structure of each level is concretized (in terms of SAA-M) by the right part of the corresponding equality. The left part of equality is separated from the right one by the chain of symbols "=". Equalities are separated from each other by a semicolon.

In the given example, only semantic identifiers appear, which are abstractions of conditions and operators. The abstractions, the identifiers of which are included in the left parts of equalities of SAA schemes, are abstractions of compound operators and conditions, and the rest are elements primary at a given level of algorithm description. Thus, in the above illustrative example, abstractions of compound operators are designated by semantic identifiers "BUBBLE", "START" and "FIN".

The prominent features of SAA/1 language are the following:

- the multilevel structure of SAA schemes represented in the form of a list of equalities; each next equality concretizes (by means of SAA-M) an abstraction of some operator or a condition, which identifier is included in one of previous equalities;
- the use of semantic and standard identifiers of operators and conditions, which allows designing algorithms both in the style close to a natural language and in the form of algebraic formulas;
- the redundancy of syntactic representation of the same objects and operations of the language;
- an arbitrary length of identifiers of conditions and operators.

Thus, the basis of SAA/1 language are the facilities of Glushkov's algorithmic algebras and their modifications, focused on formalization of sequential and parallel algorithms by means of structured schemes. The main feature of SAA/1 language is its focus on multilevel descending, ascending and combined design of classes of algorithms and programs, associated with a chosen subject domain. Synthesis of programs based on SAA schemes can be carried out in nonautomated and automated modes. In the first case, the algorithm represented as SAA scheme is translated manually to a program text in a chosen programming language (target language). SAA/1 language is the basis of the method of multilevel structured design of programs and its tools (Andon et al., 2007; Doroshenko, Zhereb, & Yatsenko, 2013; Yatsenko, 2012) providing automated and automatic (under certain conditions) synthesis of programs in a target language. During the synthesis, semantic libraries containing interpretations of basic operations of SAA/1 language are used. These interpretations are represented in terms of a target language.

Such interpretation is used not only in connection with implementation of well-known algorithmic structures, but also data structures. Thereby, it is a question of an interrelated design of algorithms and data structures. Along with semantic libraries, the libraries of basic concepts adequate to actual subject domains are constructed. The construction of semantic libraries and libraries of subject domains is associated with development of a family of SAA scheme languages based on SAA/1. So, at development of the corresponding library of basic interpretations, the construction of specialized languages of SAA schemes for a description of sequential and parallel algorithms in various subject domains (sorting, search in multilevel files, designing of language processors, etc.) (Andon et al., 2007; Doroshenko, Tseytlin, Yatsenko, & Zachariya, 2006; Doroshenko et al., 2013) is carried out.

Parameter-Driven Models for Generation of Algorithm Schemes

In this subsection, the approach to generation of sequential and parallel algorithms based on the algebra of hyperschemes is considered. Hyperscheme is a parameterized algebra-algorithmic specification intended for solving a specific class of problems. By setting parameter values with subsequent interpretation of a hyperscheme, an algorithm scheme optimized to specific conditions of its use is obtained.

The basis of the algebraic apparatus of parameter-driven scheme generation is the abstract automaton model of the parameter-driven generator of texts (Yushchenko et al., 1989) and also facilities of SAA-M. Similarly to the abstract automaton model of a computer, considered in Chapter 1, the model of the parameter-driven generator of texts works according to a feedback principle (see Figure 1). A stack automaton $\overline{\Psi}$ is used as a control automaton and an automaton $\overline{\Phi}$ with a tape $\tilde{L}$ is used as an operational one.

Figure 1. An abstract automaton model of the parameter-driven generator of texts

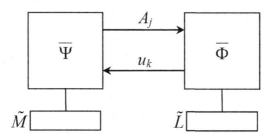

The tape $\tilde{L}$ is used for writing the text of a regular scheme being generated. The set $\overline{M}$ of states of the automaton $\overline{\Phi}$ is associated with parameters which control the generation of schemes. The elements of the information set $\overline{P} = \overline{M} \times \overline{L}$ (where $\overline{L}$ is a set of states of the tape $\tilde{L}$) are called the states of the operational structure. On each step of work of the automaton, the set of logical conditions $\{u_k | k \in I\}$ defined on the set $\overline{P}$ comes from the operational to the control automaton. According to these conditions and the content of the stack $\tilde{M}$, the control automaton initiates the execution of some operator. The set of operators $Op = \{A_j | j \in I\}$ is divided into two disjoint sets: R_T (terminal operators) and R_N (nonterminal operators). The execution of a terminal operator from the set R_T consists in a change of a current state of the operational structure, which, in particular, can be writing some text on the tape $\tilde{L}$. The execution of an operator $A \in R_N$ at the current state $p \in \overline{P}$ consists in writing some term $F_N(A,p)$ to the stack $\tilde{M}$ and its further interpretation by the control automaton. The term $F_N(A,p)$ is an analog of notions of macro definition, procedure, subroutine. The stack $\tilde{M}$ is used for processing nested and recursive terms. The generated text is a content of tape $\tilde{L}$ at a final state of the operational structure.

Algebra of Hyperschemes

The algebra of hyperschemes is the formalism, which is based on the above abstract automaton model and is applied for parameter-driven generation of regular schemes of algorithms represented in SAA-M. The algebra of hyperschemes is a two-sorted algebra

$$AHS = <\{Pr, Op\}; \Omega_{AHS}>,$$

where *Pr* is a set of predicates defined on the information set $\overline{P}$ and taking the values of four-valued logic $E_4=\{0,1,\mu,\eta\}$, where 0 is for false, 1 is for true, μ is for unknown, η is for "not computed"; *Op* is a set of operators defined on information set $\overline{P}$ and taking values in set $\overline{P}$; Ω_{AHS} is a signature of operations.

The set of predicates is associated with parameters, which control the process of generation of a regular scheme of an algorithm. The operations of the signature Ω_{AHS} are similar to the operations of SAA-M signature (see Chapter 1). In particular, the signature Ω_{AHS} includes Boolean operations, i.e. disjunction $u \vee u'$, conjunction $u \wedge u'$, negation $\bar{u}$, prediction $A \cdot u$, and operator operations: composition $A*B$, branching $([u]A,B)$, loop $\{[u]A\}$, switch operation $SELECT(u_1 \rightarrow A_1, ..., u_n \rightarrow A_n)$ and other (Yushchenko et al., 1989). The difference from SAA-M is that predicates from the set *Pr* map elements of the information set $\overline{P}$ to the elements of the set $E_4=\{0,1,\mu,\eta\}$, where the additional value η stands for "not computed". The element η is used to indicate that the value of a condition cannot be calculated due to the lack of information about parameter values. (Such condition is considered below in Example 4.) The truth tables for this four-valued logic are given in (Yushchenko et al., 1989).

The application of the operator $A \in Op$ at the state $p \in \overline{P}$ leads to a transition to the new state $A(p) \in \overline{P}$ and writing the fragment $F_h(a,p)$ of a regular scheme being generated on the tape $\tilde{L}$, where $F_h(A,p)$ is the function that specifies the generation technique for all operations of signature of *AHS* and will be considered below.

By analogy with SAA-M, an operator representation of an algorithm in *AHS* is called a *regular hyperscheme* (RHS) (Yushchenko et al., 1989). Each RHS *A*, being applied to a state $p \in \overline{P}$, generates a regular scheme $F_h(A,p)$. The hyperscheme *A* defines the class $L(A)$ of regular schemes in SAA-M: $L(A) = \{F_h(A,p) \mid p \in \overline{P}\}$.

The function $F_h(A,p)$ for the main operations of *AHS* was defined in paper (Yushchenko et al., 1989). Particularly, the composition operation $A*B$ generates the operator $C=A*B$ without changes, according to the function $F_h(C,p) = F_h(A,p)*F_h(B,p)$, where $p \in \overline{P}$.

The operation of alternative $([u]A,B)$, where $u \in Pr, A \in Op, B \in Op$ generates the operator $C=([u]A,B)$, such that for each $p \in \overline{P}$

$$F_h(C,p) = \begin{cases} F_h(A,p), \text{ if } u(p) = 1; \\ F_h(B,p), \text{ if } u(p) = 0; \\ ([u(p)] \, F_h(A,p), \, F_h(B,A(p))), \text{ if } u(p) = \cdot \, ; \\ e, \text{ if } u(p) = \frac{1}{4} \end{cases}$$

where *e* is an empty text.

According to the given definition, the result of interpretation of the operation of alternative will be the text of the operator *A*, if the value of the condition $u(p)$ is true. The text of the operator *B* is generated, if the condition $u(p)$ is false. The text of the operation of an alternative without changes is generated, if the value of $u(p)$ was not computed, and the empty text will be the result, if an error occurred during the interpretation.

Example 4. Consider the application of *AHS* to transformation of a hybrid sorting algorithm *HSort*. The algorithm reads a set of input numerical arrays and calls one of the sorting algorithms (*insertionSort*, *quickSort* or *mergeSort*) depending on the size *n* of an input array (Yatsenko, 2012). The arrays of size *n<MIN* are sorted by *insertionSort*, the arrays of size *n>MAX* are processed by *quickSort* and arrays getting to an interval [*MIN,MAX*] are sorted by *mergeSort* algorithm. The regular scheme of the algorithm is

$$HSort = INIT * \{[END\_OF\_SET] \, READ\_ARRAY(A) * ([n < MIN] \, insertionSort(A,n),$$
$$([n > MAX] \, quickSort(A,n), \, mergeSort(A,n)))\},$$

where *INIT* is the initialization operator; *END_OF_SET* is the condition, which takes true value, if all the arrays from the input set have been processed, and takes false value otherwise; *READ_ARRAY(A)* is the operator which reads the array; *A* is the input array of length *n*.

Let it is in advance known that algorithm *HSort* will be applied in conditions when the size of all input arrays is in a certain range, say, not less than *MIN*. Then the given RS becomes superfluous and for its reduction it will be considered as a hyperscheme with a parameter *n*. At the stage of interpretation of hyperscheme *HSort*, predicate *n<MIN* takes value 0, whereas *n>MAX* takes value η. The condition *n>MAX* cannot be computed, because there is not enough information about the value of parameter *n* (it is only known that $n \geq MIN$). Assuming that the function F_h is identity on a set of all basic operators and conditions of the hyperscheme, the following reduced RS will be obtained:

$$F_h(HSort, p_0) = INIT * \{[END\_OF\_SET] \, READ\_ARRAY(A) *$$
$$* \, ([n > MAX] \, quickSort(A,n), \, mergeSort(A,n)))\},$$

where $p_0 \in \overline{P}$ is the initial state of the information set *IS*.

Thus, by setting various values of the parameter *n* of the hyperscheme *HSort* (in the considered case, the value $n \geq MIN$ was set), it is possible to obtain regular scheme, optimum for given conditions.

Example 5. The paper (Yatsenko, 2011) describes a more complex hybrid sorting scheme designed with the help of machine learning technique. This algorithm can also be considered as a hyperscheme. The fragment of the algorithm scheme represented in a natural linguistic form is given below.

```
HYPERSCHEME hybridSort2(A, n)
==== IF 'size <= 30' THEN
        IF 'runs <= 0.7' THEN "insertionSort(A, n)"
        ELSE IF 'runs > 0.7' THEN
                IF 'size <= 10' THEN "insertionSort(A, n)"
                ELSE IF 'size > 10' THEN "quickSort(A, n)"
                    END IF
                END IF
            END IF
        END IF
        ELSE IF 'size > 30' THEN
                IF 'size <= 40' THEN "insertionSort(A, n)"
                ELSE IF 'size > 40' THEN "quickSort(A, n)"
                    END IF
                END IF
            END IF
        END IF
```

In the given scheme, the selection of one of the algorithms is implemented based on the size *n* of the input array *A* and its presortedness degree (*runs*). The presortedness degree of the array *A* is computed according to the formula $runs(A)=runs\_up(A)/n$, where $runs\_up(A)$ is the number of ascending substrings, or the "runs up", of the array *A*; *runs*(A) takes values in the range $(0...1]$. Let it is in advance known that the algorithm described by the given scheme will be applied in conditions when the size of all input arrays is $n<20$, and the degree of presortedness is *runs*=0.9. Then, as a result of the interpretation of the hyperscheme, the following reduced SAA scheme is obtained:

```
SCHEME hybridSort3(A, n)
==== IF 'size <= 10' THEN "insertionSort(A, n)"
     ELSE IF 'size > 10' THEN "quickSort(A, n)"
           END IF
     END IF
```

By analogy with the modified SAA, in (Yushchenko et al., 1989) the modified *AHS* was proposed, oriented on sequential and parallel generation of sequential and parallel RS represented in SAA-M. The signature of the modified *AHS*, in particular, contains the operation of asynchronous disjunction *A//B*, consisting in parallel execution of the operators *A* and *B*. For generation of asynchronous disjunction, the operation of its sequential generation *(//)(A,B)* or the asynchronous generation *(///)(A,B)* is used. For synchronization of processes initiated by asynchronous disjunctions, control points and synchronizers are used. Each control point $CP(u)$ is associated with the condition u, which is false while a computation process has not yet reached the point $CP(u)$, and true from the moment of achievement of the given point. The synchronizer $S(u)$ implements the delay of computation process at false value of u until u gets true value. The application of these constructs is considered further.

Application of Hyperschemes to Representation of Derivation Algorithms in Generative Grammars

In this subsection, the algebra of hyperschemes is applied for representation of algorithms of inference control in structured design grammars. The approach is illustrated by an example of generating an algorithm from the subject domain of linear algebra.

Structured design grammar (SDG) (Andon et al., 2007) is the 5-tuple

$$G^D = (T^D, N^D, \sigma^D, P^D, U^D),$$

where $T^D = \bar{Z} \cup \bar{R}$ is a set of terminal symbols, $\bar{Z}$ is a set of basic conditions, operators and data objects, $\bar{R}$ s a set of separators: symbols of SAA-M operations, brackets, etc.; N^D is a set of non-terminal symbols (logical, operator and object metavariables); $\sigma^D \in N^D$ is a start symbol; $P^D = \{\beta_i: v_i \to w_i | i \in I\}$ is a set of rules; U^d is a derivation control algorithm. In this work derivation control algorithm is represented in the algebra of hyperschemes.

The set $L(G^D) = \{X \mid \sigma^D \stackrel{*}{\Rightarrow} X\}$ of parallel regular schemes (PRSs) over the basis Σ, which are generated from a start symbol σ^D in SDG G^D, forms the language $L(T^D)$, associated with a class of programs being designed.

A variant of a structured design grammar is a matrix SDG. The *matrix SDG* is the SDG $G^D = (T^D, N^D, \sigma^D, P^D, U^D)$ the set of rules of which $P^D = \{m_j | j \in I\}$ consists of generalized (matrix) productions of the form:

$$m_j: \left\| \begin{matrix} \gamma_1; \gamma_2; \dots \\ \dots \quad \dots \quad \dots \\ \gamma_i; \gamma_{l+1}; \dots \end{matrix} \right\|,$$

where γ_l are productions of the form $v_l \to w_l$, $l \in I$. In the process of derivation, generalized productions can be applied both sequentially and in parallel. In the case of sequential application, the rules are written in one line and are separated by a semicolon, and at parallel application they are written in a column.

Example 6. Consider the process of generating a scheme of parallel matrix multiplication algorithm with the usage of SDG and *AHS*. The algorithm multiplies two rectangular matrices: $A = (a_{lj})_{M \times N}$ and $B = (b_{lj})_{N \times Q}$. The elements of a resultant matrix $C = (c_{lj})_{M \times Q} = A \times B$ are defined according to the formula

$$c_{lj} = \sum_{k=0}^{N-1} a_{lk} \cdot b_{kj}, \quad l = 0, \dots, M-1, j = 0, \dots, Q-1,$$

where the elements of matrices are indexed starting from a zero.

In the parallel algorithm, computations are performed by K processors in such a way that the first processor computes the first $(M \cdot Q) / K$ elements of a resultant matrix, the second one processes the following $(M \cdot Q) / K$ elements, and so on. Thus, the initial matrix A and the final matrix C are divided into horizontal blocks shown in Figure 2. The processor with the number i multiplies block A_i by matrix B and as a result, the block C_i is obtained. All blocks of matrices are also indexed beginning with zero.

Figure 2. Splitting of matrices into blocks in the parallel matrix multiplication algorithm

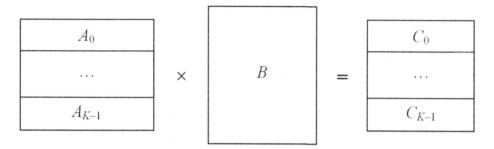

The parallel regular scheme of the algorithm is

$MatrixMultiplication(K) = START(K)$

$*(Thread(A_0, B) \; // \; Thread(A_1, B) \; // \; ... \; // \; Thread(A_{K-1}, B)) * S(PROC\_FIN) * FIN,$

where $START(K)$ is the operator of initialization of matrices and preparation for launching K parallel threads; $Thread(A_i, B)$ is the operator executing the multiplication of the i-th block of the matrix A by the matrix B; $S(PROC\_FIN)$ is the synchronizer operation, which delays the computation until all threads complete their work; FIN is the final operator which outputs the resultant matrix C.

The regular scheme of the compound operator $Thread(A_i, B)$ is presented below.

$Thread(A_i, B) =$

 $(start := M / K * i) *$

 $* (end := M / K * (i+1)) *$

 $* \; For(l, start, end-1) \; \{$

  $For(j, 0, Q-1) \; \{$

   $(value := A[l][0] * B[0][j]) *$

   $* For(k, 1, N-1) \; \{ \; value: \; = value + A[l][k] + B[k][j] \; \} *$

   $* (C[l][j] := value) \; \}$

  $\} * CP(PROC\_FIN(i)),$

where $CP(PROC\_FIN(i))$ is the control point fixing the moment of completion of computations in the thread with index i.

Consider the matrix SDG $G_1^D = (T_1^D, N_1^D, \sigma_1^D, P_1^D, U_1^D)$ intended for generating the class of parallel regular schemes *MatrixMultiplication(K)*. The SDG generates algorithms from the mentioned class with a various number of parallel threads K. The rules of the grammar G_1^D provide the generation of parallel threads *Thread(A_i, B)* by changing the values of the parameter i from 0 to $K - 1$. The set of rules P_1^D of the SDG G_1^D is the following:

$m_0: \left\| \sigma_1^D \to START(0) * PRS1 * S(PROC\_FIN) * FIN \right\|,$

$m_1: \left\| PRS1 \to Thread(A_0, B) \; // \; PRS1 \right\|,$

$m_2: \left\| \begin{array}{l} Thread(A_i, B) \; // \; PRS1 \to Thread(A_i, B) \; // \; Thread(A_{i+1}, B) \; // \; PRS1 \\ START(i) \to START(i+1) \end{array} \right\|,$

     at $i < K - 2$,

$m_3: \left\| \begin{array}{l} Thread(A_i, B) \; // \; PRS1 \to Thread(A_i, B) \; // \; Thread(A_{i+1}, B) \\ START(i) \to START(i+2) \end{array} \right\|,$

     at $i = K - 2$,

where $START(i) \in N_1^D$, $PRS1 \in N_1^D$ are operator nonterminals; $A_i \in N_1^D$ is an object nonterminal.

The process of generation of the algorithm scheme according to given rules is the following. The rule m_0 forms the general structure of the scheme. With the help of the rule m_1, the thread with the index 0 is formed. Then the rule set m_2 recursively generates the next threads of the PRS at $i<K-2$. The process completes with application of the rule set m_3 at $i=K-2$.

Further, the approach to design hyperschemes representing algorithms of derivation control in context-free SDGs (Yushchenko et al., 1989) is considered.

Let $AHS = <\{Pr,Op\};\Omega_{AHS}>$ be defined on the information set $\overline{P}$ associated with parameters of derivation control in SDG $G^D = (T^D, N^D, \sigma^D, P^D, U^D)$. The rules $\beta_i: v_i \to w_i$ of the grammar G^D with identical left parts are written as the set of equalities f_i:

$$\{f_i: v_i = w_1^i \mid w_2^i \mid ... \mid w_{t_i}^i \mid i = 1, 2, ..., n\},$$

where t_i is the number of alternative rules in the i-th equality; v_i are the operator and logical metavariables (nonterminals); $w_1^i, w_2^i, ... , w_{t_i}^i$ are the right parts of the rules, which are operators and conditions including both terminal and nonterminal symbols. The mentioned metavariables are associated with corresponding compound operators and conditions of *AHS*. Basic operators and conditions of SAA-M, included into the right parts of rules of G^D, are associated with analogous basic elements of *AHS*. The application of a basic operator or a condition of *AHS* which has the value η at the state $p \in \overline{P}$ results in writing its text without changes on the tape $\tilde{L}$. The symbol of asynchronous disjunction (if it is present) included into expressions w_j^i ($i=1,2,...,n$; $j=1,2,...,t_i$), is substituted with the symbol of operation of asynchronous or sequential generation of asynchronous disjunction. The nonterminals v_i included into the equalities f_i, which have several alternative rules, are associated with the compound operator which is the composition of some operator $O_i \in Op$ and a switch operation:

$$v_i = O_i * \text{SELECT}([u_1^i] \to w_1^i, [u_2^i] \to w_2^i, ..., [u_{t_i}^i] \to w_{t_i}^i),$$

where u_j^i are conditions, such that $\forall p \in P: u_j^i(p) \neq \cdot$ ($j=1,2,...,t_i$). The operator O_i sets true value of one of the conditions and false value of other conditions u_j^i, depending on the current state $p \in \overline{P}$. At the execution of the operator O_i, writing a text on the tape $\tilde{L}$ is not carried out. (The operator O_i can be the operator $INC(i)$ increasing the parameter i by value 1.) The operators w_j^i

in the switch operation are expressions obtained based on the right parts w_j^i of the equalities f_i.

The grammar G^D is associated with the regular hyperscheme v_1:

$$v_1 = O_1 * \text{SELECT}([u_1^1] \to w_1^1, [u_2^1] \to w_2^1, ..., [u_{t_1}^1] \to w_{t_1}^1);$$

$$v_2 = O_2 * \text{SELECT}([u_1^2] \to w_1^2, [u_2^2] \to w_2^2, ..., [u_{t_2}^2] \to w_{t_2}^2);$$

$$...$$

$$v_n = O_n * \text{SELECT}([u_1^n] \to w_1^n, [u_2^n] \to w_2^n, ..., [u_{t_n}^n] \to w_{t_n}^n).$$

The result of application of the regular hyperscheme v_1 at the state $p \in \overline{P}$ is the PRS $F_h(v_1,p)$. Here $F_h(v_1,p) \in L(G^D)$, where $L(G^D)$ is the language generated by the grammar G^D.

Example 7. Consider the regular hyperscheme *MatrixMultiHS*, which is the derivation control algorithm for SDG G_1^D constructed in Example 6 and intended for generation of the class of asynchronous PRSs of matrix multiplication. The hyperscheme was built according to the above method for designing derivation control algorithms for formal grammars and is the following:

$MatrixMultHS = (i := -1) * (K := 4)$
$*START(K) * PRS1 * S(PROC\_FIN) * FIN;$

$PRS1 = INC(i) * SELECT([i < K - 1] \to (//)(Thread(A_i, B) \; // \; PRS1),$
  $[i = K - 1] \to Thread(A_i, B)).$

Here K is a parameter of the hyperscheme (the number of parallel threads); *PRS1* is the compound operator that recursively generates a sequence of threads; *INC(i)* is an increment operator that adds 1 to the value of the index variable i.

In the given hyperscheme, the operation of sequential generation of the asynchronous disjunction is used. The start symbol σ_1^D of the grammatics

G_1^D corresponds to the compound operator *MatrixMultHS* of the hyperscheme, and the nonterminal *PRS*1 corresponds to the compound operator with the same name. The operators *START*(K), *Thread*($A_p B$) and *FIN* are identities on the information set $\overline{P}$ and their execution consists in writing on the tape $\tilde{L}$ the text of the corresponding operator with current values of the variables i and K.

The execution of the hyperscheme *MatrixMultHS* begins with initialization of the variables i and K. The parameter K, which corresponds to a number of parallel threads, is assigned the value 4. Then, the text of the operator *START*(4) is generated. After this, the compound operator *PRS*1 is applied, in which with the help of changing the value of i from 0 to $K - 1$ and a switch operation, the branches *Thread*($A_p B$) are recursively formed. The generation of PRS is finished with writing the text of basic operator *FIN* on the tape $\tilde{L}$.

The result of the application of the hyperscheme *MatrixMultHS* at the state $p \in \overline{P}$ at the value of the parameter K=4 is the PRS *MatrixMultiplication*(4), written on the tape $\tilde{L}$:

MatrixMultiplication(4) $= START(4)$
$* (Thread(A_0, B) \, // \, Thread(A_1, B) \, // \, Thread(A_2, B) \, // \, Thread(A_3, B)) * S(PROC\_FIN) * FIN.$

Thus, setting specific values of the parameter K and subsequent interpretation of the hyperscheme allows obtaining regular schemes of matrix multiplication algorithms with corresponding number of threads.

For automating the design of algorithm schemes, hyperschemes and generation of algorithms and programs, the software toolkit was developed (Yatsenko, 2012), which is considered in Chapter 5.

Parallel Computation Model for Auto-Tuning

In this subsection, the abstract model which illustrates the optimization approaches for parallel programs is considered. The model is based on a well-known abstract parallel machine with random memory access (PRAM) (Eppstein & Galil, 1988).

Figure 3. The PRAM model of parallel computation

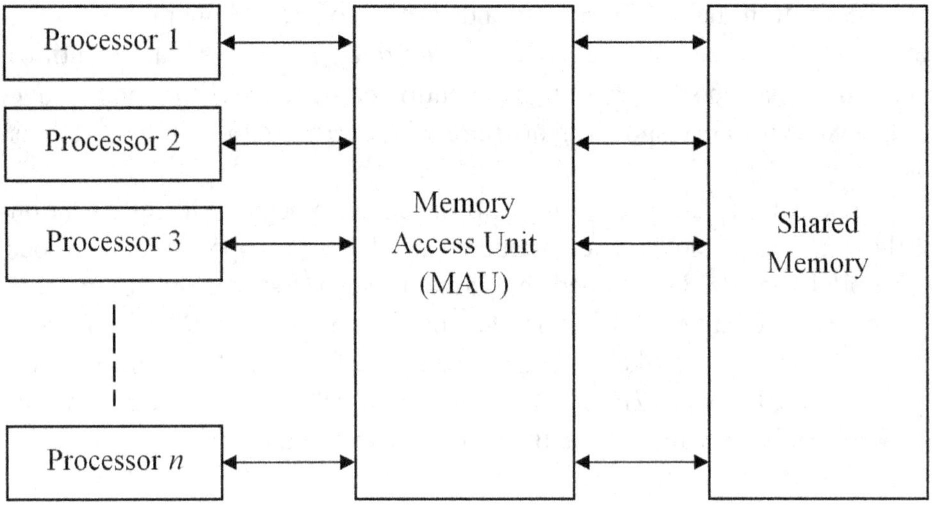

The Classic PRAM Model

The classic PRAM model (see Figure 3) consists of the following components:

- a set of n processors of the same type;
- a shared memory, through which the communication between processors is carried out;
- a memory access unit (MAU).

The main features of the PRAM model are the following:

- an unlimited number of processors $P_1, P_2, P_3, \ldots$;
- the volume of the shared memory is unlimited;
- each processor has its local memory (registers) of unlimited size;
- each processor can access any cell of the shared memory at a time;
- data are transferred to the PRAM algorithm as n elements stored in n memory cells;
- the results of PRAM algorithm consist of n elements stored in n memory cells;
- instructions of PRAM execute three-phase loops:
  - reading (if necessary) the data from a shared memory cell;
  - local computations (if they are given);

    ○   writing (if necessary) the data to a shared memory cell;
- processors execute three-phase instructions synchronously;
- the only possible method of data exchange between the processors is through the shared memory cells.

The PRAM model is useful and important for constructing parallel algorithms, since it is:

- natural — the number of operations that can be executed at a time is strictly limited by the number of processors;
- flexible — any processor can read and write to any shared memory cell at a fixed unit of time;
- simple — the model abstracts from any synchronization and communication overhead, which facilitates analysis of correctness and complexity of PRAM algorithms;
- can be used as a benchmark — if a problem has no efficient solution in PRAM, then it is not solvable on any other parallel machine;
- useful idealization and generalization of existing parallel machines with a shared memory.

The access to a shared memory in PRAM is regulated by the following strategies:

- **Exclusive Read Exclusive Write (EREW):** every memory cell can be read or written to by only one processor at a time;
- **Concurrent Read Exclusive Write (CREW):** multiple processors can read a memory cell, but only one can write at a time;
- **Concurrent Read Concurrent Write (CRCW):** multiple processors can read and write;
- **Exclusive Read Concurrent Write (ERCW):** multiple processors can write to a memory cell, but the only one can read at a time (has never been used in practice).

The semantics of the concurrent read is obvious while the concurrent write is further defined as:

- common — all processors write the same value, otherwise is illegal;
- arbitrary — only one arbitrary attempt is successful, others retire;
- priority — processor rank indicates who gets to write;

- another kind of array reduction operation like SUM, Logical AND or MAX.

The Extension of the Classic PRAM Model and Program Optimization

Consider the special PRAM* model which extends the model PRAM from the previous subsection with additional memory level and uses only one strategy for management of simultaneous access to both levels. The new model PRAM* more accurately characterizes the architecture of modern computing systems (although it is not absolutely complete) and allows to specify the nature of optimization transformations carried out by an auto-tuner (Ivanenko, Doroshenko, & Zhereb, 2014). Below, the main definitions of the model are considered.

It is assumed that the computations are executed in the parallel system which consists of N processors, where $N \in \mathbb{N}$. That is, the number of processors is unlimited, but fixed in each specific case. The *processor* is the computing unit which is able to autonomously execute computations (corresponds to the concept of a microprocessor core in contemporary computing systems). All processors of the system are considered as homogeneous.

The size of the local memory (registers) of each processor is assumed to be limited and will be designated as M_{loc}. The access time to the local memory is denoted as T_{loc}. All data that do not fit into the local memory are stored in the shared memory M_{shar}. Its size is unlimited, but the access speed is much slower: $T_{loc} \ll T_{shar}$.

The simultaneous access to the shared memory is regulated by the Exclusive Read Exclusive Write (EREW) strategy, as it is the "weakest" strategy in the sense of time complexity. The algorithm in models with "stronger" strategies CREW and CRCW will have the same or less time and computing complexity than with EREW. Therefore, optimization transformations efficient in EREW, will be efficient with any strategy.

Thus, in PRAM*, only one processor can read data from or write to a particular memory cell. All the other processors which at the same time intend to read or write data to this cell, wait in the queue. The time that processors wait for write access to the shared memory is denoted as $T_{N_{ew}}$.

Parallel programs usually contain critical sections, i.e. regions of code that cannot be executed in parallel. When such section is executed by a single processor, other processors cannot execute the same section, therefore the computations inside a critical section can be modeled by a sequential RAM model (Eppstein & Galil, 1988). Also additional time is needed to synchronize the results of critical sections execution on different processors. The execution time of all critical sections is denoted as $T_{N_{seq}}$. The time of parallel execution (i.e. non-critical sections of code) is denoted as $T_{N_{par}}$.

In the model proposed in this subsection, each instruction is executed in the following three phases.

- Read the data from the global memory to local memory, if the data is not already present in the local memory, and if it is needed for instruction execution.
- Execute the instruction using the data from the local memory.
- Write instruction results to the global memory (optional).

The time spent on memory access by the processor with number i on the first and the third phases is $T_{i_{mem}} = T_{i_{loc}} + T_{i_{shar}}$, i.e. it consists of the time of access to the local and to the global memory.

Let T_N be a total time of parallel program execution. It consists of the following parts:

$$T_N = T_{N_{par}} + T_{N_{seq}} + T_{N_{ew}}.$$

Therefore, optimizing a parallel algorithm can be aimed at one of the following three targets.

- Reducing the time of parallel execution $T_{N_{par}}$ (without increasing $T_{N_{seq}}$).
- Reducing synchronization overhead $T_{N_{ew}}$.
- Reducing sizes of critical sections and therefore the time of sequential execution $T_{N_{seq}} + T_{N_{ew}}$.

Parallel execution time can be reduced by optimizing the use of the local memory. For this purpose, the computation should be partitioned between the processors in such a way that the relevant data fits into the local memory with significantly faster access compared to global memory. In the ideal case, for each processor $i : T_{i_{shar}} \to 0$.

Figure 4. Iteration phases

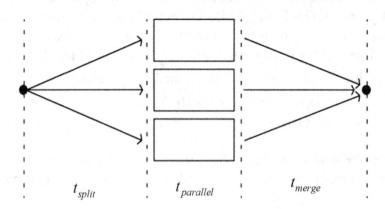

t_{split}　　　　$t_{parallel}$　　　　t_{merge}

As an example, consider a modification of the QuickSort algorithm (Sedgewick & Wayne, 2011). The modified algorithm contains a parameter responsible for switching to another algorithm for "inner" sorting. This parameter should be selected based on cache efficiency concerns. In the approach proposed in this book, the optimal value of this parameter is selected empirically by the auto-tuner. This example is considered in detail in subsection "Auto-Tuning of Programs" of Chapter 6. For now, it should be noticed that such algorithms belong to the area of cache-aware algorithms (Prokop, 1999). On the other hand, the algorithm is abstract enough: it does not depend on hardware architecture of execution environment, as this parameter is a part of a subject domain and not a parameter of cache implementation.

The synchronization overhead $T_{N_{ew}}$ can be reduced by optimal partitioning of computation tasks between processors. As an example, consider a classical coarse-grained block parallelization scheme, which provides uniform processor load using as large blocks of data as possible. In such case, the number of data exchanges between processors and the synchronization overhead is minimal. Coarse-grained block parallelization scheme provides the optimal performance for many parallel problems (Andon et al., 2007).

Another approach considers structural modification of computations performed by a program. In the following example, such transformation method is considered for the class of iterative algorithms using barrier synchronization at the end of each iteration.

Example 8 (asynchronous loops for iterative algorithms). There is a wide class of parallel programs that use iterative computation, where the outputs of a previous iteration become the inputs for the next one. Inside iterations the computations can be parallelized, e.g., by using geometrical decomposition (Andon et al., 2007).

Figure 4 shows the computations performed within the single iteration, where t_{split}, $t_{parallel}$ and t_{merge} denote the time spent on distributing data, parallel computation and collecting results, respectively. In such a computation scheme, the order of iterations cannot be changed or executed in parallel.

Now consider the concatenation of the iterations shown in Figure 5.

Figure 5. The scheme of merging several iterations into one

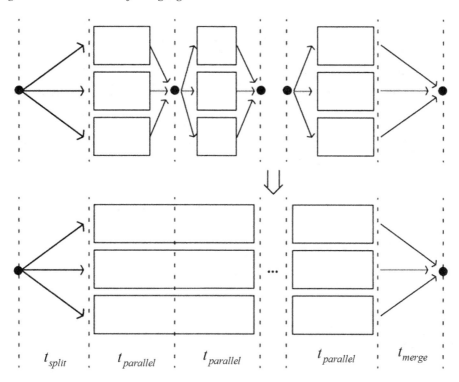

The number of merged iterations is denoted as *m*. A class of problems that allow such concatenation will be called the *problems of asynchronous loop with degree of freedom m*. Notice that such modification in computation structure can lead to slight changes in calculation result. It is out of scope to explain the details of how such inaccuracy can be estimated and analyzed, but the interested reader can find details in papers (Prusov, Doroshenko, &

Chernysh, 2009; Prusov, Doroshenko, Chernysh, & Guk, 2008). Here it should be stated only that the main idea behind such transformation is sacrificing accuracy of a result to gain an additional performance boost. And the mission of an auto-tuner is to find acceptable trade-off.

It's easy to see that the performance of the parallel algorithm is improved by modifying the computation scheme to use the asynchronous cycle. This effect is achieved because of reduced overhead on data decomposition and synchronization of intermediate iteration results.

The total execution time of the initial parallel program can be described by the following expression:

$$T_p = n \times (t_{split} + t_{exchange}),$$

where n is the total number of iterations; $t_{exchange} = t_{split} + t_{merge}$.

For simplicity, it is assumed that m is a divisor of n, $m \in [1,n]$. The estimation of the program execution time after its transformation to use the asynchronous cycle is the following:

$$T_{pm} = n \times t_{parallel} + \frac{n}{m} \times t_{echange}.$$

The estimation of the bounds on algorithm speedup s_{tuned} is

$$S_{tuned} = \frac{T_p}{T_{pm}} = \frac{t_{parallel} + t_{echange}}{\frac{1}{m} \times t_{echange} + t_{parallel}}.$$

$$\lim_{m=n \to \infty} S_{tuned} = \frac{t_{parallel} + t_{exchange}}{t_{parallel}} = 1 + \frac{t_{exchange}}{t_{parallel}}.$$

The minimum value of this expression is achieved at $m=1$, meaning that the computation scheme coincides completely with the initial one:

$$S_{tuned} = \frac{t_{parallel} + t_{exchange}}{t_{parallel} + t_{exchange}} = 1.$$

Therefore, speedup lies in the following bounds:

$$S_{tuned} \in [1,\ 1 + \frac{t_{exchange}}{t_{parallel}}].$$

Obviously, this optimization approach is the most efficient for the problems that have a large number of iterations and also a time of parallel computations and data exchange is of the same order of magnitude. As said before, for most problems the speedup s_{tuned} increases with the increase of m along with the increase of inaccuracy of a result. If there is no need to preserve the intermediate results (e.g., for visualization purposes), the optimal value of m is determined by the accuracy requirements. In Chapter 6, an example of using the asynchronous loop approach in a complex computational problem (meteorological forecasting) is considered.

Unfortunately, the approaches that target 1) optimizing a parallel section of computation and 2) reducing synchronization overhead, are usually at conflict: they require different strategies for distributing tasks between processors. The most efficient strategy depends both on a given computational problem and on parameters of hardware platform, such as shared memory access speed, cache access speed and cache size. The optimal strategy must be defined for each execution environment. The power of auto-tuning methods is that the selection of strategy is performed empirically and in automated mode.

Examples of PARALLEL Algorithms

Just as a human community can efficiently address the complex problem by dividing it into simpler subtasks, distributing the latter among the performers which make up the team, and also organizing their interaction, parallel computing systems can be regarded as groups of computers targeted at addressing complex problems in real time using well-known paradigms of parallel programming. In this subsection, formal means of organization of asynchronous parallel computation, represented in SAA-M, are considered. Asynchronous processing consists in interacting of multiple parallel branches which operate on flows of data distributed among them, exchanging of intermediate data and synchronization at certain times (for example, splitting of data into fragments and their multiprocessing).

Further, the standard multiprocessing structures taken from the forms of organization of parallel operations of human communities are considered: pipeline and slipway (Andon et al., 2007). The application of these structures is illustrated on array sorting examples.

Pipeline Multiprocessing

The *pipeline* is a parallel structure commonly used in industry: the assembled product moves over a tape (a pipeline) through the line of workers (or robots), which simultaneously perform their assembly operation at one time step. As a result of the last operation, a finished product comes off the pipeline.

Pipeline multiprocessing is the simultaneous application of an ordered sequence of generally different operators $A_1, A_2, \ldots, A_k$ to the flow of data being processed $M=(m_1, m_2, \ldots, m_c)$ so that the output result of i-th operator enters i-th queue, from the top of which the elements are transmitted to the input of $(i+1)$-th operator, $i=1, \ldots, K$:

$$m_c, m_{c-1}, \ldots, m_2, m_1 \Rightarrow A_1 \,|$$
$$\Rightarrow Q_1 \,|$$
$$\Rightarrow A_2 \Rightarrow Q_2, \ldots, Q_{k-1} \Rightarrow A_k \,|$$
$$\Rightarrow r_1 \Rightarrow R,$$

where R is the resulting data flow.

The operators $A_1, A_2, \ldots, A_k$, as the data come to their input, work in parallel, so that A_i sends its output to the input of a neighbor on the right (i.e. the operator A_{i+1}), using the queue Q_i; the operator A_k forms the flow R of resulting data. The use of queues provides independent (with respect to a time) parallel work of the operators A_i included in the pipeline.

Example 9. Consider the algorithm of asynchronous insertion sorting based on the above-considered asynchronous pipeline model. The initial marking of the array M to be sorted is the following:

$$M : H \; Y_2 \; Y_1 \; a_1 \; a_2 \; \ldots \; a_n \; K,$$

where H and K are markers fixing the beginning and the end of the array M, respectively; Y_1 and Y_2 are pointers moving along M and associated with two asynchronous processes. With the help of Y_1 the first process searches for array elements which are in the wrong place and writes them to the queue Q. The second process uses Y_2 to search for the place to insert the element from the top of the queue Q into already sorted fragment of the array.

The regular scheme of the sorting algorithm is the following:

Insertion_A = $(\{[d(Y_1,K)]\ ([l > r \mid Y_1]\ WRITE(r,Q),\ R(Y_1))\}$
* $CP(PROC\_FIN(1)) * S(PROC\_FIN(2))\ //\{[d(Y_1,K)$
$\wedge(Q = \varnothing)]\ ([Q \neq \varnothing]\ INSERT,\ E)\} * CP(PROC\_FIN(2)) * S(PROC\_FIN(1))),$

where $Q \neq \varnothing$ is the predicate which takes true value, if the queue Q is not empty; l and r are the elements immediately to the left and to the right of Y_1; $WRITE(r,Q)$ is the operator for writing the element r to the queue Q; *INSERT* is the cyclic operator moving Y_2 to the left (or to the right) in the already sorted part of the array and searching for the place to insert an element from the top of Q into the found position; the loop is executed until the queue Q is empty.

Consider the use of the algorithm *Insertion_A* on sorting of the following array:

$M : H\ Y_2\ Y_1\ 4\ 5\ 3\ 2\ 6\ 7\ 1\ 9\ 8\ K.$

First, the pointer Y_1 scans the array from left to right to the number 3; the pointer Y_2 remains in place $(Q \neq \varnothing)$. Then, the numbers 3 and 2 are written to Q and inserted into the position observed by Y_2. At the same time, Y_1 keeps moving to the right to the number 1, which is also written to the queue. The intermediate state of the array is

$M : H\ Y_2\ 2\ 3\ 4\ 5\ 6\ 7\ Y_1\ 9\ 8\ K$ (the element 1 is in Q).

Then, Y_1 is shifted to the right and the number 8 is written to Q. After this, the first process exits the loop and after passing the control point *CP(PROC_FIN(1))*, reaches the synchronizer *S(PROC_FIN(2))* and goes to a waiting state. Simultaneously, the second process inserts the number 1 from Q into the array and searches for the place to insert the number 8, which is at the top of Q. The intermediate state of the array is the following:

$M : H\ 2\ 3\ 4\ 5\ 6\ 7\ Y_2\ 9\ Y_1\ K.$

In the end, the number 8 is set at position observed by Y_2, the second process exits the loop, both synchronizers are triggered and the sorted array is obtained:

$M : H\ 1\ 2\ 3\ 4\ 5\ 6\ 7\ 8\ 9\ K.$

Slipway Multiprocessing

The above-considered pipeline structure is predominantly characterized by movement of data relatively to fixed operators processing the data flow in parallel. These operators can be both homogeneous and heterogeneous.

In the *slipway* multiprocessing, the data are fixed, while the operators are moving over the fixed data, implementing their parallel processing. Typically, operators which participate in the slipway multiprocessing, are heterogeneous; processed data are distributed between them.

The distribution of data among operators can be carried out before the start of their processing, which is called the *static slipway* multiprocessing. In the case of the *dynamic slipway*, the data are distributed between parallel branches during the multiprocessing.

Example 10. The static slipway multiprocessing is illustrated on the asynchronous shuttle sorting of the array. The initial marking of the input array M is the following:

$M : H\ Y_2\ Y_1\ a_1\ a_2\ ...\ a_i\ !\ a_{i+1}\ ...\ a_n\ Y_3\ Y_4\ K,$

where ! is the marker splitting the input array into two subarrays; Y_1, Y_2, Y_3, Y_4 are pointers.

The sorting scheme $\overrightarrow{SHUTTLE}$ consists in sorting two subarrays of the array M (subscheme $\overrightarrow{SHUT}$) and their merging (subscheme $\overrightarrow{MERGING}$):

$$\overrightarrow{SHUTTLE} = \{\overrightarrow{SHUT} * \overrightarrow{MERGING}\},$$

$$\overrightarrow{SHUT} = \overrightarrow{SHUT}\ //\ \overrightarrow{SHUT},$$

$$\overrightarrow{SHUT} = \{[d(Y_1,!)]\ R(Y_1,Y_2) * \{[l \leq r|\ Y_2]\ Transp(l,r\,|\,Y_2) * L(Y_2)\}$$
$$*SET(Y_2,Y_1)\} * CP(PROC\_FIN(1)) * S(PROC\_FIN(2)),$$

$$\overleftarrow{SHUT} = \{[d(Y_3,!)]\ R(Y_3,Y_4) * \{[l \leq r|\ Y_4]\ Transp(l,r\,|\,Y_4) * L(Y_4)\}$$
$$*SET(Y_4,Y_3)\} * CP(PROC\_FIN(2)) * S(PROC\_FIN(1)),$$

$$\overrightarrow{MERGING} = \{[l \leq r\,|\ !]\ \overrightarrow{INSERT} \,//\, \overleftarrow{INSERT}\},$$

$$\overrightarrow{INSERT} = \{[l \leq r\,|\ Y_2]\ TRANSP(l,r\,|\,Y_2) * L(Y_2)$$
$$*SET(Y_2,Y_1)\} * CP(PROC\_FIN(1)) * S(PROC\_FIN(2)),$$

$$\overleftarrow{INSERT} = \{[l \leq r\,|\ Y_4]\ TRANSP(l,r\,|\,Y_4) * R(Y_4)$$
$$*SET(Y_4,Y_3)\} * CP(PROC\_FIN(2)) * S(PROC\_FIN(1)).$$

Here $\overrightarrow{SHUT}$ and $\overleftarrow{SHUT}$ are parallel branches carrying out the left-hand and the right-hand shuttle sorting of the array, respectively; $d(Y_1,!)$ is the predicate taking true value, if Y_1 reached marker ! and false otherwise; $R(Y_1,Y_2)$ is the operator shifting the pointers Y_1 and Y_2 over the array M one symbol to the right; $l{\leq}r|Y_2$ is the predicate which takes true value, if the specified relation holds for the elements located directly to the left and to the right of the pointer Y_2; $Transp(l,r|Y_2)$ is the operator which swaps the elements adjacent to the pointer Y_2; $L(Y_2)$ is the operator shifting the pointer Y_2 over the array M one symbol to the left; $SET(Y_2,Y_1)$ is the operator placing the pointer Y_2 in a position directly to the right of the pointer Y_1; $CP(PROC\_FIN(i))$, $i{=}1,2$, are the control points fixing the moment of exit from the outer loop; $PROC\_FIN(1)$ is the predicate, which takes true value, if the compound operator $\overrightarrow{SHUT}$ completed processing, and false otherwise; $PROC\_FIN(2)$ is the predicate, which takes true value, if the compound operator $\overleftarrow{SHUT}$ completed processing, and false otherwise; $S(PROC\_FIN(i))$ is the synchronizer which delays the computation till the moment when the corresponding synchronization condition $PROC\_FIN(i)$ is true.

The body of the outer loop of the scheme $\overrightarrow{MERGING}$ consists of two asynchronous opposite directions (compound operators $\overrightarrow{INSERT}$ and $\overleftarrow{INSERT}$) for insertion of unordered elements in place, setting the pointers Y_2 and Y_4 on Y_1 and Y_3, respectively, and synchronizing the parallel processes. Functioning of the scheme $\overline{MERGING}$ ends when the condition $l \leq r$! is true, so after removing the pointers and the marker, the sorted array is obtained.

Consider the use of the scheme $\overline{SHUTTLE}$ on the process of asynchronous merging of subarrays of the array:

$$M : H \; Y_2 \; Y_1 \; 9 \; 5 \; 2 \; 8 \; 1 \; ! \; 4 \; 3 \; 7 \; 6 \; Y_3 \; Y_4 \; K.$$

With the help of the marker !, the array M is split into two fragments: 9 5 2 8 1 and 4 3 7 6, which are processed by the asynchronous parallel branches $\overline{SHUT}$ and $\overline{SHUT}$, respectively. The result of application of the scheme is the following array:

$$M : H \; Y_2 \; Y_1 \; 1 \; 2 \; 5 \; 8 \; 9 \; ! \; 3 \; 4 \; 6 \; 7 \; Y_3 \; Y_4 \; K,$$

which consists of two sorted subarrays.

Merging of the subarrays is carried out by the subscheme $\overline{MERGING}$. The compound operators $\overline{INSERT}$ and $\overline{INSERT}$ simultaneously insert the elements 3, 4 and 9, 8 in appropriate places of the subarrays. The result is the array:

$$M : H \; 1 \; 2 \; 3 \; 4 \; 5 \; Y_2 \; Y_1 \; ! \; Y_3 \; Y_4 \; 6 \; 7 \; 8 \; 9 \; K$$

After excluding the pointers Y_1, Y_2, Y_3, Y_4 and the marker !, the sorted array is obtained.

Example 11. Consider the algorithm of the dynamic slipway sorting of the array M, which is not initially divided into subarrays and is marked as follows:

$$M : H \; Y_2 \; Y_1 \; a_1 \; a_2 \; ... \; a_n \; Y_3 \; Y_4 \; K.$$

The regular scheme of dynamic slipway sorting is the following:

$$\overline{SHUTTLE\_D} = SLIPWAY\_D * \overline{MERGING\_D},$$

$SLIPWAY\_D = \overrightarrow{SHUTTLE} \, / \, /\overleftarrow{SHUTTLE},$

$\overrightarrow{SHUTTLE} = \{[d(Y_1,Y_3) = 0] \, R(Y_2,Y_1)$
$*\{[l \leq r \,|\, Y_2] \, TRANSP(l,r \,|\, Y_2) * L(Y_2)\} * SET(Y_2,Y_1)\} * CP(PROC\_FIN(1)),$

$\overleftarrow{SHUTTLE} = \{[d(Y_1,Y_3) = k] \, L(Y_3,Y_4)$
$*\{[l \leq r \,|\, Y_4] \, TRANSP(l,r \,|\, Y_4) * P(Y_4)\} * SET(Y_4,Y_3)\} * S(PROC\_FIN(1)),$

$\overrightarrow{MERGING\_D} = \{[l \leq r \,|\, Y_1] \, \overrightarrow{INSERT} \, / /\overleftarrow{INSERT}\}.$

In the given scheme, *SLIPWAY_D* is the dynamic slipway, which divides the array into two ordered subarrays with their subsequent merging. At the phase of execution of the compound operator *SLIPWAY_D*, the branch $\overrightarrow{SHUTTLE}$ implements the left-hand shuttle sorting until the condition $d(Y_1,Y_3)=0$ is true, i.e. the pointers Y_1 and Y_3 merge; at the same time, the opposite branch $\overleftarrow{SHUTTLE}$ performs the right-hand sorting until the condition $d(Y_1,Y_3)=k$ is true, i.e. the distance between Y_1 and Y_3 is reduced to k; $S(PROC\_FIN(1)$ is waiting for the control point $(d(Y_1,Y_3)=0$ is true). The compound operator $\overrightarrow{MERGING\_D}$ is the modification of the considered earlier $\overrightarrow{MERGING}$ scheme, where the condition $l \leq r$! is replaced by $l \leq r | Y_1$.

Consider the use of $\overrightarrow{SHUTTLE\_D}$ algorithm for sorting the array

$M : H \; Y_2 \; Y_1 \; 1 \; 2 \; 5 \; 8 \; 9 \; 3 \; 4 \; 6 \; 7 \; Y_3 \; Y_4 \; K.$

It is assumed that the branches $\overrightarrow{SHUTTLE}$ and $\overleftarrow{SHUTTLE}$ with identical speed scan through the sorted fragments of the array, i.e. 1 2 5 8 9 and 3 4 6 7. The value of the parameter k (in the loop condition $d(Y_1,Y_3)=k$) is 1. According to *SLIPWAY_D* scheme, the branch $\overleftarrow{SHUTTLE}$ will go to a waiting state after scanning the array 3 4 6 7 and will remain in this state until the first branch scans the number 9, after which the array will be dynamically divided into sorted subarrays:

$M : H \; 1 \; 2 \; 5 \; 8 \; 9 \; Y_2 \; Y_1 \; Y_3 \; Y_4 \; 3 \; 4 \; 6 \; 7 \; K.$

The subarrays are then merged by $\overline{INSERT}$ and $\overline{\overline{INSERT}}$ branches of $\overline{MERGING\_D}$ scheme. These branches simultaneously insert the elements 3, 4 and 9, 8 into respective positions of the subarrays. As a result, the following array is obtained:

$$M_3: H \; 1 \; 2 \; 3 \; 4 \; 5 \; Y_2 \; Y_1 \; Y_3 \; Y_4 \; 6 \; 7 \; 8 \; 9 \; K,$$

which consists of two ordered subarrays 1 2 3 4 5 and 6 7 8 9.

It should be noted that at designing sufficiently non-trivial algorithms of symbolic multiprocessing, the parallel structures which combine pipeline and slipway elements are usually applied (Andon et al., 2007).

CONCLUSION

The metarules of convolution, involution and their various combinations are focused on designing classes of algorithms and strategies of processing. The transformation metarule in combination with convolution and involution is a powerful tool for establishing connections between various algorithms and designing new algorithms, more efficient by some criteria. The transformation is the basis of analytic modifications (in particular, optimization) of schemes represented in algorithmic algebra.

The algorithmic language SAA/1 is based on Glushkov's algebra and is focused on multilevel design of algorithms and programs in a natural language form. SAA/1 is simple to learn and use and can be translated to a target programming language (such as C++, Java, etc.) by using the tools for automated software design and synthesis (Andon et al., 2007; Doroshenko et al., 2013).

Hyperschemes (parametrized meta-specifications) and auto-tuning approach are the means of increasing the adaptability of algorithms and programs to specific conditions of their use (e.g., target execution environment). The proposed extended PRAM* model is applied for explanation of program optimization approaches used in auto-tuning. The considered example of transformation method (asynchronous loops for iterative algorithms) can be applied for optimization of problems with large iterations number.

The discussed parallel computing structures (pipeline and slipway) can be applied for designing parallel algorithms in various subject domains (sorting, search, symbolic multiprocessing, etc.).

REFERENCES

Andon, P. I., Doroshenko, A. Yu., Tseytlin, G. O., & Yatsenko, O. A. (2007). *Algebra-algorithmic models and methods of parallel programming.* Kyiv: Academperiodyka. (in Russian)

Baader, F., & Nipkow, T. (1999). *Term rewriting and all that.* Cambridge: Cambridge University Press.

Bulyonkov, M. (1990). Mixed computation and compilation: New approaches to old problems. *Theoretical Computer Science, 71*(2), 209–226. doi:10.1016/0304-3975(90)90198-Q

Doroshenko, A., & Shevchenko, R. (2006). A rewriting framework for rule-based programming dynamic applications. *Fundamenta Informaticae, 72*(1-3), 95–108.

Doroshenko, A., Tseytlin, G., Yatsenko, O., & Zachariya, L. (2006). A theory of clones and formalized design of programs. In *Proceedings of the 15th International Workshop "Concurrency, Specification and Programming" (CS&P'2006)* (pp. 328-339). Berlin: Humboldt University Press.

Doroshenko, A., Zhereb, K., & Yatsenko, O. (2013). Developing and optimizing parallel programs with algebra-algorithmic and term rewriting tools. In *Proceedings of the 9th International Conference "ICT in Education, Research, and Industrial Applications" (ICTERI 2013), Revised Selected Papers (Communications in Computer and Information Science)* (Vol. 412, pp. 70-92). Berlin: Springer. 10.1007/978-3-319-03998-5_5

Durillo, J., & Fahringer, T. (2014). From single- to multi-objective auto-tuning of programs: Advantages and implications. *Scientific Programming – Automatic Application Tuning for HPC Architectures, 22*(4), 285-297.

Dybvig, R. K. (2000). From macrogeneration to syntactic abstraction. *Higher-Order and Symbolic Computation, 13*(1/2), 57–63. doi:10.1023/A:1010041423101

Eppstein, D., & Galil, Z. (1988). Parallel algorithmic techniques for combinatorial computation. *Annual Review of Computer Science, 3*(1), 233–283. doi:10.1146/annurev.cs.03.060188.001313

Ivanenko, P., Doroshenko, A., & Zhereb, K. (2014). TuningGenie: Auto-tuning framework based on rewriting rules. In *Proceedings of the 10th International Conference "ICT in Education, Research and Industrial Applications. Integration, Harmonization and Knowledge Transfer" (ICTERI 2014) (Communications in Computer and Information Science)* (Vol. 469, pp. 139-158). Cham: Springer. 10.1007/978-3-319-13206-8_7

Naono, K., Teranishi, K., Cavazos, J., & Suda, R. (2010). *Software automatic tuning: From concepts to state-of-the-art results*. Berlin: Springer. doi:10.1007/978-1-4419-6935-4

Prokop, H. (1999). Cache-oblivious algorithms. In *Proceedings of the 40th Annual Symposium on Foundations of Computer Science (FOCS'99)*, (pp. 285-299). New York: IEEE Computer Society.

Prusov, V. A., Doroshenko, A. Yu., & Chernysh, R. I. (2009). A method for numerical solution of a multidimensional convection-diffusion problem. *Cybernetics and Systems Analysis, 45*(1), 89–95. doi:10.100710559-009-9074-8

Prusov, V. A., Doroshenko, A. Yu., Chernysh, R. I., & Guk, L. N. (2008). Theoretical study of a numerical method to solve a diffusion-convection problem. *Cybernetics and Systems Analysis, 44*(2), 283–291. doi:10.100710559-008-0028-3

Sedgewick, R., & Wayne, K. (2011). *Algorithms* (4th ed.). Boston: Addison-Wesley Professional.

Tichy, W. (2014). Auto-tuning parallel software: an interview with Thomas Fahringer: The multicore transformation. *Ubiquity, 2014*, 1–9. doi:10.1145/2618409

Yatsenko, O. (2011). On application of machine learning for development of adaptive sorting programs in algebra of algorithms. In *Proceedings of the 20th International Workshop "Concurrency: Specification and Programming" (CS&P'2011)* (pp. 577-588). Bialystok: Bialystok University of Technology.

Yatsenko, O. (2012). On parameter-driven generation of algorithm schemes. In *Proceedings of the 21st International Workshop "Concurrency, Specification and Programming" (CS&P'2012)* (pp. 428-438). Berlin: Humboldt University Press.

Yushchenko, K. L., Tseytlin, G. O., & Galushka, A. V. (1989). Algebraic-grammatical specifications and synthesis of structured program schemas. *Cybernetics and Systems Analysis*, 25(6), 713–727.

KEY TERMS AND DEFINITIONS

Algebra of Hyperschemes: The formalism applied for parameter-driven generation of regular schemes of algorithms based on higher-level specifications (hyperschemes).

Glushkov's System of Algorithmic Algebras (SAA, Glushkov's Algebra): The two-sorted algebra focused on analytical form of representation of algorithms and formalized transformation of these representations.

Hyperscheme: A parameterized algebra-algorithmic specification intended for solving a specific class of problems. By setting parameter values with subsequent interpretation of a hyperscheme, an algorithm scheme optimized to specific conditions of its use is obtained.

Modified System of Algorithmic Algebras (SAA-M): The extension of the Glushkov's system of algorithmic algebras (SAA) intended for formalization of parallel algorithms.

Parallel Random-Access Machine (PRAM): A shared-memory abstract machine for modeling parallel algorithmic performance.

PRAM*: The model which extends the classic shared-memory abstract machine for modeling parallel algorithmic performance (PRAM) with additional memory level and uses only one strategy for management of simultaneous access to both memory levels.

Regular Scheme (RS): A representation of an algorithm in the system of algorithmic algebras (SAA).

SAA Scheme: A representation of an algorithm in algorithmic language SAA/1.

SAA/1: The algorithmic language based on Glushkov's system of algorithmic algebras and focused on natural linguistic representation of schemes. It is applied for multilevel structured designing and documenting of sequential and parallel algorithms and programs.

Transformation: The process of conversion of algorithm schemes based on equalities represented in algorithmic algebra.

Chapter 3
Term Rewriting–Based Programming

ABSTRACT

One of the directions of algebraic programming is the use of rewriting rules technique. This direction formalizes the transformational aspects of programming, which allows us to describe transformations of some formal objects and research properties of such transformations. The rewriting rules technique is both a powerful formal tool for transformation of formal systems and a practical tool for programming that allows implementing transformations of complex objects. In this chapter, the main definitions associated with algebraic programming based on rewriting rules are given, term rewriting systems are overviewed, and applications of these systems for processing and transformation of programs are considered.

INTRODUCTION

At present, metaprogramming problems (i.e. the development of programs, the input and/or output data of which are also programs) become increasingly relevant. Some metaprogramming tools, such as compilers and programming language editors, are necessary for programming arbitrary tasks, as without them the development becomes too difficult or impossible. The other tools are not so irreplaceable, but still form an important part of modern software lifecycle. Static analysis allows improving the quality of source code, revealing potential errors or programming style violations. Automatic transformations

DOI: 10.4018/978-1-5225-9384-3.ch003

of programs contribute to increasing their readability, performance, security, reduce development time and allow avoiding mechanical mistakes. Specialized languages reduce program size, allowing to concisely and clearly express subject domain concepts. Code generation provides the opportunity to use a higher level of abstraction and automatically obtain relevant executable code. Thus, metaprogramming plays a crucial role in development of modern software.

For solving metaprogramming problems, general-purpose programming languages such as C/C++, Java, C# can be used. However, these problems have some features which are not taken into account in general-purpose languages. Metaprograms do not require means for defining complex data structures: their working object is source code in some standard structured representation, most often it is a parse tree. Most metaprogramming problems can be presented as transformations of this tree. Traditional imperative languages contain general-purpose control structures (branching, loops) that form the basis of any imperative program. However, in metaprograms there is no need for complex control: neither in data access area (usually the whole tree is traversed in some fixed order), nor at applying transformations (which are applied while conditions of their application are present). On the other hand, metaprogramming requires operations that are not so easily implementable in imperative languages. For example, searching for a part of a tree corresponding to a given template or application of a transformation to all parts where it is applicable. Another significant requirement is a possibility to easily add or modify transformations; in traditional languages, it will require at least recompilation and maybe modification of other transformations for their correct cooperation.

Thus, application of general-purpose languages for solving the problems of processing and transforming programs is not justified. However, there are specialized programming tools that are well suited exactly for such problems. These are rewriting rules systems working with terms (Baader & Nipkow, 1999; Dershowitz & Plaisted, 2001). The term is a natural representation of a tree and rewriting rules include a search for a template and replacement of a subterm, which allows modeling any transformations. Rewriting rules system controls the process of transformations application (i.e. rewriting), so the developer has only to specify necessary transformations. The addition of new transformations consists in implementation of new rules which automatically correctly cooperate with already existing ones. Therefore, rewriting rules systems are perfectly suitable for implementation of metaprogramming problems.

So far, many rewriting rules systems have been developed; they differ in implementation features and scopes of applications. In this chapter, an overview of rule-based systems is given and their use for program processing and transformation is considered.

The Main Features of Rewriting: Definitions and Examples

Many formal systems using rewriting technique have been proposed (Baader & Nipkow, 1999). Further, several such systems are considered demonstrating various rewriting aspects.

Abstract Rewriting Systems

This subsection uses some definitions from the theory of sets and algebraic systems (Baader & Nipkow, 1999; Mal'cev, 1973).

Definition 1. The *binary relation R* on the sets A and B is a subset of the Cartesian product $R \subseteq A \times B$, i.e. the set of pairs $\{(a,b) \in R \mid a \in A, b \in B\}$. The fact that two elements $a \in A$ and $b \in B$ are in the relation R is denoted as $aRb \sim (a,b) \in R$.

The binary relation on the set A is a subset of the Cartesian square of the set A, i.e. $R \subseteq A \times A$.

Since relations are sets, usual operations over sets are defined for them: a union $R \cup S$, an intersection $R \cap S$, a difference $R \backslash S$, a subset $R \subseteq S$.

The *product* (or *composition*) *of relations* $R \subseteq A \times B$ and $S \subseteq B \times C$ is the relation $R \circ S \subseteq A \times C$ such that $R \circ S = \{(a,c) \mid a \in A, c \in C, \exists b \in B : aRb \wedge bSc\}$.

The *identity relation* on the set A is the relation $I_A \subseteq A \times A$, such that $I_A = \{(a,a) \mid a \in A\}$.

The *inverse relation* for the relation $R \subseteq A \times B$ is the relation $R' \subseteq B \times A$, such that $bR'a \sim aRb$.

The *power of relation* $R \subseteq A \times A$ for any $n \in \mathbb{N}_0$ is defined as follows:

- $R^0 = I$;
- $R^1 = R$;

- $\forall n \in \mathbb{N}: R^{n+1} = R^n \circ R$.

The relation $R \subseteq A \times A$ is called

- *reflexive*, if $I \subseteq R$ (i.e. xRx);
- *symmetric*, if $R' = R$ (i.e. yRx follows from xRy);
- *transitive*, if $R^2 \subseteq R$ (i.e. xRz follows from xRy and yRz).

The *reflexive transitive closure* of the relation $R \subseteq A \times A$ is the relation $R^* = I \cup R^+ = \bigcup_{i \geq 0} R^i$, i.e. the union of all non-negative powers of the relation.

Any formal system implementing a rewriting paradigm includes the basic operation of rewriting, i.e. the transition between objects by certain rules. Formally this operation is described as follows.

Definition 2. The pair $\langle A, \rightarrow \rangle$, where A is any set and $\rightarrow \subset A \times A$ is any binary relation on this set is called an *abstract rewriting system*.

The transitions between the elements of the set A according to the relation $\rightarrow$ are of interest, i.e. the chains of the form $a_1 \rightarrow a_2 \rightarrow ... \rightarrow a_n \rightarrow ...$, such that $\forall i: a_i \rightarrow a_{i+1}$. Definition The chain can be written in the form $a_1 \rightarrow^* a_n$. ARS can be considered as a generalization of a function: in the case of a function, for each value of an argument, the transition to a single value of a function can be made, while in the case of ARS different transitions for a given initial element are possible (the indeterminacy of ARS).

The abstract rewriting system (ARS) can be considered in two aspects: static and dynamic. In the static aspect, the elements of the set A are represented in the form of points of some space, and the chains $a \rightarrow^* b$ describe the paths between these points. In the dynamic aspect, the elements of the set A are the states of some system, and the chains $a \rightarrow^* b$ describe transitions between the states. (The dynamic aspect of ARS is also called a transition system.) Both aspects are not mutually exclusive, it is possible to speak, for example, about a path between two states, or about transitions from a point to a point.

For the paths, it is natural to raise the question about "destination", i.e. a final element of the path. In particular, the existence and uniqueness are of interest. To formalize these questions, additional properties of separate elements of ARS will be introduced as well as ARS as a whole.

Definition 3. The element b is called a *successor* of the element a, if $a{\to}b$. The element a is called *reducible*, if it has a successor: $\exists x{\in}A: a{\to}x$. The element which is not reducible is called *irreducible*, or an *element in a normal form*. The element b is called a *normal form* of the element a, if $a{\to}^*b$ and b is irreducible. If the element a has a unique normal form, it is designated $a{\downarrow}$.

At first, consider a question of the existence of a normal form.

Definition 4. ARS is called *normalizing* if for each element there is a normal form (at least one). ARS is called *terminating*, or *Noetherian*, if there are no infinite ways $a_1 \to a_2 \to ... \to a_n \to ...$ in it.

It is obvious that terminating ARS is always normalizing. The reverse is incorrect: consider, for example, the system with two elements $A=\{a,b\}$, such that $a{\to}a$ and $a{\to}b$. In this case $a{\downarrow}=b$ and $b{\downarrow}=b$, i.e. both elements have a unique normal form. At the same time, there is an infinite chain $a \to a \to ... \to a \to ...$.

To guarantee that transitions terminate, it is necessary to forbid a part of transitions. In some cases, it can be made by finding and eliminating loops in transitions. Consider a function of similarity $f: A{\to}A$, such that $f(x){\to}f(y)$ follows from $x{\to}y$. An example of such function is $f(x)=x$, and also $f(x)=setp(a,p,x)$, i.e. some construct containing x as one of its parts (see Subsection "Rewriting of Fragments"). In this case, if for some element there is a path to a similar element: $\exists a \in A, \exists n > 0: a \to^n f(a)$, then the system is not terminating: since $f(a){\to}^n f(f(a))$, then $a{\to}^{2n}f(f(a))$ and in general $\forall k > 0: a \to^{kn} f^k(a)$. At a practical implementation, the algorithm for searching a normal form should remember the "history", i.e. all the previously considered elements, and when a loop is found, it should stop the search in this direction.

Another method ensuring that transitions terminate is the selection of a proper rewriting strategy.

The verification of the termination property of a system is algorithmically unsolvable problem. However, the methods for proving the termination property for certain classes of systems were developed (Baader & Nipkow, 1999; Dershowitz & Plaisted, 2001) (see also Example 1, item 1).

Further, a question of uniqueness of normal forms is considered. The more general statement is the following question: if two paths beginning from one element have diverged, then do they converge later?

For research of this question, it is necessary to consider transitions not only in direct but also in reverse directions. For relation $\rightarrow$, the inverse relation will be denoted as $\leftarrow = \rightarrow'$. The symmetric closure will be designated as $\leftrightarrow = \rightarrow \cup \leftarrow$. Then, the paths with transitions in any directions are defined by the relation $\leftrightarrow^*$ which is a symmetric reflexive transitive closure of the relation $\rightarrow$. The following designation will be used: $C = \rightarrow^* \circ \leftarrow^*$ (convergent paths) and $D = \leftarrow^* \circ \rightarrow^*$ (diverging paths). Consider also two relations defining special cases of diverging paths: $D_s = \leftarrow \circ \rightarrow^*$ and $D_l = \leftarrow \circ \rightarrow$. It is obvious that

$$C \subseteq \leftrightarrow^* \tag{1}$$

$$D_l \subseteq D_s \subseteq D \subseteq \leftrightarrow^* \tag{2}$$

Generally, the subset relations are strict, as an example $a \rightarrow b \leftarrow c \rightarrow d$ shows: here aCc, bDd and $a \leftrightarrow^* d$, but not aCd and not aDd.

Definition 5. ARS has a *Church-Rosser property*, if $\leftrightarrow^* \subseteq C$ (from (1) follows that this property is equivalent to $\leftrightarrow^* = C$). Otherwise, this property can be written as

$$\forall n, p : n \leftrightarrow^* p \Rightarrow \exists q : n \rightarrow^* q \leftarrow^* p .$$

ARS is called *confluent*, if $D \subseteq C$, or $\forall m, n, p : n \leftarrow^* m \rightarrow^* p \Rightarrow \exists q : n \rightarrow^* q \leftarrow^* p$.

ARS is called *semi-confluent*, if $D_s \subseteq C$, or $\forall m, n, p : n \leftarrow m \rightarrow^* p \Rightarrow \exists q : n \rightarrow^* q \leftarrow^* p$.

ARS is called *locally confluent*, if $D_l \subseteq C$, or $\forall m, n, p : n \leftarrow m \rightarrow p \Rightarrow \exists q : n \rightarrow^* q \leftarrow^* p$.

ARS is called *convergent*, if it is terminating and confluent.

Theorem 1. The following statements are equivalent:
1) ARS has a Church-Rosser property;
2) ARS is confluent;
3) ARS is semi-confluent.

The proof. The equivalence according to the scheme $1 \Rightarrow 2 \Rightarrow 3 \Rightarrow 1$ will be proved. Notice that from (2) follows $1 \Rightarrow 2 \Rightarrow 3$, therefore it is necessary to prove only $3 \Rightarrow 1$, i.e. $D_s \subseteq C \Rightarrow \leftrightarrow^* \subseteq C$.

For notation simplification, the designation $\rightarrow = R$, $\leftarrow = L$, $\leftrightarrow = B$ is introduced, then $B = L \cup R$, $C = R^* L^*$, $D_s = LR^*$. Let $D_s \subseteq C$. It will be proved by induction on n that $\forall n \geq 0 : B^n \subseteq C$.

The induction basis: it is obvious that at $n=0$ the $B^0 = I \subseteq C$ is satisfied.

The induction step: let $B^k \subseteq C$. Notice that $B^{k+1} = B^k B = B^k (L \cup R) = B^k L \cup B^k R$.

Let us prove that $B^k L \subseteq C$. Indeed, $B^k L \subseteq CL = R^* L^* L \subseteq R^* L^* = C$.

Let us prove that $B^k R \subseteq C$. In this case, it will be easier to prove the equivalent inclusion for inverse relations $(B^k R)' \subseteq C' = C$. So,

$$(B^k R)' = R'(B^k)' = LB^k \subseteq LC = LR^* L^* = D_s L^* \subseteq CL^* = R^* L^* L^* = R^* L^* = C.$$

From the proved inclusions $B^k L \subseteq C$ and $B^k R \subseteq C$ follows $B^k L \cup B^k R \subseteq C$, as it was required. The theorem is proved.

Due to Theorem 1, only confluent ARS will be considered further. The following statement holds.

Theorem 2. If ARS is normalizing and confluent, there is a unique normal form for each element.

The proof. The existence of the normal form follows from that ARS is normalizing. It will be admitted that for the element a there are two normal forms b,c. Then from $a \rightarrow^* b$ and $a \rightarrow^* c$ follows bDc, from which bCc follows due to the confluence. But as b,c are irreducible, from here follows $b=c$. The uniqueness of the normal form is proved.

Thus, the confluence allows calculating the normal form, not caring about a choice of successors on each step: irrespectively of this choice, the unique normal form will be obtained. Therefore, this property is significant for rewriting systems. Unfortunately, it is difficult enough to check: for the whole set of pairs of elements which are in relation $\leftrightarrow^*$ (either D, or D_s) it is necessary to check that corresponding paths converge.

Figure 1. The confluence does not follow from the local confluence

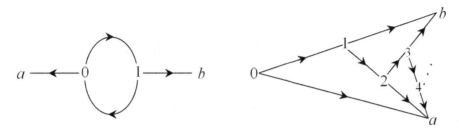

It is easier to verify the property of a local confluence, as it unites only relations → and ←, but not their transitive closures. Unfortunately, in general case, this property is not equivalent to confluence as examples $\{0 \leftrightarrow 1, 0 \rightarrow a, 1 \rightarrow b\}$ or $\{2n \rightarrow a, 2n+1 \rightarrow b, n \rightarrow n+1 \mid n \geq 0\}$ show (see Figure 1).

However, in the case of a terminating system, the following statement holds.

Theorem 3 (Newman's lemma). If ARS is terminating and locally confluent, it is confluent.

The proof can be found in (Baader & Nipkow, 1999; Huet, 1980). Below, some examples of ARS are given.

Example 1.

○ Let the relation → be the relation of strict partial order, i.e. the properties of transitivity and antisymmetry $(\rightarrow \cap \leftarrow = \varnothing)$ are satisfied for it. Then the existence of a normal form for the element $a \in A$ corresponds to the existence of a minimum of the set $\{x \in A: a \rightarrow^* x\}$. In particular, if A is a well-ordered set, the minimum (i.e. the unique normal form) always exists. Order relations can be used to prove a termination property of the system. For this purpose, the given system $(A, \rightarrow)$ is immersed into a well-ordered set $(B, >)$ by means of monotonous function $f: A \rightarrow B$, such that from $x \rightarrow y$ follows $f(x) > f(y)$. If such function exists, from the existence of the infinite chain $a_1 \rightarrow a_2 \rightarrow ... \rightarrow a_n \rightarrow ...$, the infinite chain $f(a_1) > f(a_2) > ... > f(a_n) > ...$ follows, which contradicts the definition of the system $(B, >)$. Some strategies of construction of such immersing are given in (Baader & Nipkow, 1999; Dershowitz & Plaisted, 2001).

- ◦ Let the relation $\rightarrow$ be the equivalence relation (symmetric, reflexive and transitive). Then the confluence is satisfied, but the system is not terminating, the existence of infinite chains $a \rightarrow a \rightarrow \ldots \rightarrow a \rightarrow \ldots$ follows from the reflexivity.
- ◦ Let the relation $\rightarrow$ describe the execution of some program. In this case, the set of states of the program and admissible transitions in this set are considered. Then the termination property of the system provides a program stop and convergence provides the existence of well-defined unique result (the determinacy). The normal form for the given input data is the result of the computation.

Rewriting Rules

In ARS, the binary relation $\rightarrow$ generally contains an infinite number of element pairs. Therefore, its representation in a tabular form is inconvenient. A method of representation of the relation by means of a finite number of rules will be considered.

Definition 6. Let A be a set of elements and S be a set of substitutions. Consider the following functions: *match*: $A \times A \rightarrow S$ and *subst*: $A \times S \rightarrow A$, and also the relation *ismatch* $\subseteq A \times A$. The pair of elements $(lhs_i, rhs_i) \in A \times A$ is called the *rule*.

Then the ARS $\langle A, \rightarrow \rangle$ is defined as follows:

$$a \rightarrow b \sim ismatch(a, lhs_i) \wedge b = subst(rhs_i, match(a, lhs_i)).$$

Thus, the relation is defined in the three following stages.

- The compatibility of the given element a and the left part of the rule lhs_i is checked.
- The substitution $s = match(a, lhs_i)$ which combines a and lhs_i is computed.
- The same substitution is used for the right part of the rule, and the element $b = subst(rhs_i, s)$ is computed.

In this case, the assigning of a finite number of rules allows defining an infinite relation.

Further, the rules will be designated in the form $lhs_i \rightarrow rhs_i$, when it is clear from the context that we deal with rules, not the relation $\rightarrow$ in ARS.

Example 2.

- ○ The change of states of the Turing machine is performed according to a set of rules. The set of states consists of the pairs (q,s), where q is the current state of the Turing machine, s is a current symbol on a tape, which is read by a head. The substitution consists of the triples (q,s,a), where q and s are new values of a state and a symbol on tape and a is one of the actions: to move to the right, to move to the left, to stop. The function *match* finds the necessary substitution for the given state in the table. The function *subst* modifies a state according to the substitution: changes a symbol on tape and an internal state, and also moves the head on tape and accordingly changes a visible symbol. Thus, the infinite relation of transitions between different states can be presented as a finite set of rules which in turn can be considered as input data for other programs (for example, the universal Turing machine).
- ○ In a similar way, it is possible to describe the other program models, such as various versions of automata, Petri nets, etc.
- ○ Logic programming languages, such as Prolog, use systems of implications as rules for derivation of new facts.

Rewriting of Fragments

The notation of a rewriting relation in the form of rules works well for the sets consisting of rather simple elements that are transformed completely. However, in many cases, ARS contains complex objects, and rewriting affects only their separate fragments. In this case, the application of rewriting rules to fragments of elements will be defined.

Definition 7. Let A be a set of elements and P be a set of paths, or identifiers of fragments. Consider the following functions: *getp*: $A \times P \rightarrow A$ (obtaining a fragment on a given path), *setp*: $A \times P \times A \rightarrow A$ (fragment replacement on a given path) and *listp*: $A \rightarrow P^*$ (the list of all paths to fragments of the given element). Let also the ARS $\langle A, \rightarrow \rangle$ be defined on the set A. Then it is possible to consider the ARS $\langle A, \rightarrow_p \rangle$ defined as follows:

$$a \rightarrow_p b \sim \exists p \in P, \, \exists a_p, \, b_p \in A:$$

$$p \in listp(a) \wedge a_p = getp(a, p) \wedge b_p = getp(b, p) \wedge b = setp(a, p, b_p) \wedge a_p \rightarrow b_p.$$

Thus, the relation $\rightarrow$ is applied to a fragment of the given element, and the result of rewriting is substituted instead of this fragment.

It should be noticed that fragments can intersect. In particular, there is an empty path $\varepsilon \in P$, such that $getp(a, \varepsilon) = a$ and $setp(a, \varepsilon, b) = b$. Therefore, $\rightarrow \subseteq \rightarrow_p$.

The selection of a fragment for rewriting also defines the non-determination of the transition.

Example 3.

- In the case of rewriting of strings, $A = String$, $P = \{a, b \in \mathbb{N}_0: a \leq b\}$ is the position of a substring.
- The special case of rewriting of strings is Markov's normal algorithms.
- One more special case are grammars, used for description of languages.

Term Rewriting

In this subsection, the formal model of a rewriting term system is considered.

The Alphabet of the System

The system alphabet consists of the following symbols.

1. 1. The set of constant symbols $\Sigma_c = \{c_i\}$. The constants belong to one of the primitive types

$$\Sigma_{pt} = \{\text{CHAR, INT, DECIMAL, BOOL, STRING, ATOM}\}.$$

The types CHAR, INT, DECIMAL, BOOL, STRING correspond to standard types of programming languages (symbols, integer values, decimal fractions, logic values, strings). The ATOM type contains atomic, not interpreted values. One of the atomic constants, NIL, has a special value in a system and designates an "empty" term.

2.   The set of terminal symbols $\Sigma_t = \{t_i\}$.
3.   The set of substitutable symbols (variable symbols) $\Sigma_x = \{x_i\}$.
4.   The delimiter symbols: brackets "(", ")" and a comma ",".

Terms

The terms are basic objects, which the system deals with. Informally, terms can be defined as constructs of the form $f(t_1, \ldots, t_n)$. At formal definition, two kinds of terms will be distinguished: specific (not containing variables or substitutable symbols) and substitutable (containing variables).

The set of specific terms T_c is defined recursively as follows:

- $\forall c \in \Sigma_c,\ c \in T_c$;
- $\forall f \in \Sigma_t,\ \forall t_1, \ldots, t_n \in T_c,\ f(t_1, \ldots, t_n) \in T_c$.

The set of substitutable terms T_v is defined similarly, with the addition of variable symbols:

- $\forall c \in \Sigma_c,\ c \in T_v$;
- $\forall x \in \Sigma_x,\ x \in T_v$;
- $\forall f \in \Sigma_t,\ \forall t_1, \ldots, t_n \in T_v,\ f(t_1, \ldots, t_n) \in T_v$.

It can be seen from the definition that the set of substitutable terms extends the set of specific terms: $T_c \subset T_v$. The set $T_{fv} = T_v \backslash T_c$ will be called the set of terms with free variables.

Operations on Terms

Below, some operations for the terms defined above are introduced. The definitions of operations for the set of substitutable terms T_v are formulated. Similar definitions in some cases are also applicable for specific terms from the subset $T_c \subset T_v$.

At first, the elementary properties of terms are defined: a name, an arity and a subterm.

The name: *name*: $T_v \rightarrow STRING$.

$\forall c \in \Sigma_c, \ name(c) = String(c).$

$\forall x \in \pounds_x, \ name(x) = String(x).$

$\forall f \in \pounds_t, \ \forall t_1,\ldots,t_n \in T_v, \ name(f(t_1,\ldots,t_n)) = String(f).$

The arity: *arity*: $T_v \to INT$.

$\forall c \in \pounds_c, \ arity(c) = 0.$

$\forall x \in \pounds_x, \ arity(x) = 0.$

$\forall f \in \pounds_t, \ \forall t_1,\ldots,t_n \in T_v, \ arity(f(t_1,\ldots,t_n)) = n.$

The subterm (of the first level): *subterm*: $T_v \times INT \to T_v$.

$\forall c \in \pounds_c, \ \forall j \in INT, \ subterm(c, j) = NIL.$

$\forall x \in \pounds_x, \ \forall j \in INT, \ subterm(x, j) = NIL.$

$$\forall f \in \pounds_t, \ \forall t_1,\ldots,t_n \in T_v, \ \forall j \in INT, \ subterm(f(t_1,\ldots,t_n)) = \begin{cases} 0, \ j < 1; \\ t_j, \ 1 \le j \le n; \\ 0, \ j > n. \end{cases}$$

Besides the subterms of the first level, the subterms of arbitrary levels are also needed. Such subterms are defined by the path, i.e. the sequence of integers — the positions of subterms inside a higher-level term.

The set of paths: *subterm_paths*: $T_v \to INT^{**}$.

$\forall c \in \pounds_c, \ subterm\_paths(c) = \{\mu\}$ (only the empty sequence).

$\forall f \in \pounds_t, \ \forall t_1,\ldots,t_n \in T_v, \ subterm\_paths(f(t_1,\ldots,t_n)) = \{\mu\} \cup \bigcup_{i=1}^{n} i \wedge subterm\_paths(t_i).$

The subterm (of any level): $subterm^*$: $T_v \times INT^* \to T_v$.

$\forall t \in T_v$, $subterm^*(t, \mu) = t$.

$\forall t \in T_v$, $\forall p = (p_1, ..., p_k) \in subterm\_paths(t)$, $p \neq \mu$,
$subterm^*(t, p) = subterm^*(subterm(t, p_1), (p_2, ..., p_k))$.

$\forall t \in T_v$, $\forall p \notin subterm\_paths(t)$, $subterm^*(t, p) = NIL$.

The substitution of the subterm: $subterm\_replace$: $T_v \times T_v \times INT^* \to T_v$.

$\forall t, t_r \in T_v$, $subterm\_replace(t, t_r, \mu) = t_r$.

$\forall t, t_r \in T_v$, $\forall p = (p_1, ..., p_k) \in subterm\_paths(t)$, $p \neq \mu$,
$subterm\_replace(t, t_r, p) = subterm\_replace(subterm(t, p_1), t_r, (p_2, ..., p_k))$.

$\forall t, t_r \in T_v$, $\forall p \notin subterm\_paths(t)$, $subterm\_replace(t, t_r, p) = t$.

Further, the operations of substitution and bound unification are introduced.

The substitution of free variables is a set of pairs $[x_i, t_i]$ consisting of free variables x_i and terms t_i which are substituted instead of variables:

$s = s[x_i, t_i] = substitution([x_1, t_1], ..., [x_n, t_n])$, $x_i \in \Sigma_x$, $t_i \in T_v$.

The set of substitutions will be denoted as S.

The substitution operation: $subst$: $T_v \times S \to T_v$.

$\forall t \in T_v, \forall s = s([x_1, t_1], [x_2, t_2], ..., [x_n, t_n]) \in S$,
$subst(t, s) = subst(subst(t, s([x_1, t_1])), s([x_2, t_2], ..., [x_n, t_n]))$.

The sequential application of this equality allows reducing the operation definition to substitutions with one variable.

$\forall c \in \pounds_c$, $\forall s = s[x_1, t_1] \in S$, $subst(c, s) = c$.

$$\forall x \in \pounds_x, \ \forall s = s[x_1, t_1] \in S, \ subst(x,s) = \begin{cases} t_1, x = x_1; \\ x, x \neq x_1. \end{cases}$$

$$\forall f \in \pounds_t, \ \forall t_1, \ldots, t_n \in T_v, \ \forall s \in S,$$
$$subst(f(t_1, \ldots, t_n), s) = f(subst(t_1, s), \ldots, subst(t_n, s)).$$

The bound unification: *bound_unify*: $T_v \times T_v \times S \to T_v \times S$. Based on two terms and a current substitution, the given function computes a unifier and the specified substitution.

$$\forall t \in T_v, \ \forall s \in S, \ bound\_unify(t, NIL, s) = bound\_unify(NIL, t, s) = (NIL, \varnothing).$$

$$\forall c_1, c_2 \in \pounds_c, \ \forall s \in S, \ bound\_unify(c_1, c_2, s) = \begin{cases} (NIL, \varnothing), \ c_1 \neq c_2; \\ (c_1, s), \ c_1 = c_2. \end{cases}$$

$$\forall x_1, x_2 \in \Sigma_x, \ \forall s \in S, \ bound\_unify(x_1, x_2, s) = (x_1, s \cup [x_1, x_2]).$$

$$\forall t \in T_v \setminus \Sigma_x, \ \forall x \in \Sigma_x, \ \forall s \in S,$$
$$bound\_unify(t, x, s) = bound\_unify(x, t, s) = (t, s \cup [x, t])$$

(the requirement for *t* not to be a variable is due to both equalities, in this case, would be applicable and they would give inconsistent results. The case when both terms are variables was considered in the previous subsection).

$$\forall f, g \in \pounds_t, \ \forall t_1, \ldots, t_n, \ q_1, \ldots, q_m \in T_v, \ \forall s \in S,$$

$$bound\_unify(f(t_1, \ldots, t_n), g(q_1, \ldots, q_m), s) = \begin{cases} (NIL, \varnothing), \ f \neq g \text{ or } m \neq n; \\ (f(bound\_unify1(t_1, q_1, s), \ldots, bound\_unify1(t_n, q_n, s)); \\ s \cup \bigcup_{i=1}^{n} bound\_unify2(t_i, q_i, s)). \end{cases}$$

That is, the unification occurs only if names and arities of terms coincide. In this case, the unifier is obtained by a recursive application of operation, and all the substitutions found at subterm unification are added to the substitution.

For brevity, the symbols *bound_unify*1 and *bound_unify*2 designate the first and the second component of *bound_unify*, i.e. the unifier and the substitution.

Based on the definition of the bound unification, it is possible to introduce the concept of a free unification. For this purpose, it is necessary to introduce preliminary some auxiliary concepts.

The set of free variables: $fv : T_v \to \Sigma_x^*$.

$$\forall c \in \pounds_c, \, fv(c) = \varnothing.$$

$$\forall x \in \pounds_x, \, fv(x) = \{x\}.$$

$$\forall f \in \pounds_f, \, \forall t_1, \ldots, t_n \in T_v, \, fv(f(t_1, \ldots, t_n)) = \bigcup_{i=1}^{n} fv(t_i).$$

Renaming of variables for the purpose of conflict elimination: $free\_fv : T_v \times \Sigma_x^* \times \Sigma_x^* \to T_v$.

$$\forall c \in \pounds_c, \, \forall X, Y \subset \pounds_x, \, free\_fv(c, X, Y) = c.$$

$$\forall x \in \pounds_x, \, \forall X, Y \subset \pounds_x, \, free\_fv(x, X, Y) = \begin{cases} x, x \notin X; \\ x_m : x_m \notin X \cup Y, x \in X. \end{cases}$$

$$\forall f \in \pounds_f, \, \forall t_1, \ldots, t_n \in T_v, \, \forall X, Y \subset \pounds_x,$$

$$free\_fv(f(t_1, \ldots, t_n), X, Y) = f(free\_fv(t_1, X, Z), \ldots, free\_fv(t_n, X, Z)),$$

where $Z = Y \cup fv(f(t_1, \ldots, t_n))$.

The free unification: *free_unify*: $T_v \times T_v \to S$. This function is similar to the bound unification but assumes that the variables included in input terms are not bound. Thus, for example, the variable x_1 which is included both in the first and the second term is considered different in the first and the second term. Therefore, the renaming of variables is necessary, which is carried out with the help of *free_fv*.

$$free\_unify(t_1, t_2) = bound\_unify(t_1, free\_fv(t_2, fv(t_1), \varnothing), \varnothing).$$

Rewriting Rules

Further, a concept of a rewriting rule which is used for transformation of terms is defined.

The *rewriting rule* is a pair of terms $r=(t_{in}, t_{out})$ on which the additional condition $fv(t_{out}) \subseteq fv(t_{in})$ is imposed, i.e. all free variables of a target term t_{out} are present in the input term t_{in}. The rule can be written in the form of the term $rule(t_{in}, t_{out})$.

The application of the rule to the given term $t \in T_c$ is described by the function

$$apply(t, rule(t_{in}, t_{out})) = subst(t_{out}, free\_unify(t, t_{in})).$$

It is necessary to notice that the additional condition $t_{in} \notin \Sigma_x$ is usually imposed on the input term, i.e. the input term cannot be a variable. This restriction is due to the fact that if the input term is a variable, the corresponding rule will always be applicable. Such a restriction is not imposed for reasons which will be explained further.

Usually, the rule is applied not to a term, but to some its subterm. Thus, there is not the only result of the application of a rule, but a set of results from rule application to various subterms:

$$apply(t, r) = \bigcup_{p \in subterm\_paths(t)} \{subterm\_replace(t, apply(subterm^*(t, p), r), p)\}.$$

The rewriting rule system is the ordered sequence of rules: $R=(r_1, \ldots, r_k)$. The application of the system of rules to a term is a union of results of the application of separate rules to the given term (and its subterms):

$$apply(t, R) = \bigcup_{r \in R} apply(t, r).$$

It is necessary to notice that rewriting rules allow defining an abstract rewriting system (according to the definitions (Baader & Nipkow, 1999)). Indeed, let us fix the system of rewriting rules R. Consider the set of specific terms T_c with the binary relation $\rightarrow$: $\forall x, y \in T_c$, $x \rightarrow y \Leftrightarrow y \in apply(x, R)$ defined on it. This structure can be considered as a rewriting system that will allow defining such properties as confluence, Noetherian, existence, and uniqueness of a normal form. Such properties will depend on a chosen system of rules *R*.

Rewriting Strategy

In a general case, the result of rewriting rule system applied to a term is a set of terms, instead of a unique result term, i.e. the action of a system of rules is defined ambiguously. For practical application, it is necessary to define a method of selection of one result from the set *apply(t,R)*. The rewriting strategy is such a method.

The *rewriting strategy* is an arbitrary function selecting a unique result from the set of results: $str(t,R) = t_{res} \in apply(t,R)$. From the construction of the set $apply(t,R)$, the equivalent definition follows: $str(t,R) = (p_i, r_j), p_i \in subterm\_paths(t), r_j \in R$, i.e. the strategy chooses a specific rule from the system and a subterm to which it is applied.

One of the ways to assign the strategy is ordering of sets *subterm_paths(t)* and *R*, then the strategy chooses the first (in sense of the introduced order) elements for which the rule works. For the set of paths to subterms, it is possible to use a lexicographic order, i.e. $(i_1, \dots, i_n) < (j_1, \dots j_m)$, if $i_1 < j_1$, or $i_1 = j_1, i_2 < j_2$, etc. At the same time, it will be considered that the empty subsequence precedes any number. Such order on the set *subterm_paths(t)* corresponds to a depth-first tree traversal. For a breadth-first traversal, it is necessary to use the modified order, in which the sequence length is compared at first (the shorter one comes in the beginning), and only for the sequences of identical length, the lexicographic order is used.

For the set of paths, it is possible to use a lexicographic order both in direct and opposite directions. The usage of a direct direction leads to the *TopDown* strategy, in which the subterms are checked beginning "from above", i.e. the term itself, then its first subterm, etc. The opposite direction is implemented in the *BottomUp* strategy, where checking begins "from below".

For the system of rules *R*, it is possible to use a total order, which is based on the lexicographic comparison. But such ordering has no special sense, as it is based on superficial similarity. The partial ordering, based on the fact that more specific rules have higher priority, is more intelligent. Formally, it is defined as follows. The relation of a partial order for terms $t_1 \leq_c t_2 \Leftrightarrow \exists s \in S : subst(t_2, s) = t_1$ is introduced (i.e. there is a substitution transforming a less specific term to a more specific). The order relation for rules is defined based on a comparison of their input samples:

$(t_{in}, t_{out}) \leq_c (q_{in}, q_{out}) \Leftrightarrow t_{in} \leq_c q_{in}$. For the rules incomparable over the introduced relation of a partial order, another criterion is applied, for example, the order of rules in a system.

Interaction with an Environment

The model constructed above describes the term rewriting system which can be applied for transformation of an input term into an output based on a system of rules. However, for the practical application, the additional possibilities can be demanded, such as execution of procedural actions or data access, which are not presented in an input term. In this connection, the system model will be extended by adding interaction with an external program environment.

As an environment model, the triple $E=<X, check, action>$ is considered, where E is a designation of the environment, X is an input state of the environment, $check: X \times T_c \rightarrow BOOL$ is the function allowing to request data from the environment, $action: X \times T_c \rightarrow X$ is the function modeling the influence on the environment. Thus, the state of the system at the time moment i is described now by two parameters: t_i is a current term and x_i is a current state of the environment.

The definition of a rewriting rule is also extended: the quadruple $r=(t_{in}, t_{cond}, t_{out}, t_{act})$ will be called a *rule*, with additional conditions $fv(t_{cond}) \subseteq fv(t_{in})$, $fv(t_{out}) \subseteq fv(t_{in})$, $fv(t_{act}) \subseteq fv(t_{in})$. In this definition, the following additional terms are added: t_{cond} is a condition of application of a rule and t_{act} is an additional action at rule activation. The rule application to a term (and all its subterms) is defined in the following modified manner:

$$Apply(t,r) = \bigcup_{p \in subterm\_paths(t) \wedge rule\_check(subterm^*(t,p),r)} \left\{ subterm\_replace(t, apply(subterm^*(t,p),r), p) \right\},$$

where the function of checking the applicability of the rule is

$$rule\_check(t,r) = check(x_i, subst(t_{cond}, free\_unify(t, t_{in}))) .$$

Thus, from the unification of a term and the input sample, the substitution is obtained, which is applied to a condition term, then the result is checked with the use of the environment (the *check* function). Thus, the environment can influence the activation of rules.

The transformation of terms is defined the same as earlier but taking into account the new definition of *Apply(t,r)*. If the state of the system at the moment of time *i* is known (i.e. t_i and x_i are known), then the term during the following moment of time *i*+1 is defined by the equation $t_{i+1} = str(t_i, R) \in apply(t_i, R)$. The state of the system at the moment of time *i*+1 is defined by the equation $x_{i+1} = action(x_i, subst(t_{act}, free\_unify(t_i, t_{in})))$.

Thus, the extended system is defined by the system of rules $R = \{r_1, \ldots, r_n\}$ and the environment *E=<X,check,action>*. If the input term t_0 and the initial state x_0 of the environment are set, it is possible to define the sequence $\{(t_i, x_i)\}$ of states of the system at the moment of time *i*. If for any *i* the $t_{i+1} = t_i$ is satisfied, the system *(R,E)* converges for the input data (t_0, x_0). In this case, the resulting term is t_i, which will be designated as follows: $t_i = redue(t_0, R, x_0, E)$, or, at the fixed environment, $t_i = reduce(t_0, R)$.

TermWare Language

For denoting terms and rules, the TermWare language (Doroshenko & Shevchenko, 2006) is used. Terms are written in a natural manner, i.e. $f(t_1, \ldots, t_n)$. For separate symbols from Σ_t, which designate arithmetic operations, the reduced designations are used, i.e. the expression can be written in a natural form which is then transformed into a term. For example, the expression *a+b*(c+d)* will be transformed into the term *plus(a,multiply(b,plus(c,d)))*.

For writing the rules, the following syntax is used: the rule $r = (t_{in}, t_{cond}, t_{out}, t_{act})$ is written as $t_{in}[t_{cond}] \rightarrow t_{out}[t_{act}]$. Notice that this notation is also the reduction for the term $if\_rule(t_{in}, t_{cond}, action(t_{out}, t_{act}))$. The components t_{cond} and t_{act} are unessential and can be omitted, i.e. the rule can look like $t_{in}[t_{cond}] \rightarrow t_{out}$ or $t_{in} \rightarrow t_{out}[t_{act}]$, or $t_{in} \rightarrow t_{out}$.

In TermWare, the propositional variables have identifiers that begin with the symbol $, for example, $x, $y. As an illustration, consider the rule $p(\$x,\$y) \rightarrow q(\$y,\$x)$. For example, the result of the application of this rule to the term *p(a,f(b))* is the term *q(f(b),a)*.

The TermWare language contains special facilities for expression of lists. The list $(t_1, t_2, \ldots, t_n)$ is represented in the form $cons(t_1, cons(t_2, \ldots, cons(t_n, NIL)\ldots))$. For such a construct, the reduction $[t_1, \ldots, t_n]$ is used. Also for writing the rules dealing with such lists, the reduction $[\$x:\$y] = cons(\$x\$y)$ is useful. This reduction selects the first element of the list ($x) and the rest of the list ($y). Notice that $[x:y] \neq [x,y]$: the first expression designates the list of any length, with the first element x and the rest of the list y, whereas the second expression designates the list containing two elements x and y.

Existing Software Implementations and Applications of Rewriting Rules TECHNIQUE

The *rewriting rules system* is a software system that contains a language for description of rules, a program for their application, and, probably, sets of ready-made rules or rewriting strategies. Often, such a system is a part of a more general metaprogramming platform.

Further, some examples of rewriting rules systems and applications of term rewriting technique for working with program code are considered.

Rewriting Rule Systems

The Maude system (Meseguer et al., 2002; "The Maude System", 2017; Winkler, 1993) is based on the theory of algebraic systems. The program is represented in the form of many-sorted algebra: the set of sorts (data types) and operations on objects of these sorts are defined. Rules are defined in two ways. System definition includes the equations setting correlations between operations. These equations can be used for reduction of terms to an elementary form (which contains only basic operations). Besides, the rules, which are used for transition between terms and cannot be simplified with the use of the equations, are defined separately. Formally, the unique distinction between the equations and the rules consists in that the equations are symmetric (i.e. the transition is possible from the left part to the right, and vice versa). Nevertheless, it is recommended to use these means for different purposes: the equations for defining the general structure of a problem, and a rule for defining specific transformations.

The Stratego system (Bravenboer et al., 2008; "Stratego Program Transformation Language", n.d.) uses the standard model of rewriting systems: working object is the term to which rules of the form $LHS{\rightarrow}RHS$ are applied. The feature of the Stratego is that rewriting strategy plays a key role in the system (in particular, it can be seen from its name too). The rewriting strategies are used in all systems of rewriting rules, as for practical application it is necessary to set a certain order of action of rules. However, most systems contain one or several predetermined strategies, and, probably the means for implementation of new strategies. In Stratego, a different approach is provided: the set of elementary strategies and the means of their combination, which gives the possibility to declaratively define any strategy. The means of definition of strategies actually are basic in the system: even rewriting rules are implemented as a strategy of a special kind.

As it can be seen from its name, ASF+SDF system ("The Meta-Environment", n.d.; van den Brand et al., 2000) consists of two parts (formalisms): the means for description of SDF language syntax (Syntax Definition Formalism) (Heering et al., 1989) and facilities for description of ASF transformations (Algebraic Specification Formalism) (van den Brand et al., 2000). ASF+SDF is used only for solving the problems of source code transformation, therefore the code analysis means are an integral part of the system. This is the difference of ASF+SDF from other rewriting rule systems, such as Stratego, where SDF means are also used, but they are independent of rewriting rules. Therefore, the Stratego system can be used for solving the problems which are not concerned with processing of source code of programs. For such problems, it is possible to use ASF+SDF too, but at that, it will be necessary to implement a special language for a problem description that will allow using SDF means.

As well as ASF+SDF, the TXL system (Cordy, 2006; "The TXL Programming Language", n.d.) is intended for description of transformations of source code of programs. Therefore, the TXL rules contain two parts: the description of the language syntax and the description of transformations. Unlike ASF+SDF, where these descriptions are placed in different files and basically can be used independently, in TXL syntax and transformations are described in a shared file and use one language for their notation.

Rules in TXL are written in the syntax of the source language (similarly to ASF+SDF).

The Jess system (Friedman-Hill, 2003; "Jess, the Rule Engine for the Java Platform", 2013) was initially developed as a platform for the development of expert systems, therefore it has certain differences from other rewriting rule systems. The working object in Jess is the set of facts, each of which is represented in the form of a term. Rules, as well as in other systems, consist of the left part defining a condition of application of a rule, and the right part describing the action of a rule. However, unlike the other systems, in Jess the left part of a rule can contain several samples; thus the rule works, if each sample is present among the current set of the facts. The right part is not necessarily rewriting (fact updating): other actions, such as addition or fact removal, an output of the debugging information or a call of any function, are possible.

The APS system ("APS and IMS are best for rewriting and modelling", n.d.; Letichevsky, Kapitonova, & Konozenko, 1993) unites various programming paradigms: besides rewriting, there can be used imperative and functional paradigms for implementing strategies, as well as logic paradigm in the form of unification during rewriting. In this regard, APS is close to Stratego or TXL. As well as the Maude system, APS supports the implementation of additional possibilities with the use of the built-in language (in the case of APS it is the APLAN language). The APS system is a part of the insertion modeling system IMS (A. A. Letichevsky, O. A. Letychevskyi, & Peschanenko, 2012; A. Letichevsky, O. Letichevskyi, Peschanenko, Blinov, & Klionov, 2011).

The TermWare system (Doroshenko & Shevchenko, 2006; "TermWare", n.d.) mainly uses the standard model of rewriting rules. Rules are defined in the form *LHS→RHS*. Basically, the notation in the form of terms is used, although the reduced form of notation is available for standard arithmetic and logic operations. Also, it is possible to attach additional parsers for supporting the syntax of various languages. Several built-in rewriting strategies are available, and additional strategies can be implemented with the use of Java program interfaces. Though TermWare can be used as an independent application (with the command line interface), the basic variant of the usage of this system consists in its embedding in Java applications. Every system of rules can specify the so-called facts database — the Java class implementing a certain interface. In this case, the system of rules can receive information from the facts database and carry out the actions provided in the facts database. Thus, the interaction of a declarative system of rules and the imperative Java program is achieved.

The Main Directions of Use

Rewriting rules systems are a natural way of representation of transformations of program source code. Therefore, there are many works describing the use of term rewriting technique for working with source code. The main directions of research in this area are the following:

- **analysis of code:** for the purpose of finding errors and inconsistencies with programming standards);
- **transformation of code:** depending on the transformation purpose, the following directions are possible:

- ○ **refactoring**, which includes the transformations preserving a behavior of a program, but improving code readability, conformity to coding standards and eliminating code duplication;
- ○ **optimization**, which involves the transformations aimed at increase in performance of an application;
- ○ **security**, which contains the transformations raising the security of a program by detection and elimination of potentially dangerous code fragments;
- ○ **legacy code**, which is the transition from legacy code to a similar code on more modern platforms, supporting legacy code and maintaining its interaction with new applications;
- **creation of new languages:** such languages can be implemented as independent domain-specific languages (DSLs) or as extensions of existing general-purpose languages;
- **software modeling:** creation and processing of high-level program models, transition from high-level models to source code.

The use of term rewriting systems for each of the above-mentioned directions is considered in more detail further.

The Analysis of Source Code

The static analysis of source code is an important factor in the improvement of the quality of applications. This method allows finding fragments of program code, which are syntactically correct (i.e. do not cause a compilation error) but can lead to errors during execution or complicate understanding and updating of source code. It should be emphasized that it is a question of the static analysis, i.e. the analysis of source code without the use of the information at execution time.

The input data of the algorithms of the static analysis is source code written in a high-level programming language. Some elementary errors can be already found in text representation (for example, the use of unsafe functions). However, for the full-scale analysis, it is necessary to translate source code to a more structured representation, most often a parse tree. Since trees are naturally transformed into terms, it is possible to use rewriting rules after the syntactic analysis.

There are two approaches for implementation of static analysis algorithms: more formal and more practical. Under the formal approach, a formal model of program execution is constructed, for example, with the use of linear temporal logic (LTL) (Lacey, Jones, van Wyk, & Frederiksen, 2002). Then, some properties of the program, for example, the absence of blocking (deadlocks) (Akhter & Roberts, 2006) in the case of a parallel program, are formulated. After that, the tools of automatic proof are used, which can determine whether the input program has a given property.

More applicable in practice is the approach based on a search of standard templates of erroneous code. Such an approach cannot guarantee the detection of all errors; besides, false positives are possible, when correct code corresponds to the defined pattern of an error. Nevertheless, such an approach does not require a search of a large number of states, therefore it is applicable to code of any size. An example of such an approach is the JavaChecker system, intended for searching standard errors in Java code ("JavaChecker", n.d.). The system is based on TermWare and uses rewriting rules for searching the defined patterns of errors. The input code is not modified: when the error is detected, the system reports the message with the use of means of interaction with an environment.

Refactoring

Refactoring is the transformation of source code preserving behavior of a program but changing the structure of code (Garrido & Meseguer, 2006). Refactoring can be applied for simplification of code and improvement of its readability, elimination of code duplication and alignment with chosen programming standards. Classical examples of refactoring are renaming of a method (and all references to it), allocation of reusable code into a separate method.

The proof of correctness of transformations, i.e. that transformations do not change a program behavior, is very important for refactoring. For this purpose, as well as in a case with the code analysis, formal methods are applied. In paper (Garrido & Meseguer, 2006), Maude is applied for formal representation of some transformations of Java programs and proof of their correctness. For this purpose, the specification of execution time semantics for Java, constructed in (Farzan, Chen, Meseguer, & Rosu, 2004) is used. It is necessary to notice that the proof requires human intervention, although it intensively uses the possibilities of Maude. Similar results for a preprocessor of C language were obtained in (Garrido, Meseguer, & Johnson, 2006).

Optimization

One more important class of transformations are optimizing transformations, i.e. transformations which preserve a program behavior (a result for given input data), but increase the performance of the program, for example, concerning the execution time. Optimizing transformations can be applied both at the level of source code and at the level of intermediate representation in the compiler. The latter variant is used most often, as in this case transformations are carried out automatically, and the source code does not contain the special optimized constructs which hide the purpose of code and complicate its understanding. For the implementation of optimizing transformations inside the compiler, rewriting rules systems can also be used, as shown in (Visser, Benaissa, & Tolmach, 1998). The mentioned work proposes to use Stratego for implementation of optimizers. It is supposed that optimizing transformations for the given language are defined in the form of rules and strategies of Stratego. The strategies are interpreted at debugging of transformations and compiled into C code for final use that increases the performance of the optimizer.

Security

Increasing the security of applications is becoming more and more important in connection with the development of Internet technologies and widespread harmful programs. The use of rewriting rules systems may improve the security of applications, for example, due to detection of errors at the static analysis. Besides, the rules can be used for implementation of transformations raising the security.

Examples of such transformations are described in (Wang, Cordy, & Dean, 2005), where TXL rules for automatic inclusion of additional assumptions (assertions) in C code are used. Assumptions check correctness of execution of certain operations. For example, at accessing an array, it is checked that the index does not exceed the array dimensions. If the assumption is not satisfied, the execution of a program is interrupted with an error message that allows the developer to find an error. Besides, the execution of a program in an incorrect state that leads to vulnerability, such as buffer overflow, is prevented.

Legacy Code

When working with legacy code, there are a lot of problems concerned with the absence of documentation, loss of information on system architecture, usage of no longer supported technologies. Rewriting rules can extract additional information from source code and also carry out transformations to simplify interaction of old applications with new platforms. The transfer of a whole application or its part to new technology is also possible.

Extraction of information from legacy code is described, for example, in (Ceccato, Dean, Tonella, & Marchignoli, 2008). It is a matter of recovery of data structures from code for languages not supporting abstract data structures. TXL rules find sets of variables that are used together; such sets correspond to data structures in modern programming languages. A similar approach is used in (Hunold et al., 2008), where TXL rules are used for the extraction of information on system architecture.

Domain-Specific Languages

At present, there is considerable interest in domain-specific languages (Visser, 2007). Such languages allow developing programs in a given subject domain easier and faster than general-purpose languages, as they contain language constructs implementing the concepts of a subject domain. But there is a need to create the corresponding language (or a set of languages) for each subject domain, unlike general-purpose languages, where one language can be applied for solving various problems. Therefore, the problem of automation of development of DSLs is actual.

Most often, the transformation to one of the general-purpose languages is used for DSLs instead of development of a full-scale compiler. For the implementation of such a transformation, it is possible to use rewriting rules. For example, paper (Hamey & Goldrei, 2007) describes the Apply language for solving computer vision tasks. This language is translated to C by means of Stratego rules. Paper (Fabry, Tanter, & D'Hondt, 2007) considers the implementation of aspect-oriented domain-specific language KALA for description of transactions.

Extensions of Languages

Besides independent domain-specific languages, it is possible to implement languages that are built into existing general-purpose language, extending its facilities. Actually, such languages extend libraries of some subject domain, adding convenient syntax for method calls. In (Bravenboer, Dolstra, & Visser, 2007), the StringBorg platform for the development of such built-in languages is proposed. Grammars of both languages (basic and built-in) are defined independently, after which the parser of conjoint language is automatically generated. Constructs of built-in language are converted to API calls with the use of Stratego rules. Automatic generation of API for the construction of safe string representation of built-in language is possible (for example, in the case of SQL, the replacement of special symbols is made, which prevents SQL code injections). Another advantage of the StringBorg platform is the possibility to use any combination of basic and built-in languages. The special case of language extension is presented in (Kats, Bravenboer, & Visser, 2008), where Java was chosen as the basic language, and a bytecode, i.e. a low-level representation of the same language, was used as the extension.

Software Modeling

For many problems, it is convenient to use high-level program models (the "high level" refers to a level higher than source code). Such models can have various presentations: specialized languages, UML diagrams, formal specifications. But in any case, elements of a model can be represented in the form of terms. Therefore, rewriting rules can be applied to models as well as to source code.

There are the following classes of problems concerned with program models.

- Transition from source code to a model.
- Transition from a model to source code.
- Model transformation.

In the first case, it is a matter of recovery of some information implicitly present in code. Rewriting rules are well suited for solving this task, since the necessary information can be represented in the form of source code templates. This approach is applied in (Alalfi, Cordy, & Dean, 2008), where UML entity-relationship diagram is recovered from data description in SQL language. The recovery is implemented using TXL. A similar approach is used in (Hunold et al., 2008) for recovery of the architecture of the legacy system.

The transition from a model to a source code actually means the generation of code from a model. This approach is provided in model-driven development (MDD) and model-driven architecture (MDA) (Miller et al., 2003). Rewriting rules can be used directly for implementation of such transformation. Model-based approaches, proposing general-purpose modeling languages, allow handling the dynamism and particularly the deðnition of reconðguration rules managing the evolution of an application in run-time (Eichler, Monteil, & Stolf, 2013). They provide a very intuitive and visual formal or semi-formal description of structural properties (for example, designing and describing software models using UML). Nevertheless, the generic ðtness of model-based approaches implies poor means of describing speciðc issues like behavioural properties. The models still need to be formally checked against incoherencies or inconsistencies. In the paper (Chama, Elmansouri, & Chaoui, 2013), a framework and a tool based on graph transformation allowing an automatic translation of some UML diagrams to equivalent Maude formal specifications are described. Work (Eichler, Monteil, & Stolf, 2013) proposes a formal approach for integrating the consideration of constraints, non-trivial attributes, and their propagation within the framework of graph rewriting systems. In (Boronat, Carsi, & Ramos, 2005), a framework for model management, called MOMENT, is described that supports automatic formal model transformations in MDA based on the algebraic specification of models and uses term rewriting system. The formal transformation mechanism is applied between platform-independent models, such as UML models and relational schemas. In (Karsai, Agrawal, & Ledeczi, 2003), a meta-programmable tool GRE (Graph Rewriting Engine) for implementing model transformations is applied. GRE is programmed through a high-level language, called GReAT (Graph Rewriting And Transformations) and captures metamodels of transformations as explicitly sequenced rewriting rules graph. Paper (Hemel, Kats, & Visser, 2008) describes generation of code for Java platforms Seam and JavaServer Faces from high-level descriptions of data. The project uses Stratego and is a part of the implementation of the WebDSL language (Visser, 2007). The transformation of models with the use of TXL is described in (Paige & Radjenovic, 2003).

Rewriting rules can also be used for the development of additional tools that transform models. For example, paper (Arnoldus, Bijpost, & van den Brand, 2007) proposes the construction of code generator based on templates, which comprehends the syntax of a target language. The SDF grammar is used, which extends the syntax of a target language with a set of metaconstructs for designing templates (such as a reference to model elements or traversal of a model). Generation is implemented with the use of ASF+SDF rules which interpret metaconstructs, extracting the data from a model.

CONCLUSION

Rewriting rules systems are popular means for implementing the tasks of data processing and transformation. They have the following advantages.

- The data format used (terms) complies with a tree structure of program representation.
- Built-in capabilities for searching the required pattern.
- The order of application of transformations is separated from actual transformations.
- Declarative representation facilitates addition and modification of transformations.
- Many systems contain built-in support for term parsing and code generation based on terms.
- It is possible to specify rules as transformation samples using the syntax of a target language.
- There is a possibility of extending a system using traditional imperative languages.

The disadvantages of rewriting rules systems include the following.

- The unusual programming model complicates learning.
- Debugging of rules is often absent or not sufficiently supported.
- Rule editors and graphical user interface are often absent.
- Different systems use different syntax for the same concepts.
- The performance can be lower than that of similar systems implemented in a traditional way.

In general, it can be noted that despite all the disadvantages, rewriting rules systems are optimal means for solving many problems related to processing and transformation of programs. However, it is necessary to further develop such systems, applications that use them and make standardization efforts in this field.

REFERENCES

Akhter, S., & Roberts, J. (2006). *Multi-core programming: Increasing performance through software multi-threading.* Santa Clara, CA: Intel Press.

Alalfi, M., Cordy, J. R., & Dean, T. R. (2008). SQL2XMI: Reverse engineering of UML-ER diagrams from relational database schemas. In *Proceedings of the 15th Working Conference on Reverse Engineering (WCRE'08)* (pp. 187-191). Washington: IEEE Computer Society. 10.1109/WCRE.2008.30

APS and IMS are best for rewriting and modelling. (n.d.). Retrieved from http://apsystems.org.ua

Arnoldus, J., Bijpost, J., & van den Brand, M. (2007). Repleo: A syntax-safe template engine. In *Proceedings of the 6th International Conference on Generative Programming and Component Engineering* (pp. 25-32). New York: ACM.

Baader, F., & Nipkow, T. (1999). *Term rewriting and all that.* Cambridge: Cambridge University Press.

Boronat, A., Carsi, J. A., & Ramos, I. (2005). An algebraic baseline for automatic transformations in MDA. *Electronic Notes in Theoretical Computer Science, 127*(3), 31–47.

Bravenboer, M., Dolstra, E., & Visser, E. (2007). Preventing injection attacks with syntax embeddings. A host and guest language independent approach. In *Proceedings of the 6th international conference on Generative Programming and Component Engineering (GPCE'07)* (pp. 3-12). New York: ACM. 10.1145/1289971.1289975

Bravenboer, M., Kalleberg, K. T., Vermaas, R., & Visser, E. (2008). Stratego/XT 0.17. A language and toolset for program transformation. *Science of Computer Programming. Special issue on experimental software and toolkits, 72*(1-2), 52-70.

Ceccato, M., Dean, T. R., Tonella, P., & Marchignoli, D. (2008). Data model reverse engineering in migrating a legacy system to Java. In *Proceedings of the 15th Working Conference on Reverse Engineering (WCRE 2008)* (pp. 177-186). Washington: IEEE Computer Society. 10.1109/WCRE.2008.27

Chama, W., Elmansouri, R., & Chaoui, A. (2013). A modeling and verification approach based on graph transformation. *LNSE, 1*(1), 39–43. doi:10.7763/LNSE.2013.V1.9

Cordy, J. R. (2006). The TXL source transformation language. *Science of Computer Programming, 61*(3), 190–210. doi:10.1016/j.scico.2006.04.002

Dershowitz, N., & Plaisted, D. A. (2001). Rewriting. In A. J. Robinson & A. Voronkov (Eds.), *Handbook of automated reasoning* (pp. 537–608). Cambridge, MA: Elsevier. doi:10.1016/B978-044450813-3/50011-4

Doroshenko, A., & Shevchenko, R. (2006). A rewriting framework for rule-based programming dynamic applications. *Fundamenta Informaticae, 72*(1-3), 95–108.

Eichler, C., Monteil, T., & Stolf, P. (2013). *Modelling constrained dynamic software architecture with attributed graph rewriting systems.* Retrieved from https://hal.archives-ouvertes.fr/hal-00798391/document

Fabry, J., Tanter, E., & D'Hondt, T. (2007). ReLAx: Implementing KALA over the Reflex AOP kernel. In *Proceedings of the 2nd Workshop on Domain-Specific Aspect Languages (DSAL'07)* (pp. 3-12). New York: ACM. 10.1145/1255400.1255403

Farzan, A., Chen, F., Meseguer, J., & Rosu, G. (2004). Formal analysis of Java programs in JavaFAN. In *Proceedings of the International Conference on Computer Aided Verification (CAV'2004) (LNCS)* (Vol. 3114, pp. 501-505). Berlin: Springer. 10.1007/978-3-540-27813-9_46

Friedman-Hill, E. (2003). *Jess in action.* Greenwich: Manning Publications Co.

Garrido, A., & Meseguer, J. (2006). Formal specification and verification of Java refactorings. In *Proceedings of the 6th IEEE International Workshop on Source Code Analysis and Manipulation (SCAM'06)* (pp. 165-174). Washington: IEEE Computer Society. 10.1109/SCAM.2006.16

Garrido, A., Meseguer, J., & Johnson, R. (2006). *Algebraic semantics of the C preprocessor and correctness of its refactorings.* Retrieved from http://www.ideals.illinois.edu/handle/2142/11162

Hamey, L., & Goldrei, S. (2007). Implementing a domain-specific language using Stratego/XT. In *Proceedings of the 7th Workshop on Language Descriptions, Tools, and Applications (LDTA 2007)* (pp. 32-46). Amsterdam: Elsevier Science.

Hemel, Z., Kats, L. C. L., & Visser, E. (2008). Code generation by model transformation: A case study in transformation modularity. In *Proceedings of the 1st International Conference on Model Transformation (ICMT 2008)* (pp. 183-198). Berlin: Springer.

Huet, G. (1980). Confluent reductions: Abstract properties and applications to term rewriting systems. *Journal of the Association for Computing Machinery, 27*(4), 797–821. doi:10.1145/322217.322230

Hunold, S., Korch, M., Krellner, B., Rauber, T., Reichel, T., & Rünger, G. (2008). Transformation of legacy software into client/server applications through pattern-based rearchitecturing. In *Proceedings of the 32nd Annual IEEE International Conference on Computer Software and Applications (COMPSAC'08)* (pp. 303-310). Washington: IEEE Computer Society. 10.1109/COMPSAC.2008.158

JavaChecker. (n.d.). Retrieved from http://www.gradsoft.kiev.ua/products/javachecker_eng.html

Jess, the Rule Engine for the Java Platform. (2013). Retrieved from http://www.jessrules.com

Karsai, G., Agrawal, A., & Ledeczi, A. (2003). A metamodel-driven MDA process and its tools. *Proceedings of Workshop in Software Model Engineering, UML 2003 Conference.* Retrieved from https://www.isis.vanderbilt.edu/sites/default/files/Karsai_G_10_0_2003_A_Metamode.pdf

Kats, L. C. L., Bravenboer, M., & Visser, E. (2008). Mixing source and bytecode: A case for compilation by normalization. In *Proceedings of the 23rd ACM SIGPLAN Conference on Object-Oriented Programming, Systems, Languages, and Applications (OOPSLA'08)* (pp. 91-108). New York: ACM. 10.1145/1449764.1449772

Lacey, D., Jones, N. D., van Wyk, E., & Frederiksen, C. C. (2002). Proving correctness of compiler optimizations by temporal logic. In *Proceedings of the 29th ACM SIGPLAN-SIGACT Symposium on Principles of Programming Languages (POPL'02)* (pp. 283-294). New York: ACM. 10.1145/503272.503299

Letichevsky, A., Letichevskyi, O., Peschanenko, V., Blinov, I., & Klionov, D. (2011). Insertion modeling system and constraint programming. In *Proceedings of the 7th International Conference "ICT in Education, Research and Industrial Applications. Integration, Harmonization and Knowledge Transfer" (ICTERI 2011)* (pp. 51-64). Berlin: Springer.

Letichevsky, A. A., Kapitonova, Yu. V., & Konozenko, S. V. (1993). Computations in APS. *Theoretical Computer Science, 119*(1), 145–171. doi:10.1016/0304-3975(93)90343-R

Letichevsky, A. A., Kapitonova, Yu. V., Kotlyarov, V. P., Letichevsky, O. A., Nikitchenko, N. S., Volkov, V. A., & Weigert, T. (2008). Insertion modeling in distributed system design. *Problems in Programming,* (4), 13-38.

Letichevsky, A. A., Kapitonova, Yu. V., Volkov, V. A., Letichevsky, O. A., Baranov, S. N., Kotlyarov, V. P., & Weigert, T. (2005). Systems specification by basic protocols. *Cybernetics and Systems Analysis, 41*(4), 479–493. doi:10.100710559-005-0083-y

Letichevsky, A. A., Letychevskyi, O. A., & Peschanenko, V. S. (2012). Insertion modeling system. In *Proceedings of the 8th International Conference on Perspectives of System Informatics (PSI'11)* (pp. 262-273). Berlin: Springer.

Mal'cev, A. I. (1973). *Algebraic systems.* Berlin: Springer. doi:10.1007/978-3-642-65374-2

Meseguer, J., Olveczky, P. C., Stehr, M.-O., & Talcott, C. (2002). Maude as a wide-spectrum framework for formal modeling and analysis of active networks. In *Proceedings of the DARPA Active Networks Conference and Exposition (DANCE'02)* (pp. 494-510). Washington: IEEE Computer Society. 10.1109/DANCE.2002.1003516

Miller, G., Evans, A., Jacobson, I., Jondell, H., Kennedy, A., Mellor, S. J., & Thomas, D. A. (2003). Model driven architecture: How far have we come, how far can we go? In *Proceedings of the 18th Annual ACM SIGPLAN Conference on Object-oriented programming, systems, languages, and applications (OOPSLA'03)* (pp. 273-274). New York: ACM. 10.1145/949344.949409

Paige, R., & Radjenovic, A. (2003). Towards model transformation with TXL. In *Proceedings of the Metamodelling for MDA Workshop 2003* (pp. 162-177). Academic Press.

Stratego Program Transformation Language. (n.d.). Retrieved from http://strategoxt.org

TermWare. (n.d.). Retrieved from http://www.gradsoft.com.ua/products/termware_eng.html

The Maude System. (2017). Retrieved from http://maude.cs.uiuc.edu

The Meta-Environment. (n.d.). Retrieved from http://www.meta-environment.org

The TXL Programming Language. (n.d.). Retrieved from http://www.txl.ca

van den Brand, M., Heering, J., Klint, P., & Olivier, P. (2000). Compiling language definitions: The ASF+SDF compiler. *ACM Transactions on Programming Languages and Systems*, *24*(4), 334–368. doi:10.1145/567097.567099

Visser, E. (2007). WebDSL: A case study in domain-specific language engineering. In *Proceedings of the International Summer School on Generative and Transformational Techniques in Software Engineering (GTTSE 2007) (LNCS)* (Vol. 5235, pp. 291-373). Berlin: Springer.

Visser, E., Benaissa, Z.-A., & Tolmach, A. (1998). Building program optimizers with rewriting strategies. In *Proceedings of the 3rd ACM SIGPLAN International Conference on Functional Programming (ICFP'1998)* (pp. 13-26). New York: ACM.

Wang, L., Cordy, J. R., & Dean, T. (2005). Enhancing security using legality assertions. In *Proceedings of the IEEE 12th International Working Conference on Reverse Engineering (WCRE'05)* (pp. 35-44). Washington: IEEE Computer Society. 10.1109/WCRE.2005.36

Winkler, T. (1993). Programming in OBJ and Maude. *Functional Programming, Concurrency, Simulation and Automated Reasoning, International Lecture Series 1991-1992. LNCS*, *693*, 229–277.

KEY TERMS AND DEFINITIONS

Abstract Rewriting System (ARS): A set of objects with a binary relation called the rewrite relation defined on it.

Optimization: The transformation which preserves a program behavior (a result for a given input data) and increases program performance, for example, in regard to execution time.

Rewriting Rules System: A software system which contains a language for description of rules, a program for their application, and also, probably, sets of ready-made rules or rewriting strategies.

Rewriting Rules Technique: A formal tool for transformation of formal systems based on term rewriting and a practical tool for programming, which allows implementing transformations of complex objects. Rewriting covers a wide range of methods of replacing sub-terms of a formula with other terms.

Rewriting Strategy: A function selecting a unique result term from the set of results of application of a rewriting rule system to a term.

TermWare: An open-source implementation of rewriting rules engine written in Java. It provides a language for describing rewriting rules that operate on data structures called terms and also a rule engine that interprets rules to transform terms.

Term Rewriting Rule: A pair of terms (left-hand side and right-hand side) divided by an arrow. The left-hand side is replaced by the right-hand side.

Chapter 4

Algebra–Dynamic Models for CPU– and GPU–Parallel Program Design and the Model of Auto–Tuning

ABSTRACT

This chapter considers algebra-dynamic models of parallel programs, which are based on concepts of transition systems theory and algebra of algorithms. The models of sequential and parallel multithreaded programs for multicore processors and program models for graphics processing units are constructed. The authors describe transformations of programs aimed at transition from sequential to parallel versions (parallelization) and improving performance of parallel programs in respect to execution time (optimization). The transformations are based on using rewriting rules technique. The formal model of program auto-tuning as an evolutional extension of transition systems is proposed, and some properties of programs are considered.

INTRODUCTION

Development of multicore processors leads to increasing importance of parallel programming aimed at standard, widely accessible computers, and not just for specialized high-performance systems (Akhter & Roberts, 2006). However, there is one more direction of parallel programming which

DOI: 10.4018/978-1-5225-9384-3.ch004

has received especial development recently, namely, the programming of general-purpose tasks for graphics processing units (GPUs) ("General-Purpose Computation on Graphics Hardware", n.d.). Market requirements have led to rapid development of GPUs and, at present, their computing capacity considerably exceeds the capabilities of usual processors. Therefore, GPUs were applied for solving the problems not concerned directly with graphics processing. Research in these directions is supported by GPU developers: in particular, NVIDIA company provides CUDA platform for general-purpose computations on GPUs ("NVIDIA CUDA technology", n.d.).

Despite the presence of specialized facilities for CUDA, development of GPU programs remains a labor-consuming work, which requires from a developer a knowledge about low-level details of hardware and software platform. Therefore, there is a need of research in the area of automation of software development process for GPUs. This chapter describes the development of formal design methods, based on concepts of transition systems theory, algebraic programming and algebra-dynamic models of programs (Andon, Doroshenko, Tseytlin, & Yatsenko, 2007; Doroshenko, Zhereb, & Yatsenko, 2010) with the use of rewriting rules technique (Doroshenko & Shevchenko, 2006; "TermWare", n.d.) for automated development of efficient programs for GPUs. High-level models of programs and models of program execution are developed for central processing unit (CPU) and GPU. Application of rewriting rules and high-level models for automated parallelization and optimization of programs for GPUs is described. The method of automated transition between a high-level model of a program and a source code, which is based on the use of special rewriting rules is proposed. This chapter also considers the formal model of program auto-tuning constructed as an evolutional extension of transition systems and properties of programs.

Currently there is a significant amount of research in the area of automation of software development for graphics processors. Research community examines problems of transition from sequential to parallel programs as well as problems of optimization of existing parallel programs with the use of GPUs. Particularly, the paper (Lee, Min, & Eigenmann, 2009) considers the automatic transition from a multithreaded program implemented using OpenMP technology ("OpenMP Application Programming Interface", 2015) to implementation of the same program on CUDA platform. Paper (Baskaran et al., 2008) describes a platform for loop optimization in GPU programs. Systems for automatic parallelization and optimization of programs from a specific subject domain, for example, data mining (Ma & Agrawal, 2009) or image processing (Allusse, Horain, Agarwal, & Saipriyadarshan, 2008), are developed. Paper (Lefohn, Sengupta, Kniss, Strzodka, & Owens, 2006) describes the library of high-level data structures for GPUs. Programming platforms for GPUs providing the facilities of a level higher than CUDA are also developed, such as hiCUDA (Han & Abdelrahman, 2009) and BSGP (Hou, Zhou, & Guo, 2008). The difference of the research presented in this chapter consists in the use of formal models and methods that allows combining brevity of description and efficiency of implementation of transformations.

The Concept of a transition System

For description of program execution, general concepts of the theory of transition systems are used (Andon et al., 2007; Keller, 1975). We consider here the *transition system* as a triple

$$(S_0, S, d),$$

where S is the state space; $S_0 \subseteq S$ is the set of initial states; $d \subset S \times S$ is the binary transition relation over the state space. The system can move from the state S_i into the state s_j, if $(s_i, s_j) \in d$.

Let $P(S_0)$ designate the set of all finite processes, i.e. sequences of states $p = s_0 s_1 \ldots s_n \ldots$, beginning at S_0, $s_0 \in S_0$, $n \geq 1$, then d can be represented as the relation

$$d \subseteq P(S_0) \times S. \tag{1}$$

The transition relation d and the set of initial states S_0 unambiguously define the set of admissible processes F of the system as the union $F = \bigcup_{t=0}^{\infty} F_t$, where F_t is a set of admissible processes of length t.

The sets F_t can be defined recursively as follows:

$$F_0 = S_0;$$

$$\forall t > 0, F_t = \{ps \mid p \in F_{t-1}, (p,s) \in d\}$$

(i.e. the processes of the length t are obtained from the processes of the length $t-1$ by adding the states defined by the transition relation).

Therefore, the system (S_0,S,d) can be defined in an alternative way as a pair (S,F).

Below, some general properties of transition systems (Doroshenko, 2000) are described.

The system (S_0,S,d) is called *finite-state automaton*, if $(ps_1,s_2) \in d \Leftrightarrow (s_1,s_2) \in d$. For the finite-state automaton system, admissible transitions depend only on a current state and do not depend on a prehistory. All the systems considered in this chapter are a finite-state automaton. Therefore, instead of relation (1), $d \subseteq S \times S$ will be used further.

The system is called *deterministic*, if $\forall p \in P(S_0)$, $\exists! s \in S$: $(p,s) \in d$, i.e. the transition is defined unambiguously. For the deterministic finite-state automaton systems the relation d is a function $d: S \rightarrow S$.

The transition system is called *multicomponent*, if the set of its states S is contained in the Cartesian product $S \subseteq S_1 \times ... \times S_m$.

Sets $S_1,...,S_m$, which make the least Cartesian product containing S, are called *system components*.

If system components are multicomponent transition systems, then the system is called *multilevel*.

Multicomponent multilevel systems are used as a model of execution of parallel programs in this chapter.

Execution Model of a Sequential Program

Algebra-dynamic models of programs consist of two parts: a model of program structure and a model of program execution. For modeling a program code, Glushkov's algebra of algorithms (see Chapter 1 and also (Andon et al., 2007; Doroshenko, Tseytlin, Yatsenko, & Zachariya, 2006; Yatsenko, 2012)) is used. It should be reminded that Glushkov's algebra is the two-sorted algebra $GA=<\{Pr,Op\}; \Omega_{GA}>$ containing the set of conditions (predicates) Pr and the set of operators Op.

The operations defined in GA are the following.

- Logic operations of conjunction, disjunction and negation:

$AND: Pr \times Pr \rightarrow Pr;$

$OR : Pr \times Pr \rightarrow Pr;$

$NOT : Pr \times Pr \rightarrow Pr.$

- Checking a condition after operator execution (prediction):

$AFTER : Op \times Pr \rightarrow Pr.$

- Sequential composition of operators:

$THEN : Op \times Op \rightarrow Op.$

- Branching:

$IF : Pr \times Op \times Op \rightarrow Op.$

- Iteration (a loop construct):

$WHILE : Pr \times Op \rightarrow Op.$

In this chapter, the following program model is considered. The program consists of a set of components corresponding to specific programming language functions (methods, procedures) $P=\{P_1,...,P_k\}$. It is regarded that the component is described by an identifier (a name unique within the program) and also by the model of a code:

$P_i=(name_i, code_i),\ name_i \in STRING,\ code_i \in Op.$

Procedural code is represented as an expression in Glushkov's algebra.

On the sets of operators and conditions, basic elements are defined, and then it is possible to build various algebra expressions which will be described by compound conditions and operators. Basic conditions and operators usually depend on a subject domain. One basic operator common for all subject domains is selected: a call of a function $call(P_i)$.

A particular feature of programs for GPUs is their division into two parts: a code executed on CPU and a specialized code for GPU. These parts can be implemented in different languages. For example, in (Doroshenko & Zhereb, 2009) programs are considered, in which CPU code was implemented in C#, whereas GPU code was developed in C for CUDA, a special extension of C language.

In GPU program model, this feature is considered as follows. The program is considered as a set of components; however, now each component belongs either to CPU or to GPU code. Thus, for CPU and GPU sets of basic operators can differ.

To construct the execution model, the interpretation of Glushkov's algebra expressions that describe a program must be defined. Let V be the set of program variables. For simplicity, it is assumed that variables are typeless and take values in some universal set D. *Memory states* are partial mappings b: $V{\rightarrow}D$ from variables to their values. The *information environment* is the set of memory states: $B=\{b: V{\rightarrow}D\}$. Then, the operators of Glushkov's algebra are interpreted as a function over the set B, and conditions are interpreted as predicates on the same set. The interpretation of basic operators and conditions is defined for each subject domain.

For compound expressions the interpretation is defined as follows.

- For logical operations:

$$(u \ AND \ v)(b) = (uv)(b) = u(b) \wedge v(b) \ ;$$

$$(u \ OR \ v)(b) = (u + v)(b) = u(b) \vee v(b) \ ;$$

$$(NOT \ u)(b) = \bar{u}(b) = \neg u(b) \ .$$

- For prediction operation (checking a condition after operator execution):

$$(u \ AFTER \ P)(b) = (Pu)(b) = u(P(b)) \ .$$

- For sequential composition of operators:

$$(P \ THEN \ Q)(b) = (PQ)(b) = Q(P(b)) \ .$$

- For branching:

$$(IF\ u\ THEN\ P\ ELSE\ Q)(b) = ((u)P,Q)(b) = \begin{cases} P(b),\ u(b) = 1, \\ Q(b),\ u(b) = 0. \end{cases}$$

- For iteration:

$$(WHILE\ u\ P)(b) = (\{u\}P)(b) = \begin{cases} (\{u\}P)(P(b)),\ u(b) = 1, \\ b,\ u(b) = 0. \end{cases}$$

Here $u \in Pr$, $v \in Pr$ are conditions; $P \in Op$, $Q \in Op$ are operators.

Now, the transition system which models a sequential program execution can be described. The states of the transition system have the form $s=(b,R,F)$, where $b \in B$ is the current memory state, $R \in Op$ is the current control state (a residual program, i.e. operator describing a part of a function that has not been yet executed (Andon et al., 2007)), $F \in (P \times Op)^*$ is a function call stack, i.e. a sequence of function identifiers and operators describing control state of a given function. The initial state of the given program is $s_0 = (b_0,\ Op(P_m),\ (P_m \to \varnothing))$, where P_m is the main function (entry point of the program).

The transition relation d^{seq} is described by the following transition rules:

$(b,\ yR,\ F) \to (y(b),\ R,\ F)$, where $y \in Op$ is a basic operator;

$$(b,\ if(u,P,Q)R,\ F) \to \begin{cases} (b,\ PR,\ F),\ u(b) = 1, \\ (b,\ QR,\ F),\ u(b) = 0; \end{cases}$$

$$(b,\ while(u,P)R,\ F) \to \begin{cases} (b,\ Pwhile(u,P)R,\ F),\ u(b) = 1, \\ (b,\ R,\ F),\ u(b) = 0; \end{cases}$$

$(b,\ call(P_j)R,\ (...,P_i \to \varnothing)) \to (b,\ Op(P_j),\ (...,\ P_i \to R,\ P_j \to \varnothing))$;

$(b,\ \mu,\ (...,\ P_i \to R,\ P_j \to \varnothing)) \to (b,\ R,\ (...,\ P_i \to \varnothing))$.

Rule 1 defines the execution of basic operators. Rules 2 and 3 describe branching and loop operators. The execution of a function is described by rules 4 (function call) and 5 (return from a function).

Final states (from which no transition is possible) are $s_f = (b,\ \mu,\ \varnothing)$.

The described transition system for sequential programs will be denoted as S^{seq}. Notice that this system is deterministic, as for each state there is an unambiguously deterministic transition.

EXECUTION MODEL OF A PARALLEL PROGRAM

Based on the previously constructed sequential program model, this subsection describes similar models for multithreaded programs executed on CPU and GPU.

Execution Model of a Multithreaded Program

The execution model of a multithread program S^{mt} uses the paradigm of a shared memory (Akhter & Roberts, 2006) and is an extension of the model S^{seq}. The program in S^{mt} is executed by several threads, which can work simultaneously or in turns. All threads have access to a shared memory and there is no need for additional means of communication between threads — reading and writing shared variables can be used for this. However, for correct work of a program, the synchronization of threads is necessary to prevent a race condition. Furthermore, correct use of synchronization allows avoiding deadlocks.

The model S^{mt} consists of the two levels — low and high. On the low level, it is S^{seq} model extended by additional operators of creation ($call\_thread(P_i, P_j)$, where P_i in an identifier of a procedure to be launched and T_j is an identifier of a thread which will execute the procedure) and synchronization of threads. This level is also called a thread level. On the high level, which is called a program level, the states are partial mappings of a set of threads to a set of states of the low level:

$$s^2 = \{T_1 \rightarrow s_1^1, \ ..., \ T_k \rightarrow s_k^1\} \ .$$

Consider the operators of thread synchronization. The operators of a critical section $lock(cs_i)$ and $unlock(cs_i)$ define the fragments of code, which can be executed in only one thread at a time. These operators are identical to a classic concept of binary semaphores (Akhter & Roberts, 2006) and the critical section is modeled as follows:

$critical(cs,R) = lock(cs)\ THEN\ R\ THEN\ unlock(cs)$

where cs is an identifier of a critical section. As mentioned before, for any cs_i only one thread can execute the operators R_i. The operators of other critical sections are executed independently.

Threads interact by executing operators $wait(ev_i)$, $signal(ev_i)$, $signal\_all(ev_i)$ and $reset(ev_i)$, where ev_i is an identifier of a synchronization point. After executing $wait(ev_i)$, a thread remains in a waiting state until the operator $signal(ev_i)$ (one thread is unlocked) or $signal\_all(ev_i)$ (all threads are unlocked) is executed in any other thread. The operator $reset(ev_i)$ resets the state of a synchronization point, as a result of which any next call of operator $wait(ev_i)$ leads to a transition to a waiting state.

As in the sequential case, the execution model is defined by a transition system. Model states are partial mappings $s^2 = \{T_i \rightarrow s_i^1\}$ of the set T of all threads to states of separate threads. The starting thread is designated as $T_0 \in T$. The set of all threads T consists of the starting thread and all threads T_j which occur in operators $call\_thread(P_j, T_j)$ in a program. The states of separate threads $s_i = (b, R_i, F_i) \in S^{mt}$ are similar to those in the sequential model, i.e. they are defined by a memory state b, control state R_i and a stack of calls F_i. In the model with a shared memory, the memory state b is shared by all threads. Therefore, the state of a multithreaded program can be defined in a more compact form, as a pair $s' = (b, \{T_i \rightarrow (R_i, F_i)\})$. Further, the more general form is used, which significantly facilitates the definition of transition relations.

The initial state of a program is $s_0^2 = \{T_0 \rightarrow s_0^1\} = \{T_0 \rightarrow (\varnothing, Op(P_m), (P_m \rightarrow \varnothing))\}$. Only one thread is executed and its state coincides with a state of a sequential program. All other threads are explicitly created by program operators at further execution. Such a model is used in most multithreaded platforms.

The transition relation d^{mt} extends the relation d^{seq} previously defined for the sequential model. The following rules for new operators are added to the set of rules 1–5 from the previous subsection:

$(b, call\_thread(P_i, T_j)R, F) \rightarrow (b, R, F);\ T_j \rightarrow (b, Op(P_i), (P_i \rightarrow \varnothing));$

$\{T_i \rightarrow (b, lock(cs)R, F)\} \rightarrow \{T_i \rightarrow (b \cup \{cs \rightarrow T_i\}, R, F)\}$, at $b(cs) = \varnothing$ or $b(cs) = T_i;$

$\{T_i \rightarrow (b \cup \{cs \rightarrow T_i\}, unlock(cs)R, F)\} \rightarrow \{T_i \rightarrow (b \cup \{cs \rightarrow \varnothing\}, R, F)\};$

$$(b,\ wait(ev)R,\ F) \rightarrow \begin{cases} (b,\ R,\ F),\ state(ev) = 1, \\ (b',\ waiting(ev)R,\ F),\ state(ev) = 0, \end{cases}$$

where $b' = b \cup \{queue(ev) \rightarrow queue(ev) \cup T_i\}$;

$(b,\ waiting(ev)R,\ F) \rightarrow (b,\ R,\ F)$, at $T_i \notin queue(ev)$;

$(b,\ signal(ev)R,\ F) \rightarrow (b \cup \{state(ev) \rightarrow 1,\ queue(ev) \rightarrow q'\},\ R,\ F)$, where $q' = queue(ev) \setminus T_j$;

$(b,\ signal\_all(ev)R,\ F) \rightarrow (b \cup \{state(ev) \rightarrow 1,\ queue(ev) \rightarrow \varnothing\},\ R,\ F)$;

$(b,\ reset(ev)R,\ F) \rightarrow (b \cup \{state(ev) \rightarrow 0\},\ R,\ F)$.

Rule 6 describes the behavior of the operator $call\_thread(P_i, T_j)$. It creates the new thread T_j for executing the procedure P_i, but the state of the initial thread does not change.

Rules 7–8 describe the behavior of a critical section. For each critical section cs_i, the state $b(cs_i)$ is stored in a shared memory. The state can be empty ($b(cs_i) = \varnothing$) when the critical section is free or coincide with a thread identifier ($b(cs_i) = T_j$), i.e. the critical section is occupied by a thread T_j. The operator $lock(cs_i)$ "occupies" the critical section, i.e. it associates the state of a critical section cs_i with an identifier of a current thread. The operator $lock$ can be executed only in the case when the critical section is free or occupied by the same thread, which tries to occupy it again. The operator $unlock$ relieves the critical section, after which the other threads can execute it.

Rules 9–13 describe the behavior of operators working with events or synchronization points. As in the case of a critical section, the state of each synchronization point ev_i is stored in the memory. The state is defined by two components: $state(ev_i)$ describes an active or passive state of the synchronization point, and $queue(ev_i)$ specifies the queue of threads waiting for execution at this synchronization point.

Rule 9 defines the behavior of the operator $wait(ev_i)$. This operator is executed only in the case when the synchronization point ev_i is active, otherwise a thread transits to a waiting state and is appended to the queue. Rule 10 specifies the condition of exiting from a waiting state, namely, removing the current thread from the queue. Rules 11 and 12 describe the operators *signal(ev$_i$)* and *signal_all(ev$_i$)*, which are executed in other thread to complete waiting. As mentioned before, the main difference between these operators is that *signal(ev$_i$)* relieves one thread and *signal_all(ev$_i$)* relieves all threads from the waiting queue. The operator *reset(ev$_i$)* sets the current synchronization point *ev$_i$* to a passive state, after which it can be used for further synchronization.

The transition relation for the entire multithreaded program integrates the transitions of separate threads. This is done as follows: a subset of active threads is selected and for each of them the transition is made according to the inner relation *d^{mt}* and a new state of the program is obtained as a result of combining the states of separate threads. Formally, the transition relation *S^{mt}* is described in the following way:

$$\{T_{i_1} \to s_{i_1}, ..., T_{i_k} \to s_{i_k}, T_{i_{k+1}} \to s_{i_{k+1}}, ..., T_{i_n} \to s_{i_n}\}$$
$$\to \{T_{i_1} \to p_{i_1}, ..., T_{i_k} \to p_{i_k}, T_{i_{k+1}} \to s_{i_{k+1}}, ..., T_{i_n} \to s_{i_n}\}.$$

Here the first *k* threads are active and change their state. New states are defined as $p_i = (merge(b_i), R_i, F_i)$ where $(s_i, (b_i, R_i, F_i)) \in d^{mt}$. Since a memory state in the model is common to all threads, it is necessary to combine changes of states of separate threads. For that, the function *merge*: $B \times B^* \to B$ is used. This function changes the states of each variable which were modified in any of active threads. It is defined as follows:

$$merge(b_0, b_1, ..., b_k) = \left\{ v_i \to \begin{cases} !\{b_j(v_i) \mid b_j(v_i) \neq b_0(v_i), j = \overline{1,k}\} \\ b_0(v_i) \end{cases} \right\}, \tag{2}$$

where an arbitrary element of some set *A* is denoted as *!A*.

Function *merge* works in the following way: for each variable, one of the new values is selected which is different from the value of this variable in an initial state. If there are no such values (in all threads the variable did not change the value), then its new value coincides with an initial in combined memory state.

The following rule of thread work completion is added to the constructed transition relation:

$$\{T_1 \to s_1,...,T_{k-1} \to s_{k-1}, T_k \to (b,\mu,\varnothing), T_{k+1} \to s_{k+1},...,T_n \to s_n\}$$
$$\to \{T_1 \to s_1,...,T_{k-1} \to s_{k-1}, T_{k+1} \to s_{k+1},...,T_n \to s_n\}.$$

That is, after a thread attains a final state in the sense of transition system S^{seq}, it completes its work and is removed from the list of active threads.

The final states for a multithreaded system can be of two types. In case of successful completion of all threads, the transition system transits to a state $s_f' = (b,\{\})$ (the empty set of active threads). Such state will be called final and will be equated with the final state of the last thread $s_f = (b,\mu,\varnothing)$. There may also be a situation where one or several threads are still working, but any of them cannot make a transition because the following operator is *lock* or *wait* Such states will be called *deadlock states*.

It should be noted that such a definition of final threads does not take into account the category of background threads (the threads for which the completion criterion is not defined). Real-world multithreaded programs usually are completed when not all background threads finished (Akhter & Roberts, 2006). However, for formalization of optimization transformations considered in this book, the proposed definition is sufficient enough.

The transition system constructed in this subsection and intended for interpretation of execution of parallel multithreaded programs with shared memory will be denoted as S^{mt}.

Program Model for GPUs

In this model, the execution of CPU and GPU programs are considered separately; each of these cases is modeled as a transition system (S^{cpu} and S^{gpu}, respectively). Then, the model of the entire program S^{gc} is built as a union of the GPU and CPU models.

CPU Program Model

For modeling a part of program code intended for execution on CPU, one of the previously constructed models S^{seq} or S^{mt} can be used. In this work, to model CPU code execution, the extended sequential model S^{seq} is used. It means that the CPU part of a program is executed sequentially and does not use multithreading.

The following new operators intended for interaction with GPU are added to the S^{seq} model:

- *init_gpu* is GPU initialization;
- *copy_gpu*(m_G, m_C) is copying the data to GPU memory;
- *copy_back*(m_C, m_G) is copying the results from GPU memory to CPU memory;
- *call_gpu*($P_i, block, grid$) is the call of GPU function (CUDA kernel) P_i.

Accordingly, it is necessary to add the transition rule, which will change the state of the transition system S^{gc} as a whole, rather than only one of its components. Formal description of these rules is given further after the consideration of the GPU component.

GPU Program Model: Block Level

The GPU code execution model S^{gpu} is built as a multilevel transition system (Andon et al., 2007). The states of the multilevel system combine multiple lower-level states, which are themselves represented as transition systems. At the lowest level, execution of separate threads is modeled using the modified sequential system S^{seq}. Transitions of separate thread models are unified as a transition of the higher-level transition system.

The model S^{gpu} contains three levels of states hierarchy: a thread level, a block level and a grid level. Separate threads (the first level) are united in blocks (the second level), which in turn form the grid that describes the GPU program as a whole (the third level).

The important feature of the model S^{gpu} compared to the sequential model S^{seq} is a memory hierarchy. In CUDA, there are five kinds of memory: the registers, shared memory, constants cache, texture cache and global memory. In the model, only two most frequently used kinds of memory are considered, namely, shared memory and global memory.

Various kinds of memory in the model can be represented as additional components of a state. For the lowest level (threads) the state is $s=(b_g, b_s, R, F)$, where $b_g \in B_g$ is a global memory state; $b_s \in B_s$ is a shared memory state. However, to simplify the model, all kinds of memory are combined into a single information environment $b = b_g \cup b_s$, $b \in B = B_g \times B_s$. It is also assumed that all predicates and operators of Glushkov's algebra operate over the combined set B.

Thread level transition relation is described by rules 1–5 (rule 4 has the additional restriction — the called function P_j should work on GPU, which is described by __device__ modifier in C for CUDA).

Block level state is the set of threads with their states: $s^2 = \{T_i \rightarrow s_i^1\}$. A number of threads per block is fixed and determined by thread call parameters. Block level transitions are combinations of thread level transitions. This procedure is performed as follows: some subset of threads is selected; the transition is performed for each of the selected threads according to the thread level transition relation; a new state of the block is obtained as a combination of new states of individual threads. In this new state, the control states of individual threads are determined by the transition relation for S^{seq}. However, it is needed to merge individual memory states, as all threads operate over common memory. Therefore, the defined earlier function $merge: B \times B^* \rightarrow B$ (2) is used. It changes the value of each variable which has been changed in at least one of threads. This function is applied to both kinds of memory b_g, b_s (or to the combined memory b).

There is an important restriction on block level transitions: all threads that perform transitions simultaneously, should execute the same operator (although over different data). This models the hardware restriction of current NVIDIA devices, namely, that there is only one instruction unit per block, and therefore only threads that execute the same instruction can be performed simultaneously ("NVIDIA CUDA technology", n.d.).

For thread synchronization, the *_Barrier* operator is added. This operator is used to synchronize threads within the block: each thread that reaches this operator waits for all other threads. To model the execution of the *_Barrier* operator, the following transition rules are added:

$(b,\ \_Barrier;\ R,\ F) \rightarrow (inc(b),\ waiting\_Barrier;\ R,\ F);$

$(b,\ waiting\_Barrier;\ R,\ F) \rightarrow (zero(b),\ R,\ F)$, if $bc=threads$.

The additional variable $bc \in b_s$ describing a number of waiting threads is used. Two operators $inc(b): bc \leftarrow bc+1$ and $zero(b): bc \leftarrow 0$ increase the number of waiting threads and clear the waiting list. In C for CUDA, the *_Barrier* operator is implemented as __syncthreads() primitive.

GPU Program Model: Grid Level

The grid level model is constructed from multiple block level models in the same way as the block level model is constructed from thread level models.

Grid level states are collections of blocks with their states: $s^3 = \{B_j \to s_j^2\}$. The number of blocks per grid is fixed and determined by thread call parameters, in the same way as in block level.

Grid level transitions are combined from block level transitions in the same way as for block level. One difference from the block level model is that shared memory is specific for each block, therefore *merge* function is only used for global memory b_g.

CUDA platform provides some synchronization facilities that work at grid level (such as atomic operations). However, such facilities are not supported by all devices, have a negative effect on program performance and contradict CUDA best design practices that suggest independent execution of blocks ("NVIDIA CUDA technology", n.d.). Therefore, these facilities are not included in the model under consideration.

Interaction of CPU and GPU

Interaction of CPU and GPU programs is achieved from CPU code using the operators *copy_gpu*, *copy_back* and *call_gpu* (the operator *init_gpu* is used once at the beginning of the program and does not influence the further execution). The first two operators copy the data between CPU memory and GPU global memory. Formally, this is described as a mapping between certain subsets of CPU memory b_c and global memory b_g.

The *call_gpu* operator actually starts GPU code execution. Its work is described by two transition rules:

$$(s^c, (b_g, \varnothing)) \to (s^c, s_0^g(P_i, block, grid)) ;$$

$$(s^c, s_f^g) \to ((b, R, F), (b_g', \varnothing)) .$$

Here, the designation $s^c = (b,\ call\_gpu(P_i,\ block, grid)R,\ F)$ is used for a current state of CPU model. Rule 16 describes the creation of the initial state of the model S^{gpu}, when the operator *call_gpu* is executed. The parameters of this state, such as a number of blocks and threads and the kernel to execute, are taken from operator parameters. Notice that this rule does not change CPU control state: from a CPU point of view, the program execution is suspended during execution of the GPU kernel. Rule 17 is applied when GPU computations are completed (i.e. GPU model achieves its final state s_f^g). It

Figure 1. The structure of the GPU program model

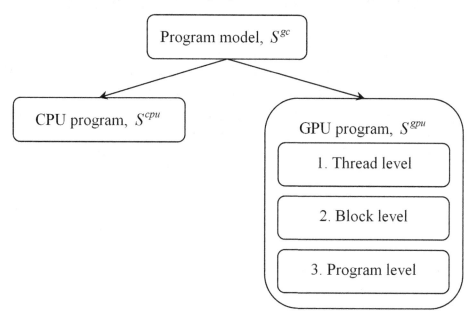

clears GPU control state and completes execution of the *call_gpu* operator in the CPU model. The state of CPU memory is not changed during GPU computations: results should be explicitly copied using the *copy_back* operator.

All the components of the S^{gc} model are shown in Figure 1.

The algebra-dynamic models of program execution described in this chapter can be used to perform a formal analysis and transformation of programs for GPUs. In (Andon, Doroshenko, & Zhereb, 2011) authors utilize algebra-dynamic models to prove program transformation correctness for multithreaded programs. Certain program properties (equivalence, absence of conflicts and deadlocks) can be formulated in terms of the developed models. Then, the correctness of transformation is proved for programs having such properties. The same approach is applicable to GPU.

Program Transformations Based on Rewriting Rules

This subsection considers the application of the algebra-dynamic models for designing program transformations that can increase performance by parallelizing and optimizing of programs for GPUs. To automate program transformations, TermWare rewriting rules system described in Chapter 3 is used (see also (Doroshenko & Shevchenko, 2006; "TermWare", n.d.)).

The Transition from Sequential Program to GPU Program

Rewriting rules are used to automate program transformations, such as a transition from a sequential program for CPU to a parallel program executing on GPU. For this purpose, a sequential program is represented as a high-level model described above. The code of each component ($code_i$) is modeled as an expression in Glushkov's algebra which has a natural term representation. These terms are then transformed with TermWare rewriting rules.

Consider the parallelizing transformations for loop expressions. Let the fragment of the initial sequential program be the following:

$$Seq1 = for(i, 0, m, body(i)) \tag{3}$$

Here, the loop operator $for(var, min, mac, body)$ with a counter is used, which can be expressed using the general *while* operator. The compound operator $body(i)$ describes the loop body. Consider the transformation of Seq_1 to the parallel equivalent:

$$
\begin{aligned}
Gpu1 = \ &init\_gpu; \\
&copy\_gpu; \\
&call\_gpu(gbody1, block1d, grid1d); \\
&copy\_back.
\end{aligned}
\tag{4}
$$

Here, GPU interaction operators described earlier are used. The loop body $body(i)$ is moved to the new GPU component $gbody1$:

$$
\begin{aligned}
gbody1 = \ &assign(i, \_GetCoor(x)); \\
&\_CpuToGpu(body(i)).
\end{aligned}
\tag{5}
$$

The first operator computes the iteration number i from thread parameters using the $\_GetCoor(x)$ function. Then, the loop body is executed with $\_CpuToGpu$ used for transformation between CPU and GPU operators.

The transformation from the sequential program $Seq1$ to the parallel version for graphics processing units $Gpu1$ is described by the following rewriting rules:

for($iter$, 0, $itlm$, $body$)
$\rightarrow$ [*init_gpu*; *copy_gpu*; *call_gpu*(*gbody*1, *block*1*d*, *grid*1*d*($itlm$)); *copy_back*] $^;$

[_ *AddMethod*(*gbody*1, _ *CreateKernel*1*d*($iter$, $body$))] ;

_*CreateKernel*1*d*($iter$, $body$) $\rightarrow$ *assign*($iter$, _*GetCoor*(*x*));
_*CpuToGpu*($body$)*grid*1*d*($itlm$) $\rightarrow$ ($itlm$ + *block*1*d* − 1) / *block*1*d* $^\cdot$

Rule 1 describes the transition of the fragment of the program from *Seq*1 to *Gpu*1. Notice that the rule contains the action _*AddMethod* which creates a new component of the program. Rule 2 generates the body of the new component *gbody*1. Rule 3 sets the size of a grid for kernel call based on the iteration count $itlm$ of the original loop.

Notice that the rewriting rules which specify the transition are simple enough and follow directly from algebraic equalities (3)–(5). This is possible because high-level algebraic program models are used. Similar transformations were implemented in (Doroshenko & Zhereb, 2009) for low-level program model (a parse tree), however, those transformations used more rules and were less comprehensible.

Now consider the more complex case of parallelization. Let the sequential consists of the following nested loops:

$$Seq2 = for(i, 0, m, \qquad \qquad \qquad (6)$$
$$for(j, 0, n,$$
$$body(i, j)))$$

where the iterations of the outer loop are noncommutative, while the iterations of the inner loop are commutative.

In this case, the corresponding parallel program is

$$Gpu2 = copy\_gpu;$$
$$for(i, 0, m, \qquad \qquad \qquad (7)$$
$$call\_gpu(gbody2, block1d, grid1d));$$
$$copy\_back,$$

where the kernel *gbody2* is called inside the loop and conforms to the inner loop:

$$gbody2 = assign(j, \_GetCoor(x));$$
$$\_CpuToGpu(body(i, j)).$$

It is worth considering one other case, where the iterations of both the outer and the inner loop of the sequential program *Seq2* are independent. This allows parallelization of both loops. For GPU, it is possible to use the capabilities of the CUDA platform to work with two-dimensional objects. In this case, the outer and the inner loops correspond to two dimensions, and the program is parallelized by both dimensions. The transformed program is the following:

$$Gpu3 = copy\_gpu;$$
$$call\_gpu(gbody3, block2d, grid2d); \qquad (8)$$
$$copy\_back,$$

where the new kernel *gbody3* and two-dimensional structures of the blocks and the grid are used. The block size *block2d=bs×bs* is defined by hardware limitation on the maximum block size. In accordance with this limitation, let *bs*=16, so that the block size is *bs×bs*=256. Consequently, the size of the grid is defined based on the number of iterations of the initial loops:

$$grid2d = (m/bs) \times (n/bs).$$

The kernel *gbody3* is the following:

$$gbody3 = assign(i, \_GetCoor(x));$$
$$assign(j, \_GetCoor(y));$$
$$\_CpuToGpu(body(i, j)),$$

where the indexes of the iterations of both loops are computed based on x and y coordinates of a thread in a block and a block in the grid.

GPU Program Optimization

Rewriting rules can also be used to automate optimizing transformations. In this case, they are applied to the models of parallel GPU programs, either obtained manually or as a result of prior parallelizing transformations. In this subsection, examples of two optimizing transformations are considered: modification of a loop structure and transition from a global to a shared memory.

Loop Structure Modification

A particular feature of GPU programs is that each iteration of a sequential program is executed on a separate thread in GPU. In the general case, this allows to achieve high efficiency, as hardware planner of GPU can effectively distribute simple threads among available hardware resources. However, the situation is possible when it is more advantageous to place several loop iterations in one thread. It may be needed if the number of iterations of an initial loop is so large that hardware limits on a size of block and grid do not allow to execute each iteration on a separate thread. Furthermore, the situation is possible when close iterations share some memory areas, in this case joining close iterations in one thread allows using shared memory more efficiently.

The initial program for the transformation is $Gpu1$ (4). In the transformed program, both CPU and GPU code are modified. The new kernel is the following:

$$gbody1.1 = assign(k, \_GetCoor(x));$$
$$for(i, min(k), max(k),$$
$$\_CpuToGpu(body(i))).$$

Now, the thread index defines not a specific iteration, but some section of iterations defined by limits $min(k)=k*ls$, $max(k)=min(m,(k+1)*ls)$, where ls is a parameter determining the number of iterations executed in one thread. This parameter is set according to problem features.

CPU program for kernel call is also modified. The general form remains the same:

$Gpu1.1 = init\_gpu$;

  $copy\_gpu$;

  $call\_gpu(gbody1.1, block1d, grid1d.1)$;

  $copy\_back$.

The difference from program *Gpu*1 consists in call of the kernel *gbody*1.1 and change of the grid size. The size of the grid is still defined in such a way that the number of blocks is sufficient for executing all iterations: $grid1d=m/(bs*ls)$. It should be noticed that the block size is not changed: $block1d=bs$, as it is defined by hardware limits.

Programs *Gpu*1 and *Gpu*1.1 return the same result, if iterations in *Gpu*1 are independent.

The Transition from a Global to a Shared Memory

Another type of optimizing transformation for GPU program consists in using shared memory. This type of memory is notable for high access speed, though it is limited by size ("NVIDIA CUDA technology", n.d.). In many cases, the transition to shared memory allows increasing program efficiency sufficiently.

Below, this transformation is considered for the one-dimensional case (program *Gpu*1 (4)). The two-dimensional case (program *Gpu*3(8)) is transformed in a similar way.

The initial program for the transformation is *Gpu*1 (4). The transformation only affects GPU components of a program (kernels). The general form of the transformed program *Gpu*1.2 remains the same, except that the call of the kernel *gbody*1.1 is replaced with the call of the modified kernel *gbody*1.2:

$Gpu1.2 = init\_gpu$;

  $copy\_gpu$;

  $call\_gpu(gbody1.2, block1d, grid1d.1)$;

  $copy\_back$.

The kernel *gbody*1 (5) is transformed into the following kernel *gbody*1.2:

$gbody1.2 = assign(i, \_GetCoor(x));$

$\qquad copy\_shared(i);$

$\qquad \_Barrier;$

$\qquad \_GlobalToShared(gbody(i));$

$\qquad \_Barrier;$

$\qquad copy\_global(i).$

Here, the operator $gbody(i)=\_CpuToGpu(body(i))$ denotes the computations performed in each GPU thread. The transformed kernel uses two operators $copy\_shared(i)$ and $copy\_global(i)$ to copy data between global and shared memory. These operators are similar to $copy\_gpu$ and $copy\_back$ operators that copy data between CPU and GPU memory. The difference is that $copy\_gpu$ and $copy\_back$ operators copy all data at once, whereas in $copy\_shared(i)$ and $copy\_global(i)$ each thread copies a part of data. Therefore it is necessary to synchronize threads by using the $\_Barrier$ operator. The transformation also uses the function $\_GlobalToShared$ for transition from the operators working above the global memory B_g to operators above the shared memory B_S.

The rules implementing this transformation are similar to the rules used for transformation of the CPU program $Seq1$ to the GPU program $Gpu1$.

The Transition Between High-Level and Low-Level Program Models

As mentioned before, high-level program models allow for more brief and expressive representation of program transformations. However, there is a need for means of transition between a program model and a source code. When low-level program models (parse trees) are used, such transition is carried out using a parser and a code generator for a given programming language. Such an approach has been used, for example, in (Doroshenko & Zhereb, 2009). However, to construct high-level models, an additional knowledge of a subject domain is needed. Such knowledge can be expressed in the form of basic predicates and operators of Glushkov's algebra. For transition between source code and its high-level algebraic model, a special kind of rewriting rules called patterns (described in detail in subsection "The Rewriting Rules System TermWare" of Chapter 5) is used.

An important feature of the high-level models is language independence. A single high-level program model can be transformed into low-level models for multiple languages. For example, consider an implementation of the operator *init_gpu* in two languages, C and C#. In the first case, this operator is represented as a function call:

$$t_g^c = FunctionCall(InitCUDA, NIL),$$

which produces the code fragment InitCUDA().

For C#, the same operator results in the creation of an object:

$$t_g^{cs} = DeclarationAssignment(cuda, CUDA, New(CUDA, [0, true])).$$

The respective code fragment is CUDA cuda = new CUDA(0, true).

Therefore, high-level models allow describing program transformations independently of implementation language.

The examples of use of the proposed approach are given in subsection "Development of Programs for Graphics Processing Units" of Chapter 6.

Evolutionary Model of an Auto-Tuner and Properties of Programs

As discussed in Chapter 1, the auto-tuning consists in empiric evaluation of various modifications of an initial version of a program P. These modifications are defined by a set of configurations C. Since all the modifications in the proposed auto-tuning approach are obtained by introducing changes to P and each modification corresponds to a single auto-tuning iteration, then the auto-tuning can be considered as a sequential evolution of P.

The Model of an Auto-Tuner

In this subsection, the auto-tuner as evolutionary transition system for parallel programs is considered. This transition system is denoted as S^{true}. An execution of a parallel program in S^{true} is identical to its execution in the considered earlier model S^{mt}. In S^{true} model, variables also do not have a type and take values of some universal set D from a normed space.

Let P be a program and $P*$ be its modification transformed by the auto-tuner S^{true}. The computation execution time is designated as $T*$. The *auto-tuning system* is a 5-tuple

$$<PRAM^*, EV, OUT, E, P>$$

where *PRAM** is the parallel computation model considered in Chapter 2; P is an initial version of a program; OUT is a "benchmark" computation result of the program P, which is used for analysis of accuracy of evolutional versions of P and comes to the input of the auto-tuning system; E is an admissible error of computation which is defined by an expert in a subject domain of the algorithm; $EV(OUT^*, OUT, E, T^*) \to \mathbb{Z}$ is the function of empirical numerical evaluation of performance of the program from a current auto-tuning iteration, OUT^* is the result of the program P^*, T^* is the execution time of the program.

The function EV is specified by a developer of a program being optimized, but in a general case it is defined as follows:

$$EV(OUT^*, OUT, E, T^*) = \begin{cases} T^*, & \Delta(OUT, OUT^*) = 0, \\ T^* * g(\Delta(OUT, OUT^*), E), & \Delta(OUT, OUT^*) > 0, \end{cases}$$

where Δ is the difference between OUT and OUT^*.

In cases when different versions of a program being optimized return the same result (e.g., different sorting algorithms), EV returns the execution time (for example, in milliseconds). In other cases EV should reflect a possible balance between decreasing the execution time and loss of result accuracy, for which an auxiliary function g is used. For most computational problems this function just discards too inaccurate versions P^*, $\Delta(OUT, OUT^*) > E$.

Hence, the task of the auto-tuner is the minimization of EV. That is, the auto-tuner selects the fastest evolutional version of a program, which satisfies the defined conditions of result accuracy. Each auto-tuning iteration qualitatively evaluates the program version being generated:

$$<P, C_i> \to P^*, EV_i,$$

where i is a number of iteration; P^* is a new version of the initial program P characterized by configuration C_i; EV_i is an evaluation of performance of P^* from i-th iteration.

On the first iteration of auto-tuning, the initial version of the program is considered optimal $P^{opt} = P$. The transformation of the program on a current iteration of auto-tuning is considered *efficient*, if $0 < EV(P^*) < EV(P^{opt})$. If the applied transformation has been efficient, then the obtained version of the initial program is considered improved and is taken as P^{opt}.

Typically, the auto-tuner just iterates through the set of configurations C until all configurations are evaluated or time quota is over. In partial/complex cases the decision to continue or stop auto-tuning iterations is taken by an expert developer. After the completion of all auto-tuning iterations, the obtained program P^{opt} is considered optimal for a target execution environment and is stored for further use. For problems with high computational complexity and a large number of configurations, sequential iteration through a set of configurations is often replaced by the use of search algorithms (Ivanenko, 2011; Hutter, Hoos, & Leyton-Brown, 2011). Moreover, a part of tuning iterations can be replaced with evaluation from a model developed with the help of machine learning methods (Doroshenko, Ivanenko, Novak, & Yatsenko, 2018).

Program Properties

The constructed model S^{true} can be used for a formal definition of some program properties which facilitate the analysis of correctness and efficiency of optimization transformations being performed by an auto-tuner.

The correctness of transformations means that initial and transformed program return the same result. Formally, this condition can be formulated as follows. Let $V_R \subset V$ be as a subset of *resulting variables*. Two programs P^1 and P^2 will be called *result equivalent*, if for equal initial data b_0 the programs simultaneously attain or do not attain the final states $s_f^1 = (b^1, \mu, \varnothing)$ and $s_f^2 = (b^2, \mu, \varnothing)$, and these final memory states coincide by the resulting variables $b_{V_R}^1 = b_{V_R}^2$.

The result equivalence is quite general property, but it is almost impossible to implement its verification, as this requires the analysis of all paths of program execution depending on input data and versions of execution of different threads. Therefore, it is necessary to define more partial properties for a description of transformation correctness which can be verified in practice.

First, some properties of operators of Glushkov's algebra are considered. For each operator $y \in Op$, the set of variables $R(y) \subset V$ is defined, on which the result of operator application depends, and the set of variables $W(y) \subset V$, which change the value as a result of operation execution. Two operators $y_1, y_2 \in Op$ will be called *dependent* (by data), if $R(y_1) \cap W(y_2) \neq \varnothing$ or $W(y_1) \cap R(y_2) \neq \varnothing$, or $W(y_1) \cap W(y_2) \neq \varnothing$. Two operators $y_1, y_2 \in Op$ are *commutative* (with regard to composition operation), if $y_1 y_2 = y_2 y_1$. It is obvious that independent operators are commutative, but the reverse is not true, for example, two copies of the same operator $y \in Op$ are always commutative, but they are dependent if $W(y) \neq \varnothing$.

Below, the following program properties are defined: deadlock-freeness, absence of conflicts and equivalence by operators.

The program P will be called *deadlock-free*, if no deadlock states (the states when further execution of the program in the transition system is impossible) appear in the process of its execution. It is evident that all sequential programs in model S^{seq} are deadlock-free.

In model S^{mt}, the situation when there exist dependent operators which are executed simultaneously in different threads will be called a *conflict transition*.

The program P will be called *conflictless*, if no conflict transitions appear during its execution. For conflictless programs, function *merge* (2) may not be used. Instead of combining the results of simultaneous execution of several operators, these operators can be executed sequentially in any order.

If a sequence of program execution (a sequence of system transitions) is known, then it is possible to determine the history of basic operators usage (Mazurkiewicz, 1995). To do so, one more component $h \in Op$ will be added to the state of the transition system. In the initial state, $h = \varepsilon$. The transition rule 1 from subsection "Execution Model of a Sequential Program" is also modified: $(b, Yr, F, h) \rightarrow (y(b), R, F, hy)$. At simultaneous application of several such rules in different threads, respective operators y in arbitrary order will be added. Operator h in a final state will be called the *history of operator usage*.

Two histories h_1, h_2 are considered *equivalent* (with regard to the defined system of equivalence of operators of Glushkov's algebra), if h_2 can be obtained from h_1 by successive application of equivalence operation to operators of the history. In particular, the equivalence system always includes all relations defining the commutativity of operators. That is, h_2 can also be obtained from h_1 by successive permutations of commutative pairs of operators. Two programs P^1 and P^2 will be called *operator equivalent*, if for equal initial data b_0 they generate equivalent histories of operator execution.

Now, the following statement can be introduced.

Theorem 1. If two programs P^1 and P^2 are deadlock-free, conflictless and operator equivalent, then they are result equivalent.

Proof. Deadlock-free programs do not transit to deadlock states, so they either attain a final state or do not stop. In the latter case, the history of operators will be infinite, therefore if such situation is present in P^1, then it also exists in P^2. Hence, the first part of the definition of result equivalence is proved. Now, it will be checked that on equal initial data, programs will give the same results. Indeed, the work of a program can be presented as an action of some combined operator y_f on initial memory state b_0: $b_f = y_f b_0$. Based on the construction of transition systems S^{seq} and S^{mt}, the combined operator is a sequential composition of operators, triggering at each transition. For system S^{mt}, each transition combines a set of transitions of separate threads. However, for conflictless programs, the transition of the whole system is equivalent to a sequential composition of transitions of separate threads (taken in arbitrary order).

Thus, for conflictless programs $y_f = h$, i.e. the combined operator coincides with the history of operators application. From the definition of equivalence by operators, $\forall b \in B$, $(h^1 b)_{V_R} = (h^2 b)_{V_R}$ follows, i.e. the histories of operators act similarly on resulting data. Therefore, $b^1_{V_R} = (h^1 b_0)_{V_R} = (h^2 b_0)_{V_R} = b^2_{V_R}$, which was to be proved.

Hence, the verification of result equivalence is reduced to verification of three other properties.

CONCLUSION

The algebra-dynamic models of sequential and parallel programs for multicore central processing units and graphics processing units are constructed. The models allow formally describe the process of program execution, including hardware and software specifities affecting the design of efficient parallel computations. Program transformations focused on transition from sequential to parallel programs (parallelization) and increasing the performance of parallel programs with regard to execution time (optimization) are described. Rewriting rules enable automated program parallelization and optimization. High-level program models allow describing program transformations in more concise and comprehensible fashion, and enable a single model to describe programs in different languages. The concept of an auto-tuner is formalized as an evolutionary transition system. The properties of multithreaded programs (deadlock-freeness, absence of conflicts, equivalence) are formulated.

REFERENCES

Akhter, S., & Roberts, J. (2006). *Multi-core programming: Increasing performance through software multi-threading*. Santa Clara, CA: Intel Press.

Allusse, Y., Horain, P., Agarwal, A., & Saipriyadarshan, C. (2008). GpuCV: An open source GPU-accelerated framework for image processing and computer vision. In *Proceedings of the 16th ACM International Conference on Multimedia (MM'08)* (pp. 1089-1092). New York: ACM. 10.1145/1459359.1459578

Andon, P. I., Doroshenko, A. Yu., Tseytlin, G. O., & Yatsenko, O. A. (2007). *Algebra-algorithmic models and methods of parallel programming*. Kyiv: Academperiodyka. (in Russian)

Andon, P. I., Doroshenko, A. Yu., & Zhereb, K. A. (2011). Programming high-performance parallel computations: Formal models and graphics processing units. *Cybernetics and Systems Analysis*, *47*(4), 659–668. doi:10.100710559-011-9346-y

Baskaran, M. M., Bondhugula, U., Krishnamoorthy, S., Ramanujam, J., Rountev, A., & Sadayappan, P. (2008). A compiler framework for optimization of affine loop nests for GPGPUs. In *Proceedings of the 22nd Annual International Conference on Supercomputing (ICS'08)* (pp. 225-234). New York: ACM. 10.1145/1375527.1375562

Chernysh, R. I. (2010). *Modified additive-averaged splitting algorithm, its parallel realization and application to meteorological problems*: Abstract of the thesis for a scientific degree of a candidate of physics and mathematics sciences. Kyiv: Taras Shevchenko National University of Kyiv. (in Ukrainian)

Doroshenko, A., Ivanenko, P., Novak, O., & Yatsenko, O. (2018). Optimization of parallel software tuning with statistical modeling and machine learning. In *Proceedings of the 14th International Conference "ICT in Education, Research and Industrial Applications. Integration, Harmonization and Knowledge Transfer" (ICTERI 2018)* (pp. 219-226). Berlin: Springer.

Doroshenko, A., & Shevchenko, R. (2006). A rewriting framework for rule-based programming dynamic applications. *Fundamenta Informaticae*, *72*(1-3), 95–108.

Doroshenko, A., Tseytlin, G., Yatsenko, O., & Zachariya, L. (2006). A theory of clones and formalized design of programs. In *Proceedings of the 15th International Workshop "Concurrency, Specification and Programming" (CS&P'2006)* (pp. 328-339). Berlin: Humboldt University Press.

Doroshenko, A., Zhereb, K., & Yatsenko, O. (2010). Formal facilities for designing efficient GPU programs. In *Proceedings of the 19th International Workshop "Concurrency: Specification and Programming" (CS&P'2010)* (pp. 142-153). Berlin: Humboldt University Press.

Doroshenko, A. Yu. (2000). *Mathematical models and methods of organization of highly productive parallel computations: The algebra-dynamic approach.* Kyiv: Naukova dumka. (in Russian)

Doroshenko, A. Y., & Zhereb, K. A. (2009). Development of highly-parallel applications for graphical processing units using rewriting rules. *Problems in Programming,* (3), 3-18. (in Russian)

General-Purpose Computation on Graphics Hardware. (n.d.). Retrieved from http://www.gpgpu.org

Han, T. D., & Abdelrahman, T. S. (2009). hiCUDA: A high-level directive-based language for GPU programming. In *Proceedings of the 2nd Workshop on General Purpose Processing on Graphics Processing Units* (Vol. 383, pp. 52-61). New York: ACM. 10.1145/1513895.1513902

Hou, Q., Zhou, K., & Guo, B. (2008). BSGP: Bulk-synchronous GPU programming. In *Proceedings of the 35th International Conference and Exhibition on Computer Graphics and Interactive Techniques (SIGGRAPH'08) (ACM Transactions on Graphics)* (Vol. 27, pp. 1-12). New York: ACM.

Hutter, F., Hoos, H. H., & Leyton-Brown, K. (2011). Sequential model-based optimization for general algorithm configuration. In *Proceedings of the International Conference on Learning and Intelligent Optimization (LION 2011) (LNCS)* (Vol. 6683, pp. 507-523). Berlin: Springer. 10.1007/978-3-642-25566-3_40

Ivanenko, P. (2011). Application of various algorithms for searching optimal configuration for a parallel algorithm of numerical solving a multi-level problem of environment modeling. In *Proceedings of the International Scientific Conference of Students and Young Scientists "Theoretical and Applied Aspects of Cybernetics" (TAAC'2011)* (pp. 88-89). Kyiv: Bukrek. [in Ukrainian]

Keller, R. M. (1975). A fundamental theorem of asynchronous parallel computation. *LNCS, 24*, 102–112.

Lee, S., Min, S., & Eigenmann, R. (2009). OpenMP to GPGPU: A compiler framework for automatic translation and optimization. In *Proceedings of the 14th ACM SIGPLAN Symposium on Principles and Practice of Parallel Programming (PPoPP'09)* (pp. 101-110). New York: ACM. 10.1145/1594835.1504194

Lefohn, A. E., Sengupta, S., Kniss, J., Strzodka, R., & Owens, J. D. (2006). Glift: Generic, efficient, random-access GPU data structures. *ACM Transactions on Graphics, 25*(1), 60–99. doi:10.1145/1122501.1122505

Ma, W., & Agrawal, G. (2009). A compiler and runtime system for enabling data mining applications on GPUs. In *Proceedings of the 14th ACM SIGPLAN Symposium on Principles and Practice of Parallel Programming (PPoPP'09) (ACM SIGPLAN Notices)* (Vol. 44, pp. 287-288). New York: ACM. 10.1145/1594835.1504218

Mazurkiewicz, A. (1995). Introduction to trace theory. In V. Diekert & G. Rozenberg (Eds.), *The Book of Traces* (pp. 3–41). Singapore: World Scientific. doi:10.1142/9789814261456_0001

NVIDIA CUDA Technology. (n.d.). Retrieved from http://www.nvidia.com/cuda

OpenMP Application Programming Interface Version 4.5. (2015). Retrieved from http://www.openmp.org/wp-content/uploads/openmp-4.5.pdf

Prusov, V. A., Doroshenko, A. Yu., & Chernysh, R. I. (2009). Choosing the parameter of a modified additive-averaged splitting algorithm. *Cybernetics and Systems Analysis, 45*(4), 589–596. doi:10.100710559-009-9126-0

TermWare. (n.d.). Retrieved from http://www.gradsoft.com.ua/products/termware_eng.html

Yatsenko, O. (2012). On parameter-driven generation of algorithm schemes. In *Proceedings of the 21st International Workshop "Concurrency, Specification and Programming" (CS&P'2012)* (pp. 428-438). Berlin: Humboldt University Press.

KEY TERMS AND DEFINITIONS

Algebra-Dynamic Program Model: A model of a program which is based on the concept of a transition system. It consists of two parts: a model of program structure and a model of program execution.

CUDA: A parallel computing platform and application programming interface (API) model created by NVIDIA. It allows software developers and software engineers to use a CUDA-enabled graphics processing unit (GPU).

Evolutionary Model of an Auto-Tuner: The model constructed as an evolutional extension of transition systems which formally describes the auto-tuning system intended for adjusting (optimization) of programs.

General-Purpose Computing on Graphics Processing Units (GPGPU): The use of a graphics processing unit (GPU), which typically handles computation only for computer graphics, to perform computation in applications traditionally handled by the central processing unit (CPU).

Glushkov's System of Algorithmic Algebras (SAA, Glushkov's Algebra): The two-sorted algebra focused on analytical form of representation of algorithms and formalized transformation of these representations.

Graphics Processing Unit (GPU): A specialized electronic circuit designed to rapidly manipulate and alter memory to accelerate the creation of images in a frame buffer intended for output to a display device. Modern GPUs are very efficient at manipulating computer graphics and image processing, and their highly parallel structure makes them more efficient than general-purpose CPUs for algorithms where the processing of large blocks of data is done in parallel.

Transition System: A concept used to describe the potential behavior of discrete systems. It consists of states and transitions between states, which may be labeled with labels chosen from a set; the same label may appear on more than one transition.

Chapter 5

Software Tools for Automated Program Design, Synthesis, and Auto-Tuning

ABSTRACT

The authors consider the software tools based on algebra-algorithmic models and formal methods of constructing algorithms and programs. The algebra-algorithmic integrated toolkit for design and synthesis of programs IDS, the rewriting rules system TermWare, and the auto-tuning framework TuningGenie are presented. IDS uses algebraic specifications based on Glushkov's algebra of algorithms, which are represented in three forms: algebraic (regular scheme), natural linguistic, and graphical (flowgraphs). IDS is based on the method of dialogue design of syntactically correct algorithm schemes, which eliminates syntax errors during construction of algorithm specifications. To automate transformations of algorithms and programs being designed, the rewriting rules system TermWare is used. TuningGenie framework is applied to automate the adjustment of programs to a target computing environment.

INTRODUCTION

The algebra-algorithmic approach (Andon, Doroshenko, Tseytlin, & Yatsenko, 2007; Doroshenko, Tseytlin, Yatsenko, & Zachariya, 2006) is supported by a number of tools developed within the framework of Kyiv algebraic-cybernetic school. The first such tool was the system called MULTIPROCESSIST

DOI: 10.4018/978-1-5225-9384-3.ch005

(Yushchenko, Tseytlin, Hrytsay, & Terzyan, 1989), developed in the 1980s in the programming automation department of V. M. Glushkov Institute of Cybernetics. The system provided the multilevel design of algorithms and data structures represented in the form of schemes in Glushkov's system of algorithmic algebra (SAA) and synthesis of corresponding programs. The algebraic approach was also used at development of the system for transformation of algorithm schemes (Petrushenko, 1991). The method of controlling spaces based on algebraic approach was used in the parallel programming technology PARUS (Anisimov & Kulyabko, 1984).

In this chapter, the developed tools for programming automation are considered, which continue the aforementioned research, namely, the Integrated toolkit for Design and Synthesis of programs (IDS) (Andon et al., 2007; Doroshenko, Ivanenko, Ovdii, & Yatsenko, 2016; Doroshenko, Zhereb, & Yatsenko, 2013; Yatsenko, 2012), the term rewriting system TermWare (Doroshenko & Shevchenko, 2006; "TermWare", n.d.) (see also Chapter 3) and the auto-tuning framework TuningGenie (Ivanenko, Doroshenko, Zhereb, 2014).

The approach being considered is related to works on automated synthesis of program code from specifications (Flener, 2002; Gulwani, 2010). The important aspects of program synthesis include:

- format of inputs (specifications) — how specifications or other inputs for synthesis are provided;
- methods for supporting particular subject domains — how the proposed approach is specialized for a given domain, so that domain knowledge can be used to produce more efficient programs and/or to improve developer's productivity;
- techniques for implementing transformation from specifications to output program code.

These aspects roughly correspond to three dimensions of program synthesis discussed in (Gulwani, 2010):

- *user intent* describes specifications;
- *search space* restricts all possible programs to a manageable subset;
- *search technique* describes how transformations are implemented.

For input specification, a popular option is using domain-specific languages that allow capturing requirements of a subject domain. In (Bagheri & Sullivan,

2012), authors describe Pol, a system that transforms specifications in Alloy language (Jackson, 2002) into a platform-specific code that targets different object-oriented frameworks. A similar approach is used in (Mannadiar & Vangheluwe, 2010): domain-specific models are transformed automatically into mobile applications for Android platform. Domain-specific languages can reduce the size of specifications significantly, because many details are already accounted for in domain-specific language constructs. However, creating a new DSL can require significant effort, and learning it might be hard for a domain expert.

It is possible to make DSL easier to learn by using graphical modeling language. For instance, in (Batory, 2007) a graphical tool is described that operates on state charts and eventually generates web components. Paper (Mannadiar & Vangheluwe, 2010) also develops graphical language including state charts and models of user interface screens. Such an approach works well for small specifications, but becomes inconvenient as the size of models grows and their graphical representations do not fit into a single page.

Some more formal approaches are also used, including formal specification languages (Leonard & Heitmeyer, 2008), ontologies (Bures, Denney, Fischer, & Nistor, 2004) and algebraic specifications (Apel, Lengauer, Möller, & Kästner, 2010; Jacobs, Kuncak, & Suter, 2013). In paper (Leonard & Heitmeyer, 2008), authors describe a project to translate a requirements specification, expressed in SCR (Software Cost Reduction) notation, to C code. The translation is implemented using the Abstract Program Transformation System (APTS). In paper (Bures et al., 2004), the schema-based software synthesis system is considered, which uses general code templates called schemas to represent general knowledge about software generation in a reusable ontological format. Paper (Apel et al., 2010) proposes an algebraic specification for describing program features and provide automatic generations of a program once the needed features are described. In (Jacobs et al., 2013), programs implementing data types and their containers are generated using term algebras. Using such formalisms enables analysis and verification of specifications and generated code.

There are also approaches that provide specification not of a program or an algorithm, but of a problem to be solved, in the form of functional and nonfunctional constraints (Kneuss, Kuncak, Kuraj, & Suter, 2013; Srivastava, Gulwani, & Foster, 2010), examples of input/output pairs (Menon, Tamuz, Gulwani, Lampson, & Kalai, 2013; Kitzelmann, 2010), or natural language descriptions (Gulwani, 2010). In this case, there is no simple mapping from specification to implementation; rather, there is a need to search through a space of possible programs to find one that corresponds to given constraints. Such search is usually exponential on the size of a specification. While there are heuristics that significantly reduce search space, such approaches are still limited to small programs.

Finally, specifications could be provided in the form of existing implementation of an equivalent program but lacking some important property that should be incorporated into a new program that is synthesized. Paper (Barthe, Crespo, Gulwani, Kunz, & Marron, 2013) describes an approach for synthesis of SIMD program based on equivalent program without SIMD constructs. In (Raychev, Vechev, & Yahav, 2013), a non-deterministic parallel program is augmented with synchronization constructs to make it deterministic.

Another crucial aspect of program synthesis is a specialization for a subject domain. Some approaches are restricted to a single domain, such as statistical data analysis (Fischer & Schumann, 2003) or mobile application development (Mannadiar & Vangheluwe, 2010). Others provide facilities for changing domain-specific parts, by using ontological descriptions (Bures et al., 2004), grammars (Leonard & Heitmeyer, 2008), or by providing a general framework that is complemented by domain-specific tools (Srivastava et al., 2010).

Finally, an important aspect is a transformation from input specification into source code in a target language. The transformation algorithm can be hand-coded (Fischer & Schumann, 2003), but it reduces the flexibility of a system. Therefore, the transformation is often described in a declarative form, such as rewriting rules (Leonard & Heitmeyer, 2008), visualized graph transformations (Mannadiar & Vangheluwe, 2010), code templates (Bures et al., 2004). More complex approaches require searching the space of possible programs (Srivastava et al., 2010), possibly using genetic programming or machine learning approaches (Gulwani, 2010; Menon et al., 2013). In (Bagheri & Sullivan, 2012), partial synthesis is proposed: generic parts of application are generated, and then completed with specific details manually.

In comparison, the approach considered in this chapter uses algebraic specifications based on Glushkov's algebra of algorithms (see Chapter 1), but they can be represented in three forms: algebraic (formal language), natural linguistic and graphical, therefore simplifying understanding of specifications and facilitating achievement of demanded program quality. Another advantage of the developed IDS toolkit is the method of dialogue design of syntactically correct algorithm specifications (DSC-method) (Andon et al., 2007), which eliminates syntax errors during construction of algorithm schemes. Specialization for a subject domain is done by describing basic operators and predicates from this domain. The proposed approach uses code templates to specify implementations for predicates and operators. Program transformations, such as from a sequential to a parallel algorithm, are implemented as rewriting rules. For automation of transformations of algorithms and programs, IDS is applied together with the rewriting rules system TermWare. Application of formal methods in IDS and TermWare provides automation of manual labor of a programmer and more advanced parallelization of algorithms. However, the performance of programs being designed can be further increased by using the TuningGenie framework. TuningGenie is applied to automate adjustment of programs to a target platform. The framework works with source code of a software and performs source-to-source transformations by using TermWare.

The developed tools are also associated with database design (Teorey et al., 2008), a collection of processes that facilitate the designing, development, implementation, and maintenance of enterprise data management systems. The main objectives of database designing are to produce logical and physical designs models of the proposed database system. The logical model concentrates on the data requirements and the data to be stored independently of physical considerations. The physical data design model involves translating the logical design of the database onto physical media using hardware resources and software systems such as database management systems.

The Architecture of the Toolkit for Design and Generation of Programs

The developed integrated toolkit for design and synthesis of algorithms and programs consists of the following basic components (see Figure 1):

- the *DSC-constructor* intended for dialogue design of syntactically correct schemes of algorithms represented in the modified system of algorithmic algebra (SAA-M) and synthesis of programs in C, C++, Java languages;
- the *flowgraph editor*, which is applied for editing a graphical representation of an algorithm;
- the *generator of SAA schemes* based on higher-level schemes (hyperschemes);
- the *database* containing the description of SAA-M constructs, basic predicates and operators, and also their program implementations. It

was designed using the Microsoft Access database management system ("Database design basics", n.d.).

Figure 1. The architecture of IDS toolkit

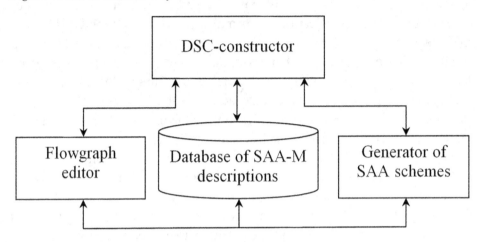

The database consists of two tables containing the description of basic elements (predicates and operators) and operations of SAA-M, respectively. The general structure of the tables is the same and is given in Table 1.

Table 1. The structure of the IDS database table

Field name	Data type	Description
Element code	Number	The key field (unique number)
Algebraic form	Text	The representation of an SAA element in algebraic form
Natural form	Text	The representation of an SAA element in natural linguistic form
Element type	Number	0 for logic element, 1 for operator element
Target programming language template	Text	The text in a target programming language (C, C++, Java, TermWare and other)
Category	Text	The subject domain of an SAA element (e.g., sorting, meteorology, general)

As it was already mentioned, the developed toolkit uses three forms of algorithm representation: analytic (a formula in the algebra of algorithms), natural linguistic (SAA scheme) and a flowgraph (based on Kaluzhnin's algebra).

The analytic representation is based on Glushkov's system of algorithmic algebras (Andon et al., 2007; Doroshenko et al., 2006) and is a compact notation of an algorithm, focused on its further transformation, e.g., minimization, improvement by various criteria, based on usage of metarules (see Chapter 2). The natural linguistic representation (an SAA scheme) is based on the algorithmic language SAA/1 (see Chapter 2). The flowgraph representation is based on the algebra of flowgraphs and is focused on the visualization of an algorithm being designed. The combination and interrelation of analytic, natural linguistic and visualized forms of representation of algorithmic schemes in IDS gives a comprehensive understanding of specifications and facilitates the achievement of demanded program quality.

Example 1. Consider the mentioned representation forms on the design of the sequential sorting algorithm *Solute* (Andon et al., 2007). Let the input array to be sorted has the following marking:

$$M : H \ Y_1 \ a_1 \ a_2 \ ... \ a_n \ K,$$

where H and K are markers fixing the beginning and the end of the array M; Y_1 is a pointer moving over the array during the processing.

The regular scheme (analytic representation) of an algorithm is the following:

$$Solute = Start * SET(Y_1, H)$$
$$*\{[d(Y_1, K)] \ ([l > r \mid Y_1] \ Transp(l, r \mid Y_1) * SET(Y_1, H), \ R(Y_1))\} * Fin,$$

where *Start* is the initialization operator; $d(Y_1, K)$ is the predicate, which takes true value, if the pointer Y_1 reached the marker K, and false otherwise; $l > r \mid Y_1$ is the predicate, which takes true value, if the specified relation holds for the elements, located to the left and to the right of the pointer Y_1; $Transp(l, r \mid Y_1)$ is the operator of transposition of the elements adjacent to the pointer Y_1; $SET(Y_1, H)$ is the operator placing the pointer Y_1 in a position directly to the right of the marker H; $R(Y_1)$ is the shift of the pointer Y_1 over the array M by one symbol to the right; *Fin* is the final operator which outputs the sorted array M.

According to the scheme of the algorithm, the first unordered pair of array elements is searched with the help of the pointer Y_1 scanning in the direction from left to right. Then, after the transposition, the pointer Y_1 is placed at the beginning of the array and scanning is repeated. The process finishes when Y_1 reaches the marker K. The flowgraph of the *Solute* algorithm is given in Figure 2.

Figure 2. The flowgraph of Solute sorting algorithm

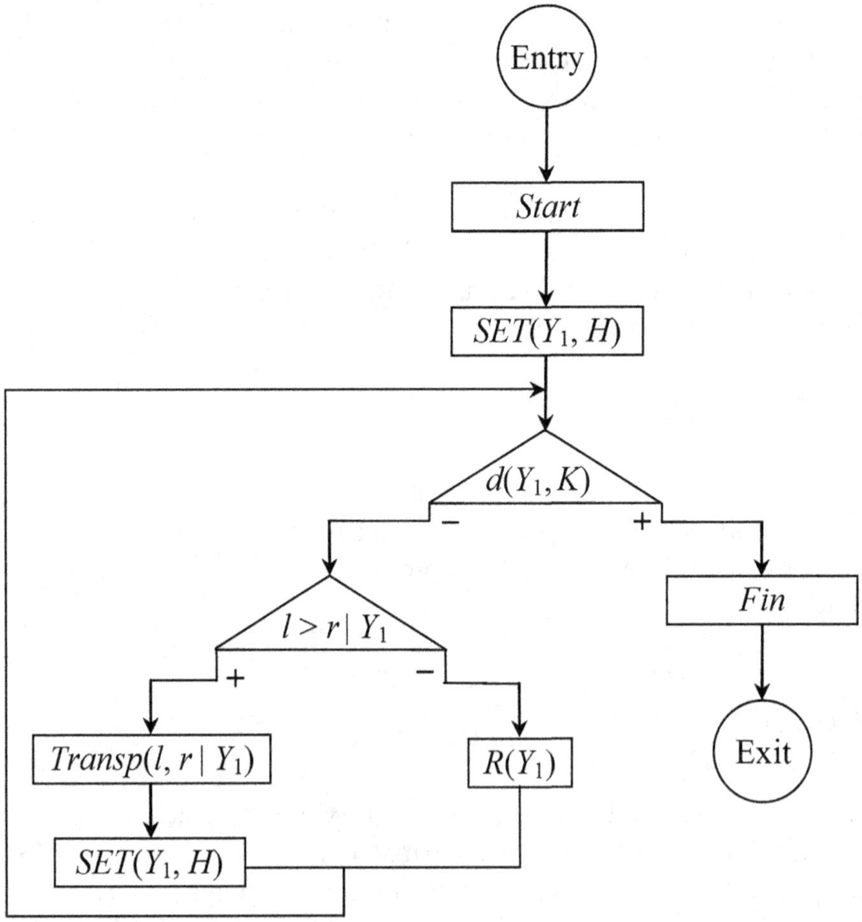

The natural linguistic representation of the algorithm is the following:

```
SCHEME SOLUTE SORT ====
      "Sequential Solute sort"
```

```
    END OF COMMENTS

"Solute"
==== "START"
     THEN
     "Place the pointer Y(1) at the beginning of the array (M)"
     THEN
     WHILE NOT 'The pointer Y(1) is at the end of the array
(M)'
     LOOP
        IF 'The elements l > r at pointer Y(1) in the array
(M)'
        THEN
           "Transpose the elements l, r at pointer Y(1) in the
array (M)"
           THEN
           "Place the pointer Y(1) at the beginning of the
array (M)"
        ELSE
           "Shift the pointer Y(1) by (1) element in the array
(M)
            to the right"
        END IF
        THEN
           "Shift the pointer Y(1) by (1) element in the array
(M)
            to the right"
     END OF LOOP
     THEN
     "FIN"
END OF SCHEME SOLUTE SORT
```

Interactive Constructing of Algorithm Specifications

One of the components of the IDS toolkit is the DSC-constructor intended for automated design and generation of schemes of algorithms and programs. The constructor is based on the method of dialogue design of syntactically correct programs (DSC-method) which is based on the interconnection of algebraic and grammatical descriptions of syntax of formal languages.

The basic idea of the DSC-constructor consists in level-by-level top-down designing of schemes by detailing language constructs of SAA-M. On each step of the design, the system allows the user to select only those constructs, the substitution of which into a scheme does not break its syntactic correctness. The DSC-constructor uses the list of SAA-M constructs and an algorithm design tree. The list consists of logic and operator operations, the superposition of which allows to create algorithms in three forms mentioned earlier. The specifications of constructs are stored in the database of the toolkit. During the design of an algorithm, the SAA-M operations chosen by the user are displayed in the tree with further detailing of their variables. Depending on a type of the chosen variable, the system offers the corresponding list of SAA-M operations or basic concepts from the database.

Figure 3. The main window of the DSC-constructor

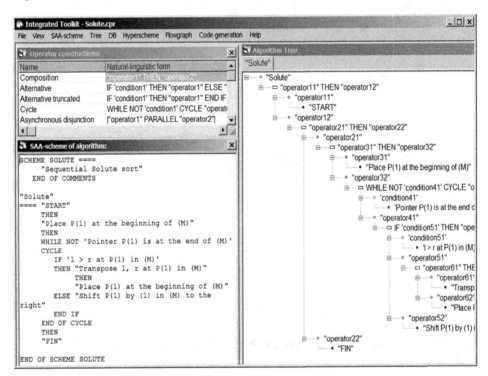

The SAA scheme corresponding to an algorithm design tree is displayed in a separate text window in an analytic or a natural linguistic form depending on the options set. It is possible to add a compound operator or a compound predicate to a scheme being designed. They are represented as an additional design tree. During the work with the DSC-constructor, the user can edit the description of the predicate and operator language constructs, and also basic conditions and operators stored in the database. The description of an element (an operation of SAA-M or a basic concept) in the database includes its representation in analytic and natural linguistic form, and also an implementation in a target programming language.

Figure 3 shows a screenshot of the DSC-constructor window with the SAA scheme of the Solute sort algorithm considered in Example 1.

The window contains three subwindows: the left upper subwindow includes a list of SAA operations, the subwindow on the right side contains the algorithm design tree, and the third subwindow shows the text of an SAA scheme. The DSC-constructor can be applied for designing both algorithms and hyperschemes. A flowgraph of an algorithm can be viewed and edited separately in the flowgraph editor.

The flowgraph editor provides the possibility to change the appearance of each component of a flowgraph representation, namely, moving flowgraph nodes, changing node text and color, setting thickness and style of lines.

Synthesis of Algorithms and Programs

Based on an algorithm tree obtained as a result of designing, IDS toolkit performs generation of programs. Besides designing SAA schemes, the toolkit supports also the automated construction of higher-level schemes called hyperschemes (the concept of a hyperscheme is considered in Chapter 2), which are applied for generation of algorithm schemes. Notice that SAA schemes and hyperschemes have an identical syntax that allows to flexibly use parameters that control the generation of schemes and are set at the level of basic conditions and operators. Figure 4 shows the sequence of program development in IDS. In the beginning, a hyperscheme is designed in the DSC-constructor. Further, the generator of SAA schemes carries out the synthesis of an algorithm scheme based on the hyperscheme. Then, DSC-constructor generates code in a target programming language based on the SAA scheme.

Figure 4. The sequence of development of algorithms and programs in IDS

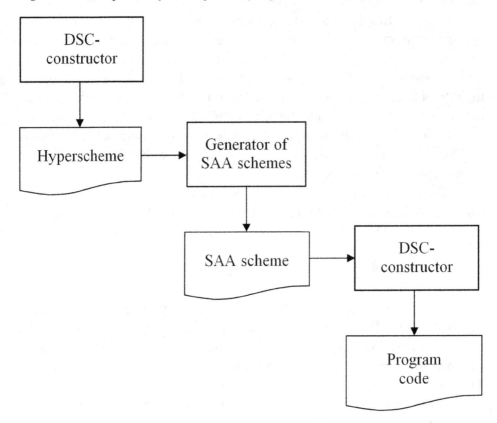

In the next subsections, the process of generation of algorithm schemes and programs is considered in more detail.

Generation of Regular Schemes Based on Hyperschemes

As it was mentioned above, the process of algorithm design in DSC-constructor consists in level-by-level designing of an algorithm scheme by detailing SAA-M constructs and is presented in the form of a tree. On each step of construction of the hyperscheme, the system allows the user to choose only those constructs, the insertion of which into the scheme does not break its syntactic correctness. The hyperscheme designed DSC-constructor is the basis for generation of an SAA scheme, and the SAA scheme is used to synthesize a program in a chosen target programming language.

Before the beginning of generation of an SAA scheme, the user can set the generation options: the name of a scheme to be generated, a comment to it, and also a name of an output file for writing the generated scheme. The hyperscheme is executed by an interpreter in interaction with a parser identifying the constructs be executed. The constructs are processed recursively according to the definition of the function F_h (see Chapter 2, Subsection "Parameter-Driven Models for Generation of Algorithm Schemes" and also (Yatsenko, 2012)). The texts of basic conditions and operators of hyperschemes are parametrized. For simplification of processing, the parameters are designated in the text of hyperschemes as $P(i)$, where i is the number of the parameter. For example, the operator assigning the value n to the parameter $P(1)$ is the following: "$P(1):=(n)$". Execution of an elementary operator or computation of an elementary condition during generation of an algorithm scheme consists in building of its text according to the values of parameters.

Table 2. The description of operator constructs of SAA-M in the database of IDS

Name	Analytic form	Natural linguistic form	Implementation in Java
Composition	"operator1" * "operator2"	"operator1" THEN "operator2"	^operator1^; ^operator2^
Branching	(['condition1'] "operator1", "operator2")	IF "condition1" THEN "operator1" ELSE "operator2" END IF	if (^condition1^) { ^operator1^ } else { ^operator2^ }
Loop	{['condition1'] "operator1"}	WHILE NOT 'condition1' LOOP "operator1" END OF LOOP	while (!(^condition1^)) { ^operator1^ }

Synthesis of Programs Based on Algorithm Schemes

DSC-constructor generates a program based on a tree obtained as a result of constructing an algorithm scheme and implementations of basic predicates and operators in a target programming language stored in the database. Compound predicates and operators can be represented as subroutines (class methods). The input of the generator is also a file which contains a skeleton description of the main class of a program (without implementations of methods), in which a substitution of the generated code is carried out. Designing program classes and their interrelations, and also generation of a skeleton program code can be done, for example, by using Rational Rose (Quatrani & Palistrant, 2006).

Table 2 gives examples of description of the main operator constructs in the database of IDS. Java is used as a target programming language.

Table 3 shows the examples of description of basic elements for sorting algorithms. The natural linguistic and analytic form of the description of a basic element includes the names of formal parameters indicated in brackets. Formal parameters specified in the text of program implementation of a basic element are replaced by corresponding actual parameters (which are set in SAA schemes) during a program synthesis.

Table 3. The examples of description in the database of basic operators and predicates for sorting algorithms

Type	Natural linguistic form	Analytic form	Implementation in Java
Operators	"Shift P(i) by (n) in (M) to the right"	R(P(i), (n))	s.moveR(%1, %2);
	"Transpose l, r at P(i) in (M)"	Transp(l, r| P(i))	s.transp(%1);
	"Place P(i) at P(j) in (M)"	Place(P(i), P(j))	s.place(%1, s.getPointerPos(%2));
Predicates	'l > r at P(i) in (M)'	l > r| P(i)	s.compare(%1, ">")
	'Distance between P(i) and P(j) in (M) is equal to (n)'	d(P(i), P(j)) = (n)	s.distance(%1, %2) == %3
	'Pointer P(i) is at the end of (M)'	d(P(i), K)	s.atEnd(%1)

Implementations of basic elements are written with the use of the Java class named Sorting, which is a reusable component developed for sorting tasks (see Figure 5). This class contains the description of data — the processed array, pointers, markers, control points, and the methods for accessing these data. The formal parameter in the text of Java implementation of basic elements is marked with the symbol % followed by a number of a parameter in a text of basic predicate or operator. For example, the basic operator "Transpose l, r at $P(i)$ in (M)" includes the parameter i, the pointer number. The value of this parameter is substituted instead of a corresponding formal parameter in the implementation of this operator, which is s.transp(%1), where s is an instance of the Sorting class; transp is the method transposing the elements of the array M, adjacent to the pointer $P(i)$. The implementations of other basic elements given in the table are also calls of methods of the Sorting class.

Figure 5. The UML class diagram for Sorting class

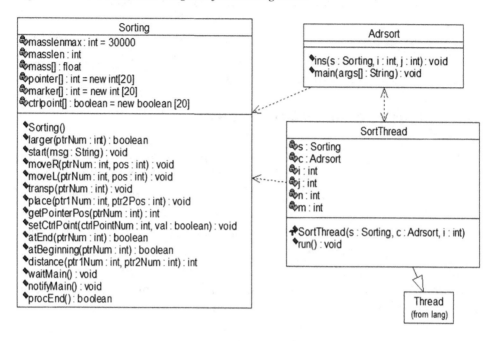

The current version of **IDS** provides generation of sequential and parallel code in C, C++, C for CUDA, Cilk++ and Java programming languages.

Table 4. The reduced notations of TermWare terms

Notation	Term
$x \rightarrow y$	*rule(x, y)*
$x[c] \rightarrow y$	*if_rule(x, c, y)*
$x[c] \rightarrow y[r]$	*if_rule(x, c, action(y, r))*
$x[c0] \rightarrow y0 \mid$ $[c1] \rightarrow y1 \mid ... \mid$ $! \rightarrow z$	*if_else_rule(x, c0, y0,* *[else_rule(c1, y1), ...],* *fail_rule(z))*
x.y	*apply(x, y)*
$[x, y, .., z]$	*cons(x, cons(y, ..., cons(z, NIL)))*
$\{x, y, ..., z\}$	*set(x, y, ..., z)*
$x + y, x - y, x * y, x / y$	*plus(x, y), minus(x, y), multiply(x, y), divide(x, y)*
$x == y, x \mathrel{!=} y, x > y, x >= y, x <$ $y, x <= y$	*eq(x, y), neq(x, y), greater(x, y),* *greater_eq(x, y), less(x, y), less_eq(x, y)*
$x \mathbin{\&\&} y, x \mathbin{\|} y, !x$	*logical_and(x, y), logical_or(x, y), logical_not(x)*

THE REWRITING RULES SYSTEM TERMWARE

To automate the transformation of programs, IDS toolkit is applied together with symbolic computation system TermWare based on rewriting rules technique (Doroshenko & Shevchenko, 2006; "TermWare", n.d.).

The Language of TermWare System

TermWare language is based on terms, i.e. expressions of the form $f(x_1,\ldots,x_n)$ with variables and data types. The variables (which are written as $var) and constants of certain data types (numerical, logic, string and atomic — unchangeable strings) are used as atomic terms. To facilitate notation and perception, simplifying reductions for many terms are used. For example, $x+y$ is used for $plus(x,y)$; $[x,y]$ — for $cons(x,y)$ (the list with the first element x and the rest of the list y); $x?y: z$ — for *if else* (x,y,z). The set of all terms is a term written with the use of these reductions. Table 4 shows the basic notations of TermWare terms.

TermWare rules have the following general form:

source[*condition*] → *destination*[*action*],

where *source* is the input sample; *destination* is the target sample; *condition* is the term defining the applicability of the rule; *action* is the operation executed when the rule triggers.

The actions being executed and the conditions being checked are optional components of the rule, which can call imperative code. For this purpose, the developer should implement the "fact base" — a class implementing the IFacts interface and providing methods that can be called from rewriting rules. Thus, the connection between declarative rules in TermWare language and imperative code in traditional object-oriented languages (such as Java or C#) is established. Besides, it is possible to write custom strategy (in the form of a class implementing the interface ITermRewritingStrategy) defining an order of application of rules.

TermWare system was initially implemented in the form of Java library intended for embedding in applications ("TermWare", n.d.). The command-line interface for interactive execution of simple rewriting rules was also developed. Later, TermWare system was transferred to Microsoft.NET platform, which allowed using rewriting rules technique for transformation of programs written in C# and other languages supported by .NET platform. The parser and code generator for C# language were developed, which enabled TermWare to work with programs represented in C#. The graphical user interface for a more convenient creation and application of rewriting rules was also implemented. The developed components constitute the toolkit intended for transformation of programs on Microsoft.NET platform, which is described in the following subsection.

The Structure of the Rewriting Rules Toolkit

The developed software toolkit Termware.NET is intended for automated transformation of programs with the use of the rewriting rules technique. The toolkit consists of the following basic components:

- the parser for translating source code from high-level languages (such as C#, C++, Java) to a model of a program in the form of terms;
- the system of application of rewriting rules for program transformation;
- the generator for translation of a program model in the form of terms to a programming language;
- the graphical user interface for viewing and editing terms and rewriting rules, and also managing other components.

The interaction between the components is schematically presented in Figure 6. The parser carries out a transition from a source text of a program in a high-level programming language (for example, C#) to its model in the form of terms. Similarly, the code generator carries out a transition from a program model to source code in a target language. Notice that the given model is low-level and explicitly describes all syntactic constructs of a programming language. For convenience of the user, the toolkit supports a transition to a high-level algebraic model. At present, the toolkit supports parsers and code generators for Java, C# 2.0 and Fortran.

Figure 6. The basic components of the Termware.NET toolkit

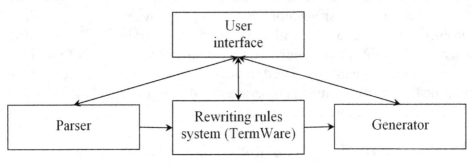

The toolkit provides the possibility of addition of new parsers and generators for other programming languages. For this purpose, it is necessary to provide the classes implementing the interfaces IParser and ICodeGenerator, which carry out transformation between a text representation of source code in a specified language and a syntactic model (a parse tree), represented in the form of terms.

For automatic application of rewriting rules to specified terms (in particular, program models), the toolkit uses the TermWare library for Microsoft.NET platform. The toolkit supports the loading and saving of systems of rules in TermWare language. Besides, there is a possibility of implementation of fact databases (containing the methods accessible for calling from rewriting rules) or additional rewriting strategies in C# language or in other languages of Microsoft.NET platform.

The graphical interface of the developed toolkit is presented in Figure 7. In the left side of the toolkit window, the tree representation of a current term (program model) is placed. The right part of the interface supports editing of rules in text or graphic (tree) representation. The graphical interface allows the user to look through and edit terms in a visual tree representation, instead of a text. Terms are edited by means of the contextual menu supporting addition and removal of nodes, change of contents of nodes, work with a clipboard. The same possibilities are accessible also at editing rules in a tree representation. Thus, the graphical interface facilitates understanding of complex program models and allows working with them without studying specific syntax of the rewriting rules system. At the same time, experienced users can work with terms in a text representation as well.

Figure 7. The graphical user interface of the Termware.NET toolkit

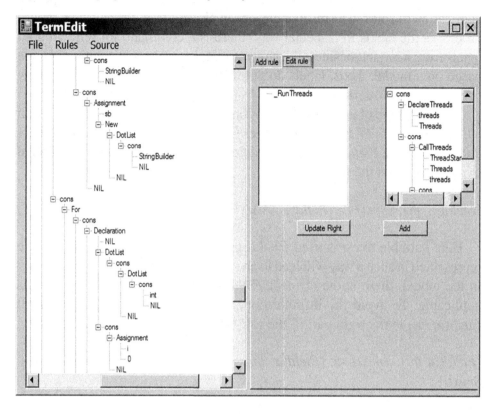

Additional Facilities of the Rewriting Rules Toolkit

Besides the basic possibilities of TermWare system ("TermWare", n.d.), the developed toolkit supports the additional facilities focused on simplification of work of the user with the system. In particular, such facilities concern labels and patterns.

Labels

labels are terms of a special kind which can be used in rewriting rules together with other terms, but also can be additionally processed by the toolkit. They look like _MARK_..., i.e. the term name begins with the symbols _MARK_ followed by any other symbols and/or subterms. Labels are used for selection of separate elements (subterms) of a model and have no independent significance in a model. Labels are used for indication of code fragments to which the transformations are applied. Besides, labels can be used to prevent repeated application of rules to terms that have been already transformed. The toolkit processes the labels in a special way: there is a command for removing all labels from a model; besides, the generator ignores labels at creation of code based on a model. Thus, labels do not influence generated code, but allow rules to work correctly.

As an example of use of the labels, consider the rules intended for addition of the element *Field(b, int)* (the integer field of a class with name *b*) directly after the element *Field(a, int)*. The simplest rule implementing the mentioned transformation is the following:

$$[Field(a, int): \$next] \rightarrow [Field(a, int): [Field(b, int): \$next]] \tag{1}$$

Here variable $next is used for designating a list tail. However, the rule represented in such a way will lead to an infinite loop: after its first triggering, in the model, there is the element *Field(a, int)*, to which the same rule is applicable. To avoid the infinite loop, it is possible to mark the element *Field(a, int)* in the right part of the rule with the label *_MARK_Processed*:

$$[Field(a, int): \$next] \rightarrow [Field(a, int, \_MARK\_Processed): [Field(b, int): \$next]] \tag{2}$$

In this case, after a single application of the rule, the resulting term differs from the initial, and the rule cannot be applied again. One more variant of an implementation of the transformation consists in marking of the initial element *Field(a, int)* with the label *_MARK_Target* and removing this label after application of the rule:

$$[Field(a, int, \_MARK\_Target): \$next] \rightarrow [Field(a, int): [Field(b, int): \$next]] \tag{3}$$

In practice, both described approaches can be applied depending on the features of a problem. If it is necessary to transform only one element of a model (for example, the field with a name *a* only in one class), a label on an initial term is used. If the transformation should work with all elements of the given kind (to add a new field after all fields with a name *a*), it makes sense to use labels on a resulting term.

Patterns

Patterns facilitate a reduction of a size of a tree representing a model. They describe the conformity between often occurring combinations of elements of a model and their reduced designation. The set of patterns allows to carry out a transition between a low-level (more detailed) model of a program and its high-level version.

As was described earlier, Termware.NET toolkit contains parser and generator of C# code, which allows building a model of a code in the form of terms based on source code, and also transit from a model to source code. However, such a model is low-level, as it contains the description of all syntactic constructs of the programming language. For example, consider a simple and widespread construct of C# language, a for-loop. This loop corresponds to a code fragment

$$for(int\ \$var=\$start;\ \$var <\$end;\ \$var++)\ \{\$body\} \tag{9}$$

Here variables $\$var$, $\$start$, $\$end$, $\$body$ are used for indicating code sections, which vary depending on a program. The fragment of the code (9) corresponds to the following low-level (syntactic) model:

$$For(cons(Declaration(NIL,\ DotList(cons(DotList(cons(int,\ NIL)),\ NIL)), \tag{10}$$

$$cons(Assignment(\$var,\ \$start),\ NIL)),\ NIL),\ less(\$var,\ \$end),$$

$$cons(PostIncrement(\$var),\ NIL),\ \$body)$$

This term is quite cumbersome and inconvenient for understanding and change. Therefore, more high-level (algebraic) representation is used instead of it:

$$ForCnt(\$var,\ \$start,\ \$end,\ \$body) \tag{11}$$

A high-level model is represented in the form of terms, as well as a low-level program model. However, unlike the low-level, the high-level model describes not syntactic constructs of a programming language, but the operators of Glushkov's algebra of algorithms (Doroshenko, Zhereb, & Yatsenko, 2010; Doroshenko et al., 2013).

The advantage of use of high-level program models consists in possibility of shorter and more expressive notation of program transformations. However, there is a necessity of transition between a program model and a source code. For low-level (syntactic) models, such transformation is carried out with the use of a parser and a generator for a given programming language. However, for construction of higher-level models, it is necessary to have an additional knowledge about a subject domain, which can be expressed in the form of sets of basic operators and predicates of Glushkov's algebra.

For automated transition from source code to a high-level program model and in the opposite direction, the rewriting rules technique is used. The transition is made in two stages: between source code and a low-level model (a parse tree), and then between a low-level model and a high-level model (operators of Glushkov's algebra). At the first stage, the parser and the generator of a given language are used. The second stage is carried out with the use of rewriting rules: as both kinds of models are representable in the form of terms, the transformations between them are written in the form of rules. The rules are represented in the form of TermWare patterns.

In the general case, the pattern is defined as a pair of systems of rules:

- R_p is for extraction of a pattern from a given term;
- R_g is for expanding the pattern into its corresponding low-level term.

In a more specific case, the pattern is defined by a pair of terms:

- t_p is a designation of the pattern (an element of a high-level model);
- t_g is an implementation of the pattern (an element of a low-level model).

In this case $R_p = \{t_g \rightarrow t_p\}$ and $R_g = \{t_p \rightarrow t_g\}$.

The pattern consisting of the operator t_p and its implementation in terms of the low-level model t_g are defined for each high-level operator. For creating a high-level model from a low-level one, rule sets R_p are applied to each pattern. Similarly, rule sets R_g are applied for transformation from a high-level to a low-level model.

For example, in the case of the for-loop, it is possible to use the expression (11) as a term t_p, and the expression (10) as a term t_g. The pattern obtained in such a way can be used for an automatic transition from a syntactic to an algebraic representation of the loop.

As a more specific example of patterns use, consider the function *_GetCoor*, which is applied for computing a number of the initial iteration of a loop based on parameters of a thread and a block in CUDA platform (see Chapter 4). In this case

$$t_p = \_GetCoor(\$c),$$

$$t_g = Dot(blockIdx, \$c)*Dot(blockDim, \$c) + Dot(threadIdx, \$c).$$

Thus, the element of a high-level model *_GetCoor(x)* can be transformed into an element of a low-level model

$$Dot(blockIdx, x)*Dot(blockDim, x) + Dot(threadIdx, x),$$

which then will be transformed into a fragment of a source code

blockIdx.x*blockDim.x + threadIDx.x.

The transformation in an opposite direction is also possible, in which the fragment of source code is translated to an element of a low-level model with the use of the parser, and then the rule R_p of a pattern is used for selection of an element of a high-level model.

Another important feature of high-level models is their independence from implementation language. Single high-level program model can correspond to low-level programs in various languages (or with the use of various platforms). To support additional language, it is necessary to add low-level model support (i.e. parser and code generator) and implement patterns for this language.

The Auto-Tuning Framework TuningGenie

TuningGenie framework is aimed at automated generation of auto-tuner applications from source code of input programs (Ivanenko, Doroshenko, & Zhereb, 2014). The idea of an auto-tuner consists in empirical evaluation of several versions of an input program and selection of the best one. The main evaluation criteria are less execution time of input program and accuracy of results obtained. The framework works with program source code using expert knowledge of a developer and automation facilities from the framework. The developer adds some metadata (parameter names and value ranges) to source code in the form of special comments-pragmas. Exploiting such expert knowledge, the developer can reduce the number of program versions to be evaluated and therefore increase optimization performance.

The Architecture of TuningGenie

The auto-tuning software implementation is based on the rewriting rules system TermWare (Doroshenko & Shevchenko, 2006). TuningGenie uses TermWare to extract expert knowledge from program source code and generates a new program version on each tuning iteration. TermWare translates source code into a term and provides transformations according to rewriting rules. The current TuningGenie version supports the optimization of Java programs. The common workflow of the TuningGenie framework is shown in Figure 8.

The input of TuningGenie is Java source code marked with so-called "pragmas". Pragmas describe configurations and transformations of a program that affect its performance. Pragmas are specified manually by program developers, using Java comments of a special form. During the parsing of source code into a term representing an abstract syntax tree, the auto-tuner builds a set of configurations based on these expert data. Then these configurations are translated into rewriting rules. Also on this "preliminary" stage, some values of program parameters are calculated. The results of this stage include a program term, a set of parameterized rewriting rules and a set of rule configurations C that specify the specific parameter values. Each of these configurations specifies a unique version of an input program.

Then TuningGenie searches for the most efficient configuration $C_{opt} \in C$ by iteratively performing the following steps.

- Select a configuration $C^* \in C$ to test. Configurations are selected sequentially from the set C. Size of C depends on values from pragmas and developers are expected to use their expert knowledge to narrow the region of search (group pragmas only if they are really related, narrow boundary values for each pragma). Additionally, the time limit can be used for cases when it's hard to estimate overall optimization time (step 4).
- Generate and compile the corresponding program version. The parameters from a given configuration are substituted into the rules; then these rules are executed on the source term of the parallel program. After the transformation is complete, the term is transformed into Java source code using TermWare facilities. The code is compiled using

common JDK tools. The result of this step is a new version of the program ready for performance measurement.

- Execute the program and evaluate its performance. A small launcher class is generated automatically. It runs the program and measures its execution time, therefore computing $f(C^*)=t$. Each configuration is executed several times (at least 3). If the time consumed for each run differs a lot (more than 10%), then a warning message is logged.
- If all configurations from the set C have been evaluated or if the optimization process has used all the allotted time, then go to step 5, otherwise go to step 1.
- The optimal configuration is selected from a set of all configurations that have been evaluated: $C_{opt}=C^*: f(C^*)=f_{min}$. For this configuration, an optimal program version is generated, as in step 2.

Figure 8. TuningGenie workflow

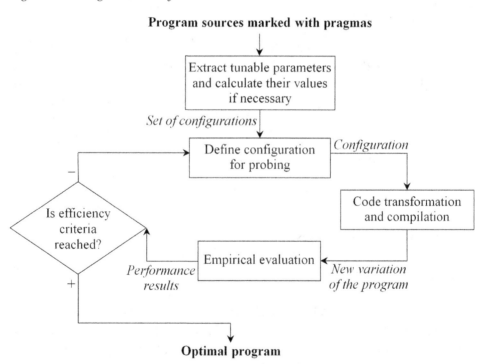

The program obtained as a result of steps 1–5 is saved and executed in a target environment. This program is considered optimal for a given architecture.

TuningGenie Pragmas

As already mentioned above, the expert knowledge about a subject domain and implementation is saved in source code as special directives called "pragmas" (by analogy with C language). Pragmas are actually the comments of a special form. Therefore, they are ignored by the Java compiler. Adding pragmas does not change the structure of computation, and such instrumented program can be compiled by any compiler without additional libraries.

Currently, the TuningGenie framework supports three kinds of pragmas: *tunableParam, calculatedValue* and *bidirectionalCycle.*

The *tunableParam* pragma specifies a search domain for an optimal value of a numeric variable. For example, the following pragma sets the possible values for a threadCount variable as a range [50…100] with a step 10:

//tunableParam name=threadCount start=50 stop=100 step=10
int threadCount = 1;

The *tunableParam* pragma is applicable to algorithms that use geometrical (data) parallelization: it allows finding the optimal decomposition of computation by estimating the size of a block that is executed on a single processor. It also can be applied when it is necessary to estimate the optimal number of some limited resources like cache size or a number of threads. Another use of the *tunableParam* pragma is to find an optimal threshold value to switch to a different algorithm.

The *calculatedValue* pragma evaluates some function in a target environment and assigns the resulting value to a given variable:

//calculatedValue name=hdReadSpeed
//method="org.tuning.EnvironmUtils.getHDReadSpeed()"
int hdKbPerSec = 1;

This pragma can be used if some algorithm parameters depend on execution environment details, such as execution time of arithmetic operations or memory access on various levels. All such values are calculated before auto-tuning process starts and saved in TermWare knowledge base. The data stored in the knowledge base is accessible from rewriting rules, so *calculatedValue* can specify the value range for the *tunableParam* pragma. In this way, the developer can run a small test program to reduce the search domain and improve auto-tuning speed.

The *bidirectionalCycle* pragma can be used to specify loops, where iterations can be run in any order. In the following example, TuningGenie will evaluate both increment (0 to SIZE-1) and decrement (SIZE-1 to 0) versions:

```
int[] data = new int[SIZE];
//bidirectionalCycle
for (int i = 0; i < SIZE; i++) {
doSomethingWith(data[i]);
}
```

This pragma is targeted at cases when multi-dimensional data is linearized into single-dimensional. Sequential iteration from the multi-dimensional point of view is not always sequential for linearized data, hence not always cache-efficient. So if the order of iteration is not important, the auto-tuner might pick up a better version.

It's worth mentioning that by default all pragmas (and corresponding parameters) are considered independent. It means that for each parameter's value from a single pragma a separate version of a program is generated and measured; parameters from other pragmas are ignored (i.e. take values specified in source code). So if there are n pragmas, with the number of configurations contributed by each pragma denoted as N_i, then the total size of search space will be $\sum_{i=1}^{n} N_i$ and not $\prod_{i=1}^{n} N_i$. To mark parameters that need to be tested in correlation, a *group* option must be specified in related pragmas.

Another important fact is that at the moment all pragma's variables have "local" scope and they are tied to demarked instruction. That's why it's impossible to gather all pragmas in one place — they have to be spread among source code and duplicated for each section of duplicated code (if such is present).

Translating Pragmas to Rewriting Rules

The rewriting rules technique is applied to transform source code of a program. For each pragma described in the previous subsection, a corresponding rewriting rule is generated. Then all the generated rules are applied to a term representing a source code of a program. In this subsection, the process of rule generation for each pragma is described in detail.

For *calculatedValue* and *tunableParam* pragmas, rewriting rules are completely identical. Both pragmas initialize some variable with a value taken from the currently tested configuration. The only difference is in the syntax of the pragmas: for *calculatedValue*, the value to be substituted is calculated before performing tuning iteration, and for *tunableParam*, it is specified in parameters.

Consider the following code fragment containing *tunableParam* pragma:

```
//tunableParam name=threshold start=1 stop=10 step=1
int threshold = 1;
```

The rule generated from this pragma (slightly simplified for readability) has the following form:

VariableDeclarator(Id("threshold"), Literal($value)) [$value!="newValue"]
   ->
VariableDeclarator(Id("threshold"), Literal("newValue"))

Notice the condition [$value!="newValue"] that was added to prevent infinite rule application. Rewriting rules are applied repeatedly until the moment when none of them is applicable. In this example, it is necessary to prevent the infinite rule application in the case when the substitution value newValue is equal to the initial $value. The actual value of "newValue" is taken from the range of values defined by the pragma. In this particular case, newValue is the range [1...10] and each value will be automatically sequentially probed and estimated by the auto-tuner.

Now consider the *bidirectionalCycle* pragma. Assume that the following loop does not depend on iteration order (i.e. it can be run both in increment and decrement order):

```
//bidirectionalCycle
for (int loopVar = 0; loopVar < 42; loopVar ++){
    ...
}
```

The pragma is translated into a rewriting rule that uses propositional variables ("TermWare Tutorial", n.d.) to invert the iteration order:

```
ForStatement(
    LoopHead(
```

```
        ForInit(VariableDeclarator(Id("loopVar"),
        Literal($initialValue))),
        RelationalExpression(Identifier("loopVar"),"<",
        Literal($endValue)),
        ForUpdate(StatementExpression(
        Identifier("loopVar "),"++"))),
    Block(.....)
 )          ->
    ForStatement(
      LoopHead(
          ForInit(VariableDeclarator(Id("loopVar"),
          Literal($endValue))),
          RelationalExpression(Identifier("loopVar"),">",
          Literal($initialValue)),
          ForUpdate(StatementExpression(Identifier("loopVar "),
          "--"))),
      Block(.....)
)
```

The above rule swaps initial and final values of the loop counter variable, changes the operator that modifies this variable on each iteration (from increment to decrement), and changes the loop exit condition.

All rewriting rules together with the strategy for their application and the knowledge base (facts database) (Doroshenko & Shevchenko, 2006; "TermWare Tutorial", n.d.), are combined into a single term system. The system performs a reduction of the initial term and obtains a new term. This term is translated back into a program source code using a target language (in this case it's Java).

The Comparison of TuningGenie to Other Auto-Tuning Frameworks

Many approaches have been proposed for the problem of auto-tuner development. Well-known examples of auto-tuners are ATLAS (Whaley, Petitet, & Dongarra, 2001) and FFTW (Frigo & Johnson, 1998), which are specialized libraries introducing the high-performance implementation of some specific functions. Unlike TuningGenie framework, which provides domain-independent optimization, they are tied to domain and language.

ABCLibScript (Katagiri, 2010) is a computer language for automatic performance tuning. It defines a language in which developers can define tuning details. Similar to the pragma-based approach used in TuningGenie, additional meta-data is inserted into source code. ABCLibScript has quite powerful capabilities that even allow performing algorithm selection based on input parameters at runtime. At the moment, TuningGenie supports only pre-execution optimization. On the other hand, pragmas used in TuningGenie are more compact and can change program structure in a declarative manner through the capabilities of rewriting rules.

TuningGenie is quite similar to Atune-IL (Schaefer, Pankratius, & Tichy, 2009), a language extension for auto-tuning. It also uses pragmas and is not tied to some specific programming language. The main difference of TuningGenie is due to the term rewriting engine that is applied for source code transformation. Representing program code as a term allows modifying program structure in a declarative way. This feature significantly increases the capabilities of the auto-tuning framework. Also, via the knowledge base, TuningGenie can exchange data between pre-tuning and tuning phases, so it can initialize program variables with values that were calculated in a target environment (micro-benchmarking (Ma et al., 2012)).

SPIRAL (Puschel et al., 2005), as well as TuningGenie, uses rewriting systems for transforming a source code. However, SPIRAL is focused on problems of digital signal processing and works with sequential code only.

The Framework of Install-time, Before Execute-time and Run-time optimization (FIBER) (Katagiri, Kise, Honda, & Yuba, 2003) works with three different phases of program lifecycle in a computing environment: installation stage, pre-execution stage, and execution phase. For automation of the optimization process, it uses compiler directives and a script language ABCLibScript (Katagiri, 2010). As with TuningGenie, the user marks out variables to be optimized and their values that must be tested. However, in general, the framework is focused on numerical variables and was not designed for optimization of general-purpose parallel programs.

Parameterized Optimizing for Empirical Tuning (POET) (Yi, Seymour, You, Vuduc, & Quinlan, 2007) uses its own language for description of code fragments that are transformed by rules defined by a program developer. In general, such an approach is very flexible, but very complex to develop large programs — the language syntax is very detailed, and therefore even simple involute of a loop requires several dozens of code lines written in POET language.

CONCLUSION

The developed IDS toolkit automates the design of high-level specifications (schemes) of algorithms, which can be represented in three equivalent forms: algebraic, natural linguistic and graphical, and therefore gives a comprehensive understanding of specifications and facilitates achievement of demanded program quality. The advantage of the toolkit consists in using the method of automated design of syntactically correct algorithm schemes, which eliminates syntax errors during construction of algorithms. The toolkit automatically translates algorithm schemes into source code in a programming language (C, C++, Java and other).

TermWare system and Termware.NET toolkit provide automated transformation of programs using the rewriting rules technique. The graphical user interface allows to create and edit rules, and also visualize a structure of a program and transformations. The developed additional facilities (labels and patterns) simplify the work of the user with the system and provide implementation of complex transformations more efficiently than in similar systems. Patterns allow using abbreviated descriptions of frequently used language constructs which are automatically transformed to complete constructs. The graphical user interface of Termware.NET supports the simplified creation of typical rules which facilitates learning of the rewriting rules technique and increases the efficiency of work with the toolkit. The presence of the parser and the generator for C# language allows to work directly with software source code, transform it into a program model and perform the reverse transformation. The architecture of Termware.NET toolkit provides the addition of other parsers and generators, in particular, for supporting other programming languages. The developed toolkit can be applied for automation of various stages of program design and development. The most often application is automatic parallelization and optimization of programs. The patterns can be applied for the transition between high-level and low-level program models. Rewriting rules can also be used for verification of program properties, both through parsing and through generation of tests.

The developed TuningGenie framework is intended for automated generation of tuner applications. It was designed with an emphasis on minimization of required source code changes in optimized programs. Most such changes are declarative and do not affect initial sources. Such flexibility is reached by utilizing the rule rewriting approach for code transformation which significantly differs from related solutions. Current TuningGenie version contains quite an extensive toolset, so reducing the time costs of optimization is the main priority in further development. Partial execution of optimized program would dramatically reduce tuning time since the current implementation of the framework fully executes target program at each tuning cycle, which may not be necessary. Adding means for software instrumentation in runtime is one of the most promising but quite challenging directions of further development. For instance, parallel applications would benefit from the ability to switch to better-performing subroutine based on input data characteristics as is presented, for example, in ABCLibScript (Katagiri, 2010). At the moment TuningGenie is used as a separate module that needs to be included and configured to tune your application. So introducing integration with project management tools like Apache Ivy, Maven or Buildr would significantly simplify the use of the framework.

REFERENCES

Andon, P. I., Doroshenko, A. Yu., Tseytlin, G. O., & Yatsenko, O. A. (2007). *Algebra-algorithmic models and methods of parallel programming*. Kyiv: Academperiodyka. (in Russian)

Anisimov, A. V., & Kulyabko, P. P. (1984). Programming of parallel processors in control spaces. *Cybernetics, 20*(3), 404–418. doi:10.1007/BF01068474

Apel, S., Lengauer, C., Möller, B., & Kästner, C. (2010). An algebraic foundation for automatic feature-based program synthesis. *Science of Computer Programming, 75*(11), 1022–1047. doi:10.1016/j.scico.2010.02.001

Bagheri, H., & Sullivan, K. (2012). Pol: Specification-driven synthesis of architectural code frameworks for platform-based applications. In *Proceedings of the 11th International Conference on Generative Programming and Component Engineering (GPCE'12) (ACM SIGPLAN Notices)* (Vol. 48, pp. 93-102). New York: ACM. 10.1145/2371401.2371416

Barthe, G., Crespo, J. M., Gulwani, S., Kunz, C., & Marron, M. (2013). From relational verification to SIMD loop synthesis. *ACM SIGPLAN Notices, 48*(8), 123–134. doi:10.1145/2517327.2442529

Batory, D. (2007). Program refactoring, program synthesis, and model-driven development. In *Proceedings of the 16th International Conference on Compiler Construction (CC'07) (LNCS)* (Vol. 4420, pp. 156-171). Berlin: Springer. 10.1007/978-3-540-71229-9_11

Bures, T., Denney, E., Fischer, B., & Nistor, E. C. (2004). The role of ontologies in schema-based program synthesis. In *Proceedings of the Workshop on Ontologies as Software Engineering Artifacts (OOPSLA 2004)* (pp. 1-6). Academic Press.

Doroshenko, A., Ivanenko, P., Ovdii, O., & Yatsenko, O. (2016). Automated program design— An example solving a weather forecasting problem. *Open Physics*, *14*(1), 410–419. doi:10.1515/phys-2016-0048

Doroshenko, A., & Shevchenko, R. (2006). A rewriting framework for rule-based programming dynamic applications. *Fundamenta Informaticae*, *72*(1-3), 95–108.

Doroshenko, A., Tseytlin, G., Yatsenko, O., & Zachariya, L. (2006). A theory of clones and formalized design of programs. In *Proceedings of the 15th International Workshop "Concurrency, Specification and Programming" (CS&P'2006)* (pp. 328-339). Berlin: Humboldt University Press.

Doroshenko, A., Zhereb, K., & Yatsenko, O. (2010). Formal facilities for designing efficient GPU programs. In *Proceedings of the 19th International Workshop "Concurrency: Specification and Programming" (CS&P'2010)* (pp. 142-153). Berlin: Humboldt University Press.

Doroshenko, A., Zhereb, K., & Yatsenko, O. (2013). Developing and optimizing parallel programs with algebra-algorithmic and term rewriting tools. In *Proceedings of the 9th International Conference "ICT in Education, Research, and Industrial Applications" (ICTERI 2013), Revised Selected Papers (Communications in Computer and Information Science)* (Vol. 412, pp. 70-92). Berlin: Springer. 10.1007/978-3-319-03998-5_5

Fischer, B., & Schumann, J. (2003). AutoBayes: A system for generating data analysis programs from statistical models. *Journal of Functional Programming*, *13*(3), 483–508. doi:10.1017/S0956796802004562

Flener, P. (2002). Achievements and prospects of program synthesis. In A. C. Kakas & F. Sadri (Eds.), *Computational Logic: Logic Programming and Beyond. LNCS* (Vol. 2407, pp. 310–346). Berlin: Springer. doi:10.1007/3-540-45628-7_13

Frigo, M., & Johnson, S. (1998). FFTW: An adaptive software architecture for the FF. *Acoustics. Speech and Signal Processing, 3*, 1381–1384.

Gulwani, S. (2010). Dimensions in program synthesis. In *Proceedings of the 12th International ACM SIGPLAN Symposium on Principles and Practice of Declarative Programming* (pp. 13-24). New York: ACM.

Ivanenko, P., Doroshenko, A., & Zhereb, K. (2014). TuningGenie: Auto-tuning framework based on rewriting rules. In *Proceedings of the 10th International Conference "ICT in Education, Research and Industrial Applications. Integration, Harmonization and Knowledge Transfer" (ICTERI 2014) (Communications in Computer and Information Science)* (Vol. 469, pp. 139-158). Cham: Springer. 10.1007/978-3-319-13206-8_7

Jackson, D. (2002). Alloy: A lightweight object modelling notation. *ACM Transactions on Software Engineering and Methodology, 11*(2), 256–290. doi:10.1145/505145.505149

Jacobs, S., Kuncak, V., & Suter, P. (2013). Reductions for synthesis procedures. In *Proceedings of the 14th International Conference on Verification, Model Checking, and Abstract Interpretation (VMCAI 2013) (LNCS)* (Vol. 7737, pp. 88-107). Berlin: Springer. 10.1007/978-3-642-35873-9_8

Katagiri, T. (2010). ABCLibScript: A computer language for automatic performance tuning. In K. Naono, K. Teranishi, & J. C. Reiji (Eds.), *Software Automatic Tuning: From Concepts to State-of-the-Art Results* (pp. 295–313). Berlin: Springer.

Katagiri, T., Kise, K., Honda, H., & Yuba, T. (2003). FIBER: A generalized framework for auto-tuning software. In *Proceedings of the International Symposium on High Performance Computing 2003 (ISHPC 2003) (LNCS)* (Vol. 2858, pp. 146-159). Berlin: Springer. 10.1007/978-3-540-39707-6_11

Kitzelmann, E. (2010). Inductive programming: A survey of program synthesis techniques. In *Proceedings of the International Workshop on Approaches and Applications of Inductive Programming (AAIP 2009) (LNCS)* (Vol. 5812, pp. 50-73). Berlin: Springer. 10.1007/978-3-642-11931-6_3

Kneuss, E., Kuncak, V., Kuraj, I., & Suter, P. (2013). *On integrating deductive synthesis and verification systems.* Technical Report. Retrieved from https://arxiv.org/pdf/1304.5661.pdf

Leonard, E. I., & Heitmeyer, C. L. (2008). Automatic program generation from formal specifications using APTS. In O. Danvy, H. Mairson, F. Henglein, & A. Pettorossi (Eds.), *Automatic Program Development* (pp. 93–113). Dordrecht: Springer. doi:10.1007/978-1-4020-6585-9_10

Mannadiar, R., & Vangheluwe, H. (2010). Modular synthesis of mobile device applications from domain-specific models. In *Proceedings of the 7th International Workshop on Model-Based Methodologies for Pervasive and Embedded Software (MOMPES'10)* (pp. 21-28). New York: ACM. 10.1145/1865875.1865879

Menon, A. K., Tamuz, O., Gulwani, S., Lampson, B., & Kalai, A. T. (2013). A machine learning framework for programming by example. In *Proceedings of the 30th International Conference on Machine Learning (ICML'13)* (pp. 187-195). Academic Press.

Petrushenko, A. N. (1991). An approach to automation of optimizing transformations of algorithms and programs. *Cybernetics and Systems Analysis, 27*(5), 744–753. doi:10.1007/BF01130548

Puschel, M., Moura, J., Johnson, J., Padua, J., Veloso, M., Singer, M., … Rizzolo, N. (2005) SPIRAL: Code generation for DSP transforms. In *Proceedings of the IEEE (Vol. 93*, pp. 232-275). 10.1109/JPROC.2004.840306

Quatrani, T., & Palistrant, J. (2006). *Visual modeling with IBM Rational Software architect and UML.* Indianapolis, IN: IBM Press.

Raychev, V., Vechev, M., & Yahav, E. (2013). Automatic synthesis of deterministic concurrency. In *Proceedings of the 20th International Static Analysis Symposium (SAS'13) (LNCS)* (Vol. 7935, pp. 283-303). Berlin: Springer.

Schaefer, C. A., Pankratius, V., & Tichy, W. F. (2009). Atune-IL: An instrumentation language for auto-tuning parallel applications. In *Proceedings of the 15th International Euro-Par Conference (Euro-Par'2009) (LNCS)* (Vol. 5704, pp. 9-20). Berlin: Springer. 10.1007/978-3-642-03869-3_5

Srivastava, S., Gulwani, S., & Foster, J. S. (2010). From program verification to program synthesis. In *Proceedings of the 37th Annual ACM SIGPLAN-SIGACT Symposium on Principles of Programming Languages (POPL'10) (ACM SIGPLAN Notices)* (Vol. 45, pp. 313-326). New York: ACM. 10.1145/1706299.1706337

Teorey, T., Buxton, S., Fryman, L., Güting, R., Halpin, T., Harrington, J., & Witt, G. (2008). *Database design: Know it all*. Burlington, MA: Morgan Kaufmann.

TermWare. (n.d.). Retrieved from http://www.gradsoft.com.ua/products/termware_eng.html

TermWare Tutorial. (n.d.). Retrieved from http://www.gradsoft.ua/rus/Products/termware/docs/tutorial_eng.html

Whaley, R., Petitet, A., & Dongarra, J. J. (2001). Automated empirical optimizations of software and the ATLAS Project. *Parallel Computing*, 27(1-2), 3–35. doi:10.1016/S0167-8191(00)00087-9

Yatsenko, O. (2012). On parameter-driven generation of algorithm schemes. In *Proceedings of the 21st International Workshop "Concurrency, Specification and Programming" (CS&P'2012)* (pp. 428-438). Berlin: Humboldt University Press.

Yi, Q., Seymour, K., You, H., Vuduc, R., & Quinlan, D. (2007). POET: Parameterized optimizations for empirical tuning. In *Proceedings of the Parallel and Distributed Processing Symposium 2007 (IPDPS 2007)* (pp. 447). Piscataway, NJ: IEEE Computer Society.

Yushchenko, K. L., Tseytlin, G. O., & Galushka, A. V. (1989). Algebraic-grammatical specifications and synthesis of structured program schemas. *Cybernetics and Systems Analysis*, 25(6), 713–727.

Yushchenko, K. L., Tseytlin, G. O., Hrytsay, V. P., & Terzyan, T. K. (1989). *Multilevel structured design of programs: Theoretical bases, tools*. Moscow: Finansy i statistika. (in Russian)

KEY TERMS AND DEFINITIONS

Glushkov's System of Algorithmic Algebras (SAA, Glushkov's Algebra): The two-sorted algebra focused on analytical form of representation of algorithms and formalized transformation of these representations.

Integrated Toolkit for Design and Synthesis of Programs (IDS): The software system intended for automated constructing of sequential and parallel algorithm schemes represented in the modified system of algorithmic algebras (SAA-M) and synthesis of programs in C, C++, Java languages.

Regular Scheme (RS): A representation of an algorithm in the system of algorithmic algebras (SAA).

Rule Patterns: The facilities of the rewriting rules framework TermWare. NET, which are applied for a transition between a low-level (more detailed) model of a program and its high-level version.

SAA Scheme: A representation of an algorithm in algorithmic language SAA/1.

SAA/1: The algorithmic language based on Glushkov's system of algorithmic algebras and focused on natural linguistic representation of schemes. It is applied for multilevel structured designing and documenting of sequential and parallel algorithms and programs.

TermWare: An open-source implementation of rewriting rules engine written in Java. It provides a language for describing rewriting rules that operate on data structures called terms and also a rule engine that interprets rules to transform terms.

TermWare.NET: The toolkit based on rewriting rules system TermWare and intended for transformation of programs on Microsoft.NET platform.

TuningGenie: The framework automating the adjustment of programs to a target computing environment.

Chapter 6

Practical Examples of Automated Development of Efficient Parallel Programs

ABSTRACT

In this chapter, some examples of application of the developed software tools for design, generation, transformation, and optimization of programs for multicore processors and graphics processing units are considered. In particular, the algebra-algorithmic-integrated toolkit for design and synthesis of programs (IDS) and the rewriting rules system TermWare.NET are applied for design and parallelization of programs for multicore central processing units. The developed algebra-dynamic models and the rewriting rules toolkit are used for parallelization and optimization of programs for NVIDIA GPUs supporting the CUDA technology. The TuningGenie framework is applied for parallel program auto-tuning: optimization of sorting, Brownian motion simulation, and meteorological forecasting programs to a target platform. The parallelization of Fortran programs using the rewriting rules technique on sample problems in the field of quantum chemistry is examined.

INTRODUCTION

In this chapter, the developed software tools described in Chapter 5 (the algebra-algorithmic integrated toolkit for design and synthesis of programs (IDS), the rewriting rules system TermWare and the auto-tuning framework

DOI: 10.4018/978-1-5225-9384-3.ch006

TuningGenie) are applied for design, generation and transformation of sample programs for multicore processors and graphics processing units. IDS toolkit (Andon, Doroshenko, Tseytlin, & Yatsenko, 2007; Doroshenko, Ivanenko, Ovdii, & Yatsenko, 2016; Doroshenko, Zhereb, & Yatsenko, 2013) uses algebraic specifications based on Glushkov's system of algorithmic algebra (SAA) (see Chapter 1), which are represented in a natural linguistic form, namely, the algorithmic language SAA/1 considered in Chapter 2. IDS is based on the method of dialogue design of syntactically correct algorithm schemes, which eliminates syntax errors during construction of algorithm specifications . To automate parallelizing and optimizing transformations of programs being designed, the rewriting rules system TermWare (Doroshenko & Shevchenko, 2006) is used. TuningGenie framework (Ivanenko, Doroshenko, Zhereb, 2014) is applied to automate the adjustment of programs to a target computing environment. The application of the mentioned software tools is illustrated by the development of programs in various subject domains (sorting, meteorological forecasting, quantum chemistry and other) written in C#, Java and Fortran languages.

It should be noted that despite being one of the first programming languages, Fortran is still widely used, in particular, for solving scientific and engineering computation-intensive problems. Its popularity is due to its relative simplicity and lack of complex facilities (e.g., pointers), closeness to mathematical description of a problem and efficiency of generated binary code. Another reason for continued use of Fortran is that in more than 50 years of its existence, a vast repository of programs, libraries and routines for solving different scientific problems has been developed. Algorithms implemented in such programs are still valuable, however, there is a need to adapt this legacy code to new parallel computing platforms. Furthermore, due to a size and a complexity of existing code, manual adaptation is not a practical option: there is a need for automated tools to facilitate conversion of legacy code to modern parallel platforms (Buttari et al., 2007).

There has been an extensive research in the area of parallelizing existing sequential code, in particular, for multicore architectures. Some approaches require manual code modification and provide facilities that help a developer to express the parallelism. Such approaches include parallel libraries (Leijen, Schulte, & Burckhardt, 2009), parallel extensions to existing languages ("OpenMP Application Programming Interface", 2015) and new parallel languages (Saraswat, Sarkar, & von Praun, 2007). Another research direction is interactive parallelization (Ishihara, Honda, & Sato, 2006), when a developer manually selects the loops to be parallelized, and the tool applies transformation automatically (the approach presented in this chapter also belongs to this category). Finally, there are numerous approaches to automated parallelization, mostly implemented as parallelizing compilers (Allen & Kennedy, 2001). Such systems use static analysis of a source code to detect possible areas of parallelism and generate parallel binary code. Some papers also use dynamic analysis to detect parallelism based on specific input data (Rus, Pennings, & Rauchwerger, 2007), or machine learning approaches to select most appropriate transformations (Tournavitis, Wang, Franke, & O'Boyle, 2009), or auto-tuning to discover optimal parameters of transformations (Datta et al., 2008).

The key difference of the approach presented in this chapter is the use of source-to-source transformations, allowing the developers to examine transformed program code, and the description of the transformations in terms of formal models and rewriting rules, making easier for developers to add new parallelizing transformations or to modify existing ones. The formal models are represented in Glushkov's algebra and are created in two steps. First, the target language parser for programming language is used to build low-level syntax model, and then rewriting rules of a special form (patterns) are applied to extract language-independent algebraic operators from language constructs. Using high-level algebraic models allows describing program transformations in a more concise manner. The additional benefit of such models when applied to a legacy code is that they aid in understanding of algorithms by hiding the (frequently obsolete) implementation details. To this end, using multiple levels of algebraic models can be useful, e.g., the highest level describes just general structure of an algorithm, while lower levels supply implementation details. After a high-level program model is created, parallelizing transformations are used to implement a parallel version of a program on a given platform. The declarative nature of rewriting rules technique simplifies adding new transformations. Also transformations work with high-level model elements (on any level of abstraction), which means they are language-independent. To automate program transformations, the rewriting rules system TermWare is used. In addition to the rewriting system, the developed tools include parsers and generators for target languages (C#, Java, Fortran) that perform transformation between source code and low-level (syntax) program model represented as TermWare term.

Design and Parallelization of Programs for Multicore Processors

In this subsection, the use of IDS and TermWare.NET systems is illustrated on design, parallelization and optimization of an algorithm finding the quantity of prime numbers in the range from 1 to some number. The algorithm checks each odd number from the range, whether is it divided by smaller odd factors. The given algorithm belongs to a class of algorithms, in which some independent computations are performed and then the result is saved to a shared memory. Such algorithms are quite easy for parallelization, however, there are some features influencing the performance of a parallel program.

IDS toolkit was applied for designing the SAA scheme of the sequential algorithm finding prime numbers. The fragment of the constructed scheme, namely, the compound operator FindPrimes, is given below.

```
"FindPrimes"
==== Locals
    (
        "Declare a variable (number) of type (long)";
        "Declare a variable (start) of type (long)";
        "Declare a variable (end) of type (long)";
        "Declare a variable (stride) of type (long)";
        "Declare a variable (factor) of type (long)"
    )
    "start:= 1";
    "end:= Number";
    "stride:= 2";
    IF 'start = 1'
    THEN "start:= start + stride"
    END IF;
    "number:= start";
    WHILE NOT 'number >= end'
    LOOP
        "factor:= 3";
        WHILE NOT 'Remainder from division of (number) by
(factor) = (0)'
        LOOP
            "factor:= factor + 2"
        END OF LOOP;
        IF 'factor = number'
        THEN "Primes[PrimeCount]:= number";
            "PrimeCount:= PrimeCount + 1"
        END IF;
        "number:= number + stride"
```

```
END OF LOOP
```

Based on the given scheme, IDS toolkit generated the following fragment of the sequential program in C# language (the method FindPrimes):

```
protected override void FindPrimes()
{
    long number;
    long start;
    long end;
    long stride;
    long factor;
    start = 1;
    end = Number;
    stride = 2;

    if (start == 1)
    {
        start = start + stride;
    };
    number = start;
    while (!(number >= end))
    {
        factor = 3;
        while (!((number % factor) == 0))
        {
            factor = factor + 2;
        };
        if (factor == number)
        {
            Primes[PrimeCount] = number;
            PrimeCount = PrimeCount + 1;
        };
        number = number + stride;
    }
}
```

The sequential program is parallelized by splitting the main loop into NUM_THREADS loops, the number of which corresponds to a number of threads. In the elementary case, each thread processes consecutive numbers. The transformation of the sequential program consists of the following steps:

- replacement of call of the FindPrimes function by operators of creation of NUM_THREADS threads;

- modification of loop parameters;
- addition of synchronization means (a critical section).

All these steps are implemented using TermWare rules. With the help of Termware.NET system, the source code of the program is transformed to a low-level model with the use of the parser for C# language, and then the low-level model is transformed to a high-level model with the use of patterns (see Chapter 5, Subsection "The Rewriting Rules System TermWare"). As a result, the following term is obtained:

```
Method(FindPrimes, void, NIL, [protected, override],
  [Declaration(number, long),
   Declaration(start, long),
   Declaration(end, long),
   Declaration(stride, long),
   Declaration(factor, long),
   Assignment(start, 1),
   Assignment(end, Number),
   Assignment(stride, 2),
   If(Equals(start, 1), Assignment(start, start+stride)),
     While(Not(number >= end),[
     Assignment(factor, 3),
     While(Not(Equals(number % factor, 0)),
             [Assignment(factor, factor+2)]),
     If(Equals(factor, number),
       [Assignment(ArrayElement(Primes, PrimeCount), number),
        Assignment(PrimeCount, PrimeCount + 1)]),
        Assignment(number, number+stride)])])
```

The given term is transformed by applying the following system of rules:

- cons(Method(FindPrimes, void, NIL, $x1, $x2), $x0) ->
- cons(Method(FindPrimes, void, NIL, $x1,
- _Parallel_For_Call (RunThreadNum, [_Index], Threads), _MARK_1), cons(Method(RunThreadNum, void, [Parameter(ThreadNum, int)], [protected, virtual], $x2), $x0));
- Assignment(start, 1) -> Assignment(start, ThreadNum * BLOCKSIZE + 1);
- Assignment(end, Number) -> Assignment(end, ThreadNum * BLOCKSIZE + BLOCKSIZE);
- If(Equals(factor, number), $x0) -> If(Equals(factor, number), Lock(This, $x0)).

185

This system operates as follows. Rule 1 replaces the method FindPrimes with a call of the new method RunThreadNum with a defined number of threads ThreadNum. Thus, the code of method RunThreadNum after application of rule 1 appears the same as the initial code of method FindPrimes. Further, rules 2–4 modify the code taking into account the introduction of multithreading. Rules 2 and 3 change the limits of the loop, which depend now on the index of a thread. Rule 4 adds locking (a critical section) for protection of access to a shared memory (namely, the variable PrimeCount and the array Primes).

The given system of rules is applied to the term of the sequential program, and as a result, the term of the parallel multithreaded program named BlockTasksThread is obtained. The new method RunThreadNum is added, limits of loops are modified and a critical section is added. The term corresponding to the new method RunThreadNum is the following:

```
Method(RunThreadNum, void, [Parameter(ThreadNum, int)],
          [protected, virtual],
  [Declaration(number, long),
  Declaration(start, long),
  Declaration(end, long),
  Declaration(stride, long),
  Declaration(factor, long),
  Assignment(start, ThreadNum * BLOCKSIZE + 1),
  Assignment(end, ThreadNum * BLOCKSIZE + BLOCKSIZE),
  Assignment(stride, 2),
  If(Equals(start, 1), Assignment(start, start+stride)),
    While(Not(number >= end), [
    Assignment(factor, 3),
    While(Not(Equals(number % factor, 0)),
            [Assignment(factor, factor + 2)]),
    If(Equals(factor, number), Lock(This,
      [Assignment(ArrayElement(Primes, PrimeCount), number),
      Assignment(PrimeCount, PrimeCount + 1)])),
      Assignment(number, number + stride)])])
```

Based on the obtained term, the source code of the following parallel program was generated (the changes in comparison with the sequential version are highlighted in bold font):

```
protected virtual void RunThreadNum(int ThreadNum)
{
    long number;
    long start;
    long end;
    long stride;
```

```
    long factor;
    start = ThreadNum * BLOCKSIZE + 1;
    end = ThreadNum * BLOCKSIZE + BLOCKSIZE;
    stride = 2;
    if (start == 1) {start = start + stride;};
    number = start;
    while (!(number >= end))
    {
        factor = 3;
        while (!((number % factor) == 0))
        { factor = factor + 2; };
        if (factor == number)
        {
            lock (this)
            {
                Primes[PrimeCount] = number;
                PrimeCount = PrimeCount + 1;
            }
        };
        number = number + stride;
    }
}

protected override void FindPrimes()
{
    Thread[] threads = new Thread[Threads];
    for (int i = 0; i < Threads; i++)
    {
        Thread t = new Thread(new
                    ParameterizedThreadStart(RunThreadNum));
        threads[i] = t;
        t.Start(i);
    }
    for (int i = 0; i < threads.Length; i++)
    {
        threads[i].Join();
    }
}
```

The obtained program BlockTasksThread allows to use a hardware of a multicore system, but not in full, as the complexity of one iteration of the loop increases depending on iteration number, and therefore different threads carry out the various amount of work. To increase the performance, it is possible to modify the loop variables, so that consecutive numbers are processed by different threads (thus, the amount of work of each thread will be approximately identical). This transformation is implemented in the form of the following TermWare rules:

- Assignment(start, plus(multiply(ThreadNum, BLOCKSIZE), 1)) ->
- Assignment(start, 2 * ThreadNum + 1);
- Assignment(end, plus(multiply(ThreadNum, BLOCKSIZE), BLOCKSIZE)) ->
- Assignment(end, Number);
- Assignment(stride, 2) -> Assignment(stride, 2 * Threads).

The result of application of these rules to the BlockTasksThread program is a more efficient InterleavedTasksThread program. The obtained program can be improved due to use of other means of synchronization, in particular, atomic functions of Interlocked type, which perform an atomic change of an argument (Guptha, 2008). In this connection, the new patterns for separate operations are used, for example:

$$\_AtomicIncrement(x) = lock(cs); Increment(x); unlock(cs).$$

This pattern can be implemented by means of combination of standard means (i.e. as a fragment of the code $lock(cs)\{x++;\}$), and in the form of one call of Interlocked function (that corresponds to the fragment *Interlocked. Increment(x)*). As a result of the transition from initial critical sections to atomic functions, more efficient program InterlockedThread was obtained, though performance change in comparison with the previous program InterleavedTasksThread appears insignificant.

Figure 1 shows the results of performance comparison of the obtained programs executed on Intel Core2 Duo E6550 CPU processor (2 cores, 2.33 GHz), 4 GB of memory. The graph shows that the elementary parallelization scheme in the initial parallel program BlockTasksThread allows using hardware resources of the processor, but not completely. The use of more correct parallelization scheme in the InterleavedTasksThread program allows to speed up the performance practically twice in comparison with the sequential case, i.e. to completely use the hardware resources. It should be noticed also that at the use of larger numbers of threads, the performance of BlockTasksThread increases, verging towards more efficient InterleavedTasksThread and InterlockedThread programs. Thus, for problems of smaller size, the correct distribution of computation between threads becomes not so essential.

Figure 1. The dependency of execution time on the quantity of numbers (2 threads)

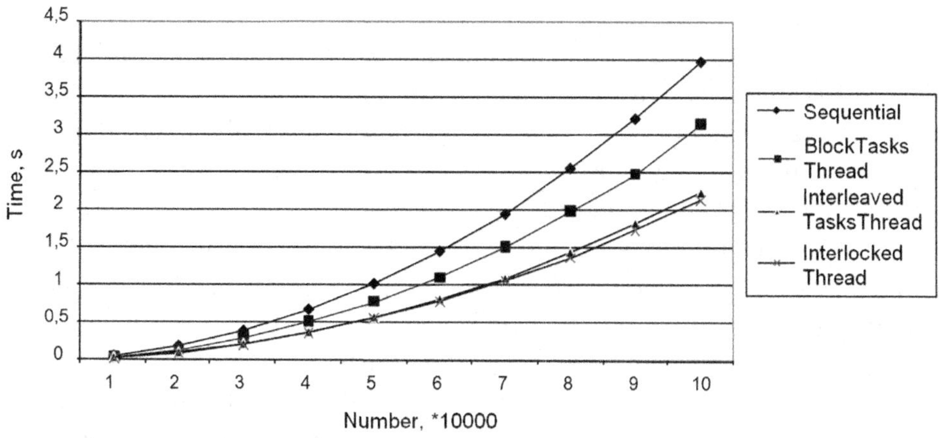

Development of Programs for Graphics Processing Units

This subsection gives the examples of use of the developed algebra-dynamic models (Chapter 4) and the rewriting rules toolkit Termware.NET for parallelization and optimization of programs for NVIDIA graphics processing units supporting the CUDA technology. The mentioned examples include the parallel matrix multiplication and the game of Life. The input data for each example is a source code of a sequential program in C# language. In the beginning, the source code is used to construct a low-level model of a program by using the parser of the Termware.NET system. Then, a high-level model is constructed with the use of patterns. For the transition from a sequential to a parallel multithreaded program, the parallelizing transformations are applied to a program model. Then, optimizing transformations are applied to a parallel program in order to increase its efficiency. For each of the obtained versions of the program, the source code is generated, which is compiled and executed at various sizes of initial data. The execution times of a sequential program T_1 and a parallel program T_n (where n is a number of GPU cores) are measured, and also the multiprocessor speedup $Sp=T_1/T_n$ is computed. All the programs being considered in this subsection were executed on the computer with the following parameters: Intel Core2 Duo E6550 CPU (2 kernels, 2.33 GHz), 4 GB of memory, NVIDIA GeForce GTS 250 GPU (128 cores, 1 GB of graphics memory).

Parallel Matrix Multiplication

Consider the parallelization and optimization of block matrix multiplication program. For transition from a sequential to a parallel multithreaded program, the parallelizing transformation $Seq2 \rightarrow Gpu3$ described in subsection "Program Transformations Based on Rewriting Rules" of Chapter 4 was applied to a program model. Then, the optimizing transformation $Gpu1 \rightarrow Gpu1.2$ (for the two-dimensional case) considered in the same subsection was applied to a parallel program in order to increase its efficiency. For each of the obtained versions of the program, source code in C# and C languages was generated. The difference between obtained programs consisted only in CPU part of the program: GPU program in both cases was the same and implemented in C for CUDA. The programs were executed on the computer with the following parameters: Intel Core2 Duo E6550 CPU (2 kernels, 2.33 GHz), 4 GB of memory, NVIDIA GeForce GTS 250 GPU (128 cores, 1 GB of graphics memory). The results of execution of various program versions are given in Figure 2. The multiprocessor speedup is computed according to the formula: $Sp=T_1/T_n$, where T_1 and T_n are execution times of a sequential program and a parallel program, respectively; n is the number of GPU cores.

Figure 2. The results of performance measurements of various versions of the matrix multiplication program

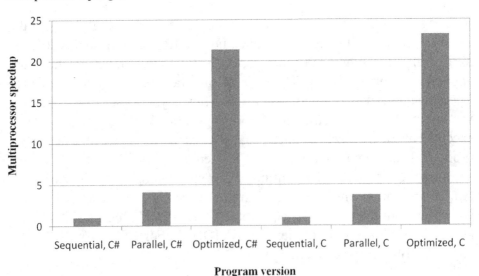

As shown in the figure, the non-optimized version of the program gives four times speedup. The optimized version reduces the execution time by more than 20 times. It should be noted that the main execution time of the GPU program is spent not on actual computation, but on copying input data and results. If the data are present in GPU memory, and a result has to be put also to GPU, the optimized version gives 124 times speedup, which is close to the number of cores (128) of the GPU used.

The Game of Life Problem

As another example of use of Termware.NET, consider the C# implementation of the game of Life ("Conway's game of life", n.d.; Doroshenko, Zhereb, & Yatsenko, 2010). First, the parallelizing transformations described in the subsection "The Transition from a Sequential Program to GPU Program" of Chapter 4 are applied to the initial sequential program . Then, the parallel program is optimized by usage of transformations considered in the subsection "GPU Program Optimization" of Chapter 4. The parallelization was applied for nested loops that compute new state of the game field. After the transformation, each game cell was computed on a separate GPU thread. The optimizing transformation consisted in using a shared memory instead of a global memory. To improve the efficiency of a shared memory use, another transformation was applied, which increased the number of cells computed by each thread. In the transformed version, each thread computed the line of 16 cells. Kernel call parameters were also modified: from 16×16 block size (corresponding to 16×16 field fragment) to 256×16 block size (256×16 field fragment). Block size was selected automatically using the knowledge of limit of 16 KB of a shared memory.

The program was transformed using the developed rewriting rules and Termware.NET system. The source code of the initial program was automatically transformed to the low-level model using the parser of the system and then into the high-level model using patterns. After that, the loop to be parallelized and the transformation (i.e. the set of rules) to be applied were selected. The transformation was executed automatically and resulted in a high-level model of the parallel GPU program which was transformed back to the low-level model and then to a source code. The optimizing transformations were applied in the same way. Thus, the transformation process is automated and user input is required only to select the developed rules which have to be applied and the part of code they should affect. To estimate the effect of transformations, the execution time for three program versions was measured: initial sequential program, program parallelized without optimization, parallelized and optimized program. The execution time of each program was measured for 1000 iterations on the 512×512 field. The obtained multiprocessor speedup is shown in Figure 3.

Figure 3. The multiprocessor speedup for the game of Life programs.

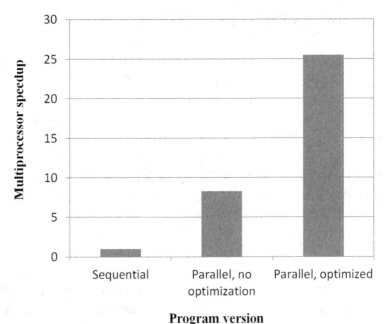

As shown in the figure, even non-optimized parallel program is 8 times faster than the initial sequential program and the optimized parallel program is 25.5 times faster.

AUTO-TUNING OF PROGRAMS

In this section, the results of optimization of some computational problems (sorting, Brownian motion simulation, meteorological forecasting) with the use of TuningGenie framework described in Chapter 5 are considered.

Optimization of QuickSort program

As a first example, consider a classic problem of number sorting. The subject of the optimization is the well-known QuickSort algorithm (Hoare, 1961). It can be considerably improved by using more efficient (in terms of memory use) internal sorting algorithm for sorting subarrays of small size. For example, the InsertionSort (Knuth, 1998), though has greater asymptotic complexity $O(n^2)$, does not need an additional memory and thus works better on small sizes of arrays when data is completely placed in a fast processor cache memory. Since the change of sorting algorithm does not influence the result of computations, the optimization of the task is carried out according to only one feature — time expenses. This idea is entirely similar to the one proposed in (McIlroy, 1993), though MergeSort algorithm was modified there.

The fragment of the modified (hybrid) version of Java source code of the QuickSort algorithm is the following:

```
public static void enhancedQuick(int[] a, int lowerBound, int
upperBound) {
   Stack<Integer> stack = new Stack<>();

   //tuneAbleParam name=threshold start=20 stop=1200 step=20
   int threshold = 1;

   addPartitionOrSort(a, lowerBound, upperBound, stack,
threshold);
   ...

private static void addPartitionOrSort(int[] array, int
lowerBound,
                  int upperBound, Stack<Integer> toSort, int
threshold) {
   if (upperBound - lowerBound >= threshold) {
      //sort parts with QuickSort
      toSort.push(lowerBound);
      toSort.push(upperBound);
   } else {
        insertionSort(array, lowerBound, upperBound);
   }
}
```

The *threshold* variable is used for switching between InsertionSort and common iterations of QuickSort; the auto-tuner is responsible for the selection of the best value of this variable. The optimal threshold value of subarray size for switching the algorithm is different for various computing environments, as it depends on the size of a processor cache.

For example, for the computer with dual-core processor Intel Core i5-2410M (3 MB L3 cache, 2.90 GHz), 4 GB DDR2 RAM (800 MHz), the auto-tuner found that at sorting integer numbers, the program should switch to InsertionSort on subarrays of the size less than 90 elements. It reduces the sorting time by 30% on average. The dependency of execution time (at sorting the array of size $2 \cdot 10^6$ elements) on the value of *threshold* is shown in Figure 4.

A similar experiment was conducted in another computing environment with quad-core Intel Core i7-6820HQ processor (8 MB L3 cache, 2.7 GHz), 16 GB LPDDR3 SDRAM (2133 MHz). The results are shown in Figure 5. This time, the program execution was much faster — depending on the value of *threshold,* sorting lasted 200–400 ms.

Figure 4. The dependency of time spent on sorting the array of $2 \cdot 10^6$ elements on the value of the threshold

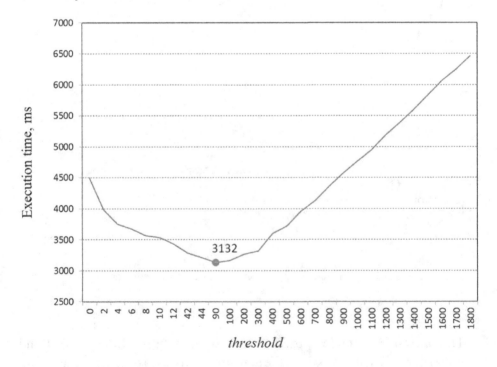

Figure 5. The dependency of time spent on sorting the array of $2 \cdot 10^6$ elements on the value of the threshold in the second computing environment

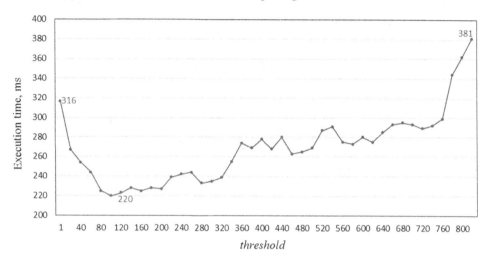

To obtain more stable measurements, the array size was increased by 10 times — to $2 \cdot 10^7$ elements. The results are shown in Figure 6.

Figure 6. The dependency of time spent on sorting the array of $2 \cdot 10^7$ elements on the value of the threshold in the second computing environment

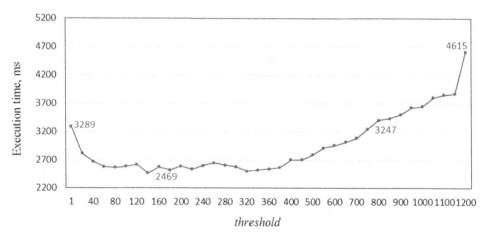

As can be seen, the effect of *threshold* value is very similar for both environments and does not depend on the size of input data — the non-optimized version of the program (*threshold*=1) is 25–30% slower. The best time is obtained at values of *threshold* close to 100 (see Table 1). At *threshold*≥800, the hybrid version is slower than the initial. Thus, the sequential program is significantly accelerated by the optimal use of CPU cache.

Table 1. The comparison of execution of common QuickSort version and its hybrid modification

Computing environment	Input array size	The execution time of common QuickSort version, ms	The best execution time of the hybrid modification, ms	Percentage difference	The optimal value of *threshold*
1	$2 \cdot 10^6$	4503	3132	30.4	90
2	$2 \cdot 10^6$	316	220	30.3	100
2	$2 \cdot 10^7$	3289	2469	24.9	140

ParallelMergeSort Optimization

In this subsection, more complex problem is considered — the optimization of parallel MergeSort algorithm. The aim of the experiment was the demonstration of parallel program optimization with several dependent parameters, not writing the quickest implementation of MergeSort. As in the previous case, the technique of switching to InsertionSort for small size arrays is applied. For performing parallel computing, the ForkJoinPool ("Class ForkJoinPool", n.d.) is used. Its main difference from the classic service of task execution ExecutorService ("Interface ExecutorService", n.d.) is the work-stealing mechanism which allows executing tasks in threads which are waiting for results of other computations. Thus, simple recursive implementation of MergeSort uses much smaller number of threads.

Besides the parameter *insertionSortThreshold* considered in the previous experiment, two new parameters are used — the number of threads in the ForkJoinPool (*parallelism*) and the minimum array size (*mergeSortBucketSize*), for which new independent computing task is spawned. The subarrays of *size<=mergeSortBucketSize* are sorted by sequential MergeSort with switching to InsertionSort at *size<=insertionSortThreshold*. The parameter *mergeSortBucketSize* was added to avoid spawning new recursive tasks for very small subarrays, because in such case the overhead may reduce the gains from parallel execution. The implementation of the sorting task executed by ForkJoinPool is the following:

```
class MergeSortTask extends RecursiveAction {

    private final int[] array;

    MergeSortTask(int arrayToSort[]) {
        this.array = arrayToSort;
    }

    @Override
    protected void compute() {
        //tuneAbleParam name=insertionSortThreshold start=10
stop=200 step=10
        int insertionSortThreshold = 100;

        //tuneAbleParam name=mergeSortBucketSize start=5000
stop=1000000
        //step=5000
        int mergeSortBucketSize = 5000;

        if (array.length <= insertionSortThreshold) {
            insertionSort(array, 0, array.length);
        } else if (array.length <= mergeSortBucketSize) {
                sequentialMergeSort(array,
insertionSortThreshold);
                }
                else {
                final int[] left = Arrays.copyOfRange(array, 0,
array.length/2);
                final int[] right = Arrays.copyOfRange(array,
array.length/2,
                                                            array.
length);
                invokeAll(new MergeSortTask(left), new
MergeSortTask(right));
                merge(left, right, array);
            }
    }
}
The ForkJoinPool is initialized in the following way:
public static void parallelMergeSort(int[] array) {
    //tuneAbleParam name=parallelism start=8 stop=16 step=2
    int parallelism = 8;

    ForkJoinPool pool = PoolCache.get(parallelism);
    ForkJoinTask<Void> job = pool.submit(new
MergeSortTask(array));
    job.join();
}
```

The experiment was performed in the following environment: 2.7 GHz Intel Core i7 processor (6820HQ) with 4 cores and 8 MB L3 cache; 16 GB 2133 MHz RAM; 512 GB Apple SSD SM0512L; MacOS 10.12.

The obtained results are given in Table 2. The following three configurations were used:

- *slow*: the default configuration that behaves almost as classical sequential merge sort;
- *optimal*: the quickest one that was automatically selected by the auto-tuner;
- *intuitive*: the values are selected intuitively with respect to known hardware specifications and algorithms details.

Table 2. The results of the ParallelMergeSort optimization experiment

Parameter	Configuration		
	slow	*optimal*	*intuitive*
parallelism	1 (one thread)	8	4
insertionSortThreshold	0 (do not switch to insertion sort at all)	120	30 (common notion is to set couple dozen as a threshold for this trick)
mergeSortBucketSize	100 000 000 (it's bigger than the test data size, so no data decomposition is applied)	50 000	10 000
Test data size	20 000 000 integers		
Average sorting time	4432 ms	898 ms	1426 ms

The *optimal* configuration is 4.93 times quicker than the *slow*. This result is quite good for a quad-core processor and was achieved primarily by a combination of two factors: optimal use of processor caches (by switching to in-place sorting for small data sets) and efficient parallelization schema (merge sort is easy to parallelize with "divide and conquer" method). The *intuitive* configuration was 3.1 times faster than the *slow*, which is also a decent result, but it was easy to guess due to the relative simplicity of the test algorithm. Usually optimal configurations are not so obvious for real-life parallel programs. The *optimal* configuration is still substantially quicker — by 58%, so it was worth to spend the time on tuning.

It should be noticed that the parameter *mergeSortBucketSize* has little effect on the speed, owing to the high efficiency of ForkJoinPool implementation. At values *mergeSortBucketSize*>100, the impact of the additional cost on spawning new recursive tasks does not sufficiently change the overall execution time of the original task. As in the previous experiment, the switch to InsertionSort on small subtasks sufficiently reduced the overall sorting time.

Auto-tuning of the parallel MergeSort algorithm using statistical modeling and machine learning is considered in (Doroshenko, Ivanenko, Novak, & Yatsenko, 2018).

Brownian Motion Simulation

Consider the results of application of TuningGenie for optimization of a parallel implementation of the problem of a simplified model of Brownian motion. The problem is formulated as follows: it is necessary to simulate a behavior of a set of particles in one-dimensional crystal of certain length (Doroshenko et al., 2013). On each step of the simulation, each particle moves to the right or to the left with a specified probability. The behavior of each particle is simulated by a separate thread. This task is a good example of using the method of asynchronous loop computations (see Chapter 2, subsection "Parallel Computation Model for Auto-Tuning", Example 8) with an interesting feature — a partial waiver of synchronization has no effect on the accuracy of results.

Let it is necessary to find out the position of a particle after a certain time interval Δt. The interval is split into n equal segments and at one time segment, the particle makes one "step", i.e. moves by one cell of the crystal. Thus, the problem is reduced to simulation of particle positions after n "steps".

The computing scheme for this problem is parallelized easily and has the property of an asynchronous loop. The degree of freedom m of asynchronous loop is determined by the need to obtain intermediate computation results. If they are not necessary (for example, a visualization is not needed), then $n=m$.

The only criterion for evaluating the quality of the performed optimization is a time spent on simulation. In fact, the influence of the value of the parameter m on the overall speed is obvious — the increase of the number of independent iterations decreases the synchronization overhead, and therefore the execution time. The configuration of the test environment and the experiment was the following: two quad-core Intel Xeon E5405 processors (2 GHz; 8 cores in total); 16 GB DDR3 RAM (1066 MHz); $n=3000000$. Figure 7 shows the dependency of the multiprocessor speedup $Sp=T_1/T_p$ (where T_1 is the execution time of the sequential program, T_p is the execution time of the parallel program on $p=8$ processor cores) on the value of the parameter m.

Figure 7. The dependency of the multiprocessor speed up on the value of the parameter m

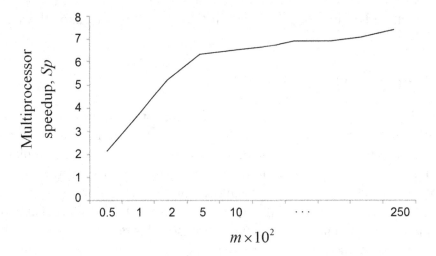

At a large value of m, the multiprocessor speedup reached the value $Sp=7.5$, which, according to the Amdahl's law, is close to the theoretical limit (i.e. 8) for the test environment.

Meteorological Forecasting Problem

This subsection presents the case study on the performance tuning of an application for short-term atmospheric circulation modeling (from hours to several days). A complete definition of the model and the method for a numerical solution can be found in (Prusov, Doroshenko, Chernysh, & Guk, 2008). The simplified problem definition is described below to give a general idea.

The model being considered describes macro-scale processes. Their usual horizontal extent is of the order of thousands of kilometers. Typical examples of such processes are equatorial and monsoonal currents, long Rossby waves (Belov, Borisenkov, & Panin, 1989), cyclones and anticyclones, ridges etc. The model is based on a spherical coordinate system. The two-dimensional simplified case which models wind characteristics (direction and force) is considered. The model consists of the following two evolution equations to calculate horizontal components of a wind velocity:

$$\frac{\partial u_1}{\partial t} + \frac{u_2}{a}\frac{\partial u_1}{\partial \varphi} + \frac{u_1}{a\cos\varphi}\frac{\partial u_1}{\partial \lambda} = -\frac{g}{a\cos\varphi}\frac{\partial h}{\partial \lambda}$$

$$+\frac{\partial}{\partial \lambda}\left(\frac{\mu_h}{\rho(a\cos\varphi)^2}\frac{\partial u_1}{\partial \lambda}\right) + \frac{\partial}{\partial \varphi}\left(\frac{\mu_h}{\rho a^2}\frac{\partial u_1}{\partial \varphi}\right) + u_2\left(\frac{u_1\ tg\ \varphi}{a} + 2\omega\sin\varphi\right),$$

(1)

$$\frac{\partial u_2}{\partial t} + \frac{u_2}{a}\frac{\partial u_2}{\partial \varphi} + \frac{u_1}{a\cos\varphi}\frac{\partial u_2}{\partial \lambda} = -\frac{g}{a}\frac{\partial h}{\partial \varphi}$$

$$+\frac{\partial}{\partial \lambda}\left(\frac{\mu_h}{\rho(a\cos\varphi)^2}\frac{\partial u_2}{\partial \lambda}\right) + \frac{\partial}{\partial \varphi}\left(\frac{\mu_h}{\rho a^2}\frac{\partial u_2}{\partial \varphi}\right) - u_1\left(\frac{u_1\ tg\ \varphi}{a} + 2\omega\sin\ \varphi\right),$$

(2)

where λ and φ are longitude and latitude, respectively; u_1, u_2 are components of the wind velocity vector $u=(u_1,u_2)$, u_1 is oriented along λ and u_2 is directed along φ; t is time; $a=6.373\times10^6$m is the Earth's radius; ρ is air density; $g=9.81$m/s^2 is gravitational acceleration; μ_h is horizontal turbulent diffusion coefficient; $\omega=7.292\times^{-5}$ is the angular speed of Earth's rotation.

The general scheme of computation is iterative. The model takes the state of the atmosphere $State(t_0)$ at some moment t_0 as an input. Suppose it is needed to get a prediction of the state at some moment $State(t_n)$ in the future, $t_n>t_0$. To compute this, the program performs a series of smaller predictions with time step $\Delta t \ll t_n - t_0$. Thus, there is a recurrence relation between iterations:

$$State(t_n) = Prediction(State(t_{n-1})),\ t_n = t_{n-1} + \Delta t.$$

The iteration step Δt should be chosen from the interval [5, 20] minutes to provide the acceptable accuracy of the result.

The use of the modified additive-averaged splitting scheme (Prusov, Doroshenko, & Chernysh, 2009) gives the property of the asynchronous loop (see Chapter 2, subsection "Parallel Computation Model for Auto-Tuning", Example 8) to the computations, provided that the number of "free" iterations is less than 10. Under this restriction, the convergence of the numerical method is preserved and the error remains within acceptable limits. In addition, the method allows to apply the geometrical decomposition of the computational domain (i.e., it is possible to adjust the number of subtasks to the number of processors) and independently compute each physical value.

Figure 8. Parallelization scheme for solving one evolution equation in the meteorological forecasting problem

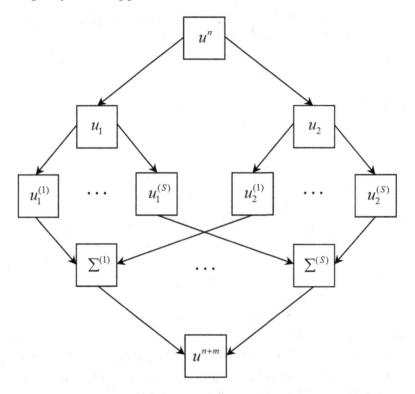

The method for the numerical solution of the described model allows to parallelize computation on three levels:

- evolution equation level. Each equation can be solved independently in the scope of one iteration;
- space directions λ and φ;
- subdomains for each space direction. The computation domain is decomposed along λ for subtasks at direction φ, and along φ for subtasks at direction λ. The number of subdomains is denoted as S.

Figure 8 shows the parallelization scheme for solving one evolution equation solution, which corresponds to computation of meteorological value u (horizontal wind velocity) during one iteration of asynchronous loop with sequence number n and degree of freedom m. Computation of u is split to calculation of u_1 and u_2.

According to the given scheme, the algorithm for computing one evolution equation consists of the following steps.

- The input is the state of the atmosphere $State(t_n)$ at moment t_n and it is necessary to compute the prediction u^{n+m} for the meteorological characteristic u. The value of this characteristic at moment t_n is defined by $State(t_n)$ and is denoted as u^n.
- By utilizing the modified additive-averaged operator splitting algorithm, prediction u^{n+m} is computed without exchanging intermediate results. Thus, these m steps are isolated from other subtasks. Such approach spares time on synchronization, but introduces additional inaccuracy of results. For the moment t_{n+m}, boundary and initial conditions are defined. They are constant for steps 3, 4 and 5. Values u_1 and u_2 are computed independently.
- Geometric decomposition is applied for each of the space directions λ and φ. Input area is split into S subdomains, so there are $2S$ independent subtasks. Each subtask iteratively calculates prognosis for moments $t_n, t_{n+1}, \ldots, t_{n+m}$.
- The average is computed based on the prognoses obtained for t_{n+m} on step 3.
- The results from step 4 are aggregated and result value u^{n+m} is obtained.

It's worth mentioning that the model is highly scalable, since subtasks with equal size (after decomposition) require an equal amount of work independently of what type of physical characteristics is computed.

The software implementation of the problem being optimized was written in C++ with the use of OpenMP ("OpenMP Application Programming Interface", 2015).

The overall performance of the parallel program mostly depends on the granularity of the data decomposition, since it defines the amount of calculation per subtask and hence the size of the plain parallel section. It's reasonable to assume that "coarse-grained" decomposition will be the most efficient one. Let N be the number of available processors. The task of the auto-tuner is to find the optimal value of the number of subdomains S. The search space of the auto-tuner can be reduced to values $S \approx N$, for example, $S \in [N\ div\ 4, 4*N]$. For tuning the program, the *tunableParam* and *bidirectionalCycle* pragmas (described in detail in subsection "The Auto-Tuning Framework TuningGenie" of Chapter 5) were used.

Figure 9. The dependency of execution time T on the number of subdomains S for parallel weather forecasting program

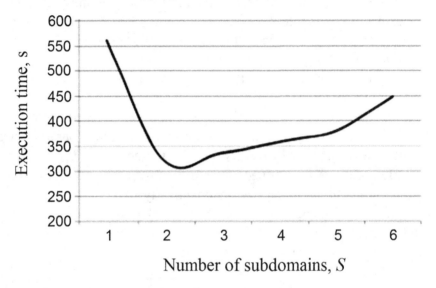

The auto-tuning experiment was performed in the environment with two quad-core Intel Xeon E5405 processors (8 cores in total; 2 GHz). The initial conditions for the model were taken from the electronic archive of regional forecasting center "Offenbach" ("Wetter und Klima – Deutscher Wetterdienst", n.d.). Size of the input grid was 600×600 points. The experiment calculated the weather forecast for 24 hours. The single run lasted 5–10 minutes and the whole optimization took about two hours. All measured times were quite stable — the deviation of execution time was 2.6% at most for the same configuration. Search for the optimal value of S was carried by TuningGenie utilizing *tunableParam* pragma. During the experiment, 14 configurations were tried: 6 for different values of S and 8 configurations were derived from *bidirectionalCycle* pragma. The optimized program showed the multiprocessor speedup $Sp(8) = T_1/T_8 = 3.82$, where T_1 is the execution time of the sequential program, T_8 is the execution time of the parallel program on 8 processors;

the efficiency was $E(8)=0.48$. Figure 9 shows the overall execution time depending on the number of subdomains S.

The experiment proved the assumption that decomposition $S=N$ is the most efficient and also revealed the other bending point of the multiprocessor speedup function $Sp(N)=T_1/T_N$. This point represented decomposition of input data into very small subdomains (about hundred elements). Such a result can be explained by the suggestion that all data entirely fit processor caches providing an additional speedup of computation. It is worth mentioning that TuningGenie simplifies the so-called program's "behavior analysis". Since it empirically evaluates all considered program variations, it is easy to discover the tuned parameter's impact on overall performance.

PARALLELIZATION OF FORTRAN PROGRAMS

In this subsection, the parallelization of Fortran programs (Doroshenko & Zhereb, 2013) using rewriting rules technique is considered. Sequential source code is transformed to parallel code for shared-memory parallel platform (such as multicore processors) using automated transformations. Parallelizing transformations are formally described as rewriting rules, which facilitates their reuse. Such an approach is aimed at two main goals: to improve runtime efficiency of programs and to increase developer's productivity. The approach is illustrated on two sample programs: a simple Gaussian elimination algorithm and an applied problem of calculating electron density from the field of quantum chemistry.

Parallelization for Shared-Memory Systems Using OpenMP

The source code of Fortran programs is parallelized by replacing suitable loops with parallel loop constructs. For developing multithreaded Fortran program, OpenMP is applied ("OpenMP Application Programming Interface", 2015). OpenMP *PARALLEL DO* directives are used to parallelize loops. For simple loops, the addition of this directive can produce quite efficient parallel code. In this case, there is an additional advantage of keeping transformed parallel code similar to existing sequential one. In more complex cases (when there is data dependency between iterations), it is necessary to apply more significant transformations, such as using OpenMP library subroutines for advanced thread management. In such cases, the transformed source code contains significant changes. However, the use of high-level algebraic models allows describing these changes in concise and understandable form.

The details of the proposed approach will be described on the example of the Fortran program implementing a Gaussian elimination algorithm for solving systems of linear algebraic equations. The Fortran source code was transformed into a low-level syntax model using the developed parser and then into a high-level algebraic model using the TermWare patterns. When working with legacy code, it is useful to apply several levels of patterns. First, general linear algebra patterns were used, such as vector and matrix operations. The obtained algebraic model was language-independent, but still quite detailed. Then, the patterns specific to the problem in question were applied. In this way, the schematic representation of the algorithm was obtained, useful for its understanding and deciding where parallelizing transformations should be applied. The high-level model of the relevant fragment of the program has the following form:

$DoCnt(K, 1, N\text{-}1,$

$FindMaxElement, CheckDetZero, SwapMaxRowColumn,$

$CalculateRow(K), UpdateElements)$

Only two of the operators present in the program will be parallelized, namely, *FindMaxElement* and *UpdateElements*. Other operators have less computational complexity, therefore their parallelization is less efficient. Out of two operators, the simplest is *UpdateElements* responsible for calculating new values for elements of a submatrix:

$UpdateElements = DoCnt(I, K + 1, N, Assign(S, A(I, K)),$

$DoCnt(J, K, N + 1, Update(A(I, J), S)))$

Here, *DoCnt* denotes the common *DO* loop with a counter. The iterations of the outer loop are independent, so this fragment is easily parallelized. The following rewriting rule is applied:

$DoCnt(\$var, \$start, \$end, \$body, \_MARK\_Parallel) \text{ -> }$

ParallelDoCnt($var, $start, $end, $body)

The loop to be transformed is marked with *_MARK_Parallel* symbol to enable the rule application. *ParallelDoCnt* operator is the high-level model element responsible for a parallel loop. In particular, for OpenMP platform, it is transformed to *OmpParallelDo* operator which describes OpenMP directive represented in Fortran as a pair of special comments: *!$OMP PARALLEL DO ... !$OMP END PARALLEL DO.*

Notice that for C language the same operator is represented as a single pragma statement: *#pragma omp parallel for.* Therefore, using multiple levels of patterns allows providing operators common for given platforms, using these general operators in most rewriting rules and then specializing them only when transforming program model back into source code.

While *UpdateElements* operator can be parallelized by simple application of OpenMP directive, the other operator *FindMaxElement* is more complex. It also has the form of a loop, but iterations of the loop update the same set of variables (value of the maximum element in a submatrix and its indices). This is the case of reduction, when some local values are calculated on each iteration and then merged into one global value. OpenMP supports such cases with REDUCTION clause, however, only a set of predefined reduction operators are supported: finding just maximum value can be accomplished using OpenMP directives, whereas finding maximum value and indices where it occurs is not directly supported. Therefore, the transformations parallelizing the loop in general reduction case need to be provided. *FindMaxElement* is represented as the following combination:

$$FindMaxElement = FindMaxElLoc1 * ... * FindMaxElLocTN * FindMaxElReduct$$

In each thread, the local version of the operator (*FindMaxElLoc1, ..., FindMaxElementLocTN*) is executed, and then the reduction operator *FindMaxElReduct* is carried out which combines local values into one global value.

Both already described parallelizing transformations are aimed at modifying the high-level structure of the algorithm. However, as was observed in (Andon, Doroshenko, & Zhereb, 2011), low-level implementation details, in particular, memory access, can have a profound impact on overall performance.

In the Gaussian elimination program, the same effect is observed. It was noticed that for certain sizes of input matrix ($N=256*M$), there was a sudden increase in execution time. The authors attribute this increase to the peculiarities of memory access: namely, caching adjacent matrix elements. For such *matrix* size, the adjacent matrix elements are put into the same cache items, which increases the number of cache misses and greatly reduces the overall performance. To overcome this peculiarity, the matrix size is declared as *N*+1 instead of *N*. The extra elements are not used in calculations, but they change the location of elements and improve the efficiency of memory access. The transformation is implemented using the following rules:

- *[Declaration(N, Integer, $val): $next] ->*
- *[Declaration(N, Integer, $val): [Declaration(MN, Integer, $val + MShift($val)): $next]]*
- *MShift($val) [$val % 32 == 0] -> 1 !-> 0*
- *Declaration(A, Array(Double, [N, N + 1])) ->*
- *Declaration(A, Array(Double, [MN, MN + 1]))*
- *Procedure($name, [N: [A: $next]]) ->*
- *Procedure($name, [N: [MN: [A: $next]]]) [Parameter(N, Integer, In): $next] ->*
- *[Parameter(N, Integer, In): [Parameter(MN, Integer, In): $next]]*
- *Call($name, [N: [A: $next]]) ->Call($name, [N: [MN: [A: $next]]])*

Rule 1 adds the new parameter *MN* denoting the declared matrix size. Rule 2 specifies the values of matrix size for which the transformation should be applied. Rule 3 modifies the matrix declaration to use new size *MN* instead of *N*. Rules 4–6 propagate new parameter to all procedures, procedure parameters and procedure calls.

Notice that rules 4–6 are applied multiple times in a single program: for each procedure definition (rules 4–5) and for each procedure call (rule 6). One of the advantages of the rewriting rules technique is that a single rule can describe changes in multiple places, reducing effort to make the changes and preventing mistakes possible when applying such changes manually. Notice also that rules 1–6 work on the lower level of abstraction compared with previously described rules. The ability to describe transformations on different model levels is another advantage of the proposed approach and it allows describing different types of transformations with the same tools.

Performance Evaluation: Test Program and the Real-World Example

To evaluate the effects of the developed transformations, the performance of different versions of the initial program of Gaussian elimination was measured. The performance of four versions was compared:

- initial sequential program (SEQ);
- parallel program with *UpdateElements* operator parallelized (PAR1);
- parallel program with both *UpdateElements* and *FindMaxElement* operators parallelized (PAR2);
- program with both operators parallelized and memory optimization applied (MEM).

The measurements were performed on the quad-core parallel system, for matrix sizes from 256 to 2048. The obtained speedup (compared with SEQ program) is shown in Figure 10.

Figure 10. The multiprocessor speedup of the transformed programs (Gaussian elimination)

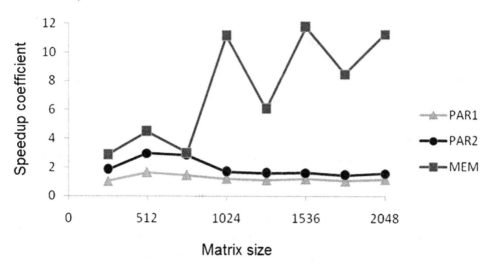

As can be seen from the diagram, all the transformations result in some performance increase, although their effect differs. For small matrix sizes, both PAR1 and PAR2 show some noticeable speedup, while MEM is not very efficient and is very close to PAR2. However, for larger matrix sizes ($N>1024$), the situation changes. PAR1 and PAR2 become less efficient and close to SEQ. However, MEM becomes much more efficient and demonstrates more than 10 times speedup. Therefore, both high-level transformations of algorithms and taking care of low-level implementation details are necessary to obtain efficient parallel programs. The measurement results also demonstrate complex dependency of execution time on real parallel systems as compared to ideal theoretical models that suggest simple $O(N^3)$ dependency.

After the development of the transformation tools for Gaussian elimination problem, they were tested on a real-world program in the quantum chemistry field. The program calculates electron and spin density in atoms of polycyclic aromatic hydrocarbons on $N{\times}N$ grid (V. D. Khavryutchenko, Tarasenko, Strelko, O. V. Khavryuchenko, & Lisnyak, 2007). The size of the program is 1680 lines of Fortran code. The source code is not well structured — actual calculations are mixed with input/output operations, debug code and some hardcoded data. Also it contains the mix of features from different versions of the language — from Fortran 77 to Fortran 95. Therefore, the use of high-level algebraic models helped to understand this legacy code and apply parallelizing transformations in the most efficient way.

The parallelizing transformations developed for the Gaussian elimination program were reused in the electron density program. Only the first most simple loop transformation was applied. However, the challenge was to select the most suitable loop for this transformation, as the program contained 54 loops and trying all of them was not a feasible option. For finding hotspots in the source code, the profiler tool Intel VTune Amplifier was used ("Intel VTune Amplifier", n.d.). Then, the rewriting rules technique was applied to detect all loops enclosing such code fragments. Thus, the number of candidate loops was significantly reduced from 54 to 6. Out of these 6 loops, the transformation was applied to a second outermost loop, since the outermost loop contained too few iterations, and parallelizing inner loops was less efficient because of repeated cost of creating and synchronizing threads each time inner loop was executed.

The execution time of the initial sequential program (SEQ) and the parallelized program (PAR) was compared for grid dimensions N from 200 to 800 (see Figure 11).

Figure 11. The comparison of the initial and the transformed program (electron density)

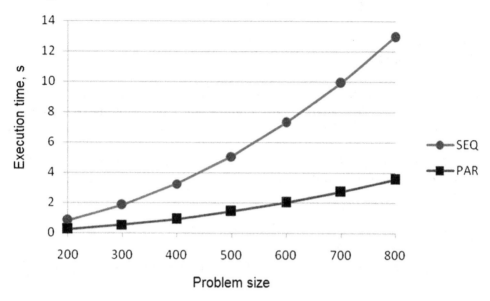

The application of transformations has resulted in quite a significant speedup — from 3.3 to 3.6 (depending on the problem size) on the quad-core system.

CONCLUSION

The examples of practical use of the proposed models and tools for automated design, synthesis and optimization of sequential and parallel programs based on algorithmic algebra, rewriting rules technique and auto-tuning methods were given. Rewriting rules enable automated program parallelization and optimization. Using high-level program models allows describing program transformations in more concise and comprehensible fashion, and also enables using a single model to describe programs in different languages. The series of practical experiments demonstrated the efficiency of applying the proposed methods and tools for software development in different subject domains.

Further research directions include the development of additional parallelizing and optimizing transformations and using them to improve the performance of various programs. The algebra-dynamic models could be extended to describe the additional hardware and software capabilities of the CUDA platform. Future plans also include the extension of tools for cloud-based platforms.

REFERENCES

Allen, R., & Kennedy, K. (2001). *Optimizing compilers for modern architectures: A dependence-based approach.* San Francisco: Morgan Kaufmann.

Andon, P. I., Doroshenko, A. Yu., Tseytlin, G. O., & Yatsenko, O. A. (2007). *Algebra-algorithmic models and methods of parallel programming.* Kyiv: Academperiodyka. (in Russian)

Andon, P. I., Doroshenko, A. Yu., & Zhereb, K. A. (2011). Programming high-performance parallel computations: Formal models and graphics processing units. *Cybernetics and Systems Analysis, 47*(4), 659–668. doi:10.100710559-011-9346-y

Belov, P. N., Borisenkov, E. P., & Panin, B. D. (1989). *Numerical methods of weather prediction.* Leningrad: Gidrometeoizdat. (in Russian)

Buttari, A., Dongarra, J., Kurzak, J., Langou, J., Luszczek, P., & Tomov, S. (2007). The impact of multicore on math software. In *Proceedings of the 8th International Workshop on Applied Parallel Computing (PARA 2006), Revised Selected Papers (LNCS)* (Vol. 4699, pp. 1-10). Berlin: Springer. 10.1007/978-3-540-75755-9_1

Class ForkJoinPool. (n.d.). Retrieved from https://docs.oracle.com/javase/8/docs/api/java/util/concurrent/ForkJoinPool.html

Conway's game of life. (n.d.). Retrieved from https://en.wikipedia.org/wiki/Conway's_Game_of_Life

Datta, K., Murphy, M., Volkov, V., Williams, S., Carter, J., Oliker, L., ... Yelick, K. (2008). Stencil computation optimization and auto-tuning on state-of-the-art multicore architectures. In *Proceedings of the 2008 ACM/IEEE conference on Supercomputing (SC'08)* (pp. 1-12). Piscataway, NJ: IEEE Press. 10.1109/SC.2008.5222004

Doroshenko, A., Ivanenko, P., Novak, O., & Yatsenko, O. (2018). Optimization of parallel software tuning with statistical modeling and machine learning. In *Proceedings of the 14th International Conference "ICT in Education, Research and Industrial Applications. Integration, Harmonization and Knowledge Transfer" (ICTERI 2018)* (pp. 219-226). Berlin: Springer.

Doroshenko, A., Ivanenko, P., Ovdii, O., & Yatsenko, O. (2016). Automated program design— An example solving a weather forecasting problem. *Open Physics*, *14*(1), 410–419. doi:10.1515/phys-2016-0048

Doroshenko, A., & Shevchenko, R. (2006). A rewriting framework for rule-based programming dynamic applications. *Fundamenta Informaticae*, *72*(1-3), 95–108.

Doroshenko, A., & Zhereb, K. (2013). Parallelizing legacy Fortran programs using rewriting rules technique and algebraic program models. In *Proceedings of the 8th International Conference "ICT in Education, Research, and Industrial Applications" (ICTERI 2012), Revised Selected Papers (Communications in Computer and Information Science)* (Vol. 347, pp. 39-59). Berlin: Springer. 10.1007/978-3-642-35737-4_3

Doroshenko, A., Zhereb, K., & Yatsenko, O. (2010). Formal facilities for designing efficient GPU programs. In *Proceedings of the 19th International Workshop "Concurrency: Specification and Programming" (CS&P'2010)* (pp. 142-153). Berlin: Humboldt University Press.

Doroshenko, A., Zhereb, K., & Yatsenko, O. (2013). Developing and optimizing parallel programs with algebra-algorithmic and term rewriting tools. In *Proceedings of the 9th International Conference "ICT in Education, Research, and Industrial Applications" (ICTERI 2013), Revised Selected Papers (Communications in Computer and Information Science)* (Vol. 412, pp. 70-92). Berlin: Springer. 10.1007/978-3-319-03998-5_5

Guptha, S. (2008). *Multithreaded programming in a Microsoft Win32* environment*. Retrieved from http://eng.harran.edu.tr/~nbesli/SP/senkronizasyon.pdf

Hoare, C. A. R. (1961). Algorithm 64: Quicksort. *Communications of the ACM*, *4*(7), 321. doi:10.1145/366622.366644

Intel VTune Amplifier. (n.d.). Retrieved from https://software.intel.com/en-us/intel-vtune-amplifier-xe

Interface ExecutorService. (n.d.). Retrieved from https://docs.oracle.com/javase/8/docs/api/java/util/concurrent/ExecutorService.html

Ishihara, M., Honda, H., & Sato, M. (2006). Development and implementation of an interactive parallelization assistance tool for OpenMP: iPat/OMP. *IEICE Transactions on Information and Systems, E89-D*(2), 399–407. doi:10.1093/ietisy/e89-d.2.399

Ivanenko, P., Doroshenko, A., & Zhereb, K. (2014). TuningGenie: Auto-tuning framework based on rewriting rules. In *Proceedings of the 10th International Conference "ICT in Education, Research and Industrial Applications. Integration, Harmonization and Knowledge Transfer" (ICTERI 2014) (Communications in Computer and Information Science)* (Vol. 469, pp. 139-158). Cham: Springer. 10.1007/978-3-319-13206-8_7

Khavryutchenko, V. D., Tarasenko, Y. A., Strelko, V. V., Khavryuchenko, O. V., & Lisnyak, V. V. (2007). Quantum chemical study of polyaromatic hydrocarbons in high multiplicity states. *International Journal of Modern Physics B, 21*(26), 4507–4515. doi:10.1142/S0217979207037946

Knuth, D. E. (1998). The art of computer programming.: Vol. 3. *Sorting and searching* (2nd ed.). Redwood City, CA: Addison-Wesley.

Leijen, D., Schulte, W., & Burckhardt, S. (2009). The design of a task parallel library. In *Proceedings of the 24th ACM SIGPLAN Conference on Object Oriented Programming Systems Languages and Applications (OOPSLA'09) (ACM SIGPLAN Notices)* (Vol. 44, pp. 227-242). New York: ACM. 10.1145/1640089.1640106

McIlroy, P. M. (1993). Optimistic sorting and information theoretic complexity. In *Proceedings of the 4th Annual ACM/SIGACT-SIAM Symposium on Discrete Algorithms (SODA'93)* (pp. 467-474). Philadelphia, PA: Society for Industrial and Applied Mathematics.

NVIDIA CUDA Technology. (n.d.). Retrieved from http://www.nvidia.com/cuda

OpenMP Application Programming Interface Version 4.5. (2015). Retrieved from http://www.openmp.org/wp-content/uploads/openmp-4.5.pdf

Prusov, V. A., Doroshenko, A. Yu., & Chernysh, R. I. (2009). A method for numerical solution of a multidimensional convection-diffusion problem. *Cybernetics and Systems Analysis*, *45*(1), 89–95. doi:10.100710559-009-9074-8

Prusov, V. A., Doroshenko, A. Yu., Chernysh, R. I., & Guk, L. N. (2008). Theoretical study of a numerical method to solve a diffusion-convection problem. *Cybernetics and Systems Analysis*, *44*(2), 283–291. doi:10.100710559-008-0028-3

Rus, S., Pennings, M., & Rauchwerger, L. (2007). Sensitivity analysis for automatic parallelization on multi-cores. In *Proceedings of the 21st Annual International Conference on Supercomputing (ICS'07)* (pp. 263-273). New York: ACM. 10.1145/1274971.1275008

Saraswat, V. A., Sarkar, V., & von Praun, C. (2007). X10: Concurrent programming for modern architectures. In *Proceedings of the 12th ACM SIGPLAN Symposium on Principles and Practice of Parallel Programming (PPoPP'07)* (p. 271). New York: ACM.

Tournavitis, G., Wang, Z., Franke, B., & O'Boyle, M. F. P. (2009). Towards a holistic approach to auto-parallelization: Integrating profile-driven parallelism detection and machine-learning based mapping. In *Proceedings of the 30th ACM SIGPLAN Conference on Programming Language Design and Implementation (PLDI'09) (ACM SIGPLAN Notices)* (Vol. 44, pp. 177-187). New York: ACM. 10.1145/1542476.1542496

Wetter und Klima – Deutscher Wetterdienst. (n.d.). Retrieved from http://www.dwd.de

KEY TERMS AND DEFINITIONS

CUDA: A parallel computing platform and application programming interface (API) model created by NVIDIA. It allows software developers and software engineers to use a CUDA-enabled graphics processing unit (GPU).

Glushkov's System of Algorithmic Algebras (SAA, Glushkov's Algebra): The two-sorted algebra focused on analytical form of representation of algorithms and formalized transformation of these representations.

Graphics Processing Unit (GPU): A specialized electronic circuit designed to rapidly manipulate and alter memory to accelerate the creation of images in a frame buffer intended for output to a display device. Modern GPUs are very efficient at manipulating computer graphics and image processing, and their highly parallel structure makes them more efficient than general-purpose CPUs for algorithms where the processing of large blocks of data is done in parallel.

Integrated Toolkit for Design and Synthesis of Programs (IDS): The software system intended for automated constructing of sequential and parallel algorithm schemes represented in the modified system of algorithmic algebras (SAA-M) and synthesis of programs in C, C++, Java languages.

Open Multi-Processing (OpenMP): An application programming interface (API) that supports multi-platform shared memory multiprocessing programming in C, C++, and Fortran. It consists of a set of compiler directives, library routines, and environment variables that influence run-time behavior.

SAA Scheme: A representation of an algorithm in algorithmic language SAA/1.

SAA/1: The algorithmic language based on Glushkov's system of algorithmic algebras and focused on natural linguistic representation of schemes. It is applied for multilevel structured designing and documenting of sequential and parallel algorithms and programs.

TermWare: An open-source implementation of rewriting rules engine written in Java. It provides a language for describing rewriting rules that operate on data structures called terms and also a rule engine that interprets rules to transform terms. Termware.NET toolkit is based on TermWare and intended for transformation of programs on Microsoft.NET platform.

TuningGenie: The framework automating the adjustment of programs to a target computing environment.

Chapter 7

Software Design Based on Using Ontologies and Algorithm Algebra

ABSTRACT

This chapter proposes an approach to the automated development of programs based on the use of ontological facilities and algebra-algorithmic toolkit for design and synthesis of programs (IDS). The program design ontology, developed using Protégé system and represented in OWL format, includes concepts from various subject domains (sorting, meteorological forecasting, and other) intended for description of main program objects: data, functions, and relations between them. IDS toolkit generates the initial (skeleton) algorithm scheme based on its ontological description extracted from OWL file. The generated scheme is the basis of further design of the algorithm and synthesis of a program in a target programming language. The approach is illustrated by examples of developing parallel sorting, meteorological forecasting, and N-body simulation programs.

INTRODUCTION

This chapter describes the approach to development of parallel programs using ontologies and algebra-algorithmic facilities. Ontology is a philosophical term that refers to the study of being, becoming, existence and reality and

DOI: 10.4018/978-1-5225-9384-3.ch007

was introduced to computer science through the field of artificial intelligence (Strmečki, Magdalenić, & Kermek, 2016).

In (Happel & Seedorf, 2006), main approaches for using ontologies in software engineering are listed:

- ontology-driven development: the use of ontologies at development time for describing the problem domain;
- ontology-enabled development: applying ontologies at development time to support developers in their tasks;
- ontology-based architectures: the use of ontologies as primary runtime artifacts;
- ontology-enabled architectures: applying ontologies as support to runtime software.

In (Calero, Ruiz, & Piattini, 2006), a broader classification of ontologies based on their subject of conceptualization is proposed:

- knowledge representation ontologies that are used to formalize knowledge under a specific paradigm;
- generic ontologies which represent reusable common-sense knowledge;
- high-level ontologies describing general concepts and notions;
- domain ontologies that offer vocabulary for concepts in a particular domain;
- task ontologies which describe the vocabulary related to a generic activity;
- domain task ontologies that are reusable only in a particular domain;
- method ontologies applicable to a reasoning process designed to perform a particular task;
- application ontologies that are dependent on the application and often specialize the vocabulary of a domain or task ontology.

Based on the moment when they are utilized, ontologies can be used during the development or in runtime. The former approach is called ontology-driven development, in which, for example, ontology's semantic content can be converted into a system component.

In (Gašević, Kaviani, & Milanović, 2009), the use of ontologies in software engineering throughout software lifecycle phases is researched. In the analysis phase, an ontology is commonly used for requirement engineering. In the design phase, ontologies are used as software models, business vocabularies and reasoning or transformation models. In the implementation phase, three possible approaches can be distinguished:

- software system implementation can be generated from an ontology created in the analysis phase and refined in the design phase;
- ontologies can be used in runtime, e.g., Jena API can be used for handling OWL ontologies in Java;
- ontologies can be used as part of the implementation logic in systems implemented using rule-based languages. In the maintenance phase, ontologies may be used as support for managing knowledge.

In the approach proposed in this chapter, the algebra-algorithmic method complements the ontologies by explicit high-level software specifications that enable the synthesis of program code. Using an ontology of a subject domain provides the description of an initial version (a skeleton) of an algorithm to be designed — the data being processed, names of functions, their input and output parameters and also interrelations between data and functions. The ontology is developed using the Protégé system ("Protégé", n.d.; "Protégé-OWL editor", 2017). The algebra-algorithmic part of the considered approach stands for formalization and automation of program development, which is implemented in the Integrated toolkit for Designing and Synthesis of programs (IDS) considered in Chapter 5 (see also (Doroshenko, Zhereb, & Yatsenko, 2013)). The ontology of a subject domain developed in Protégé and presented in OWL language is conveyed to IDS toolkit, where the corresponding skeleton scheme of an algorithm is generated and further filled with algorithmic constructs. The algorithm is represented in the modified system of algorithmic algebras (SAA-M) described in Chapter 1 (see also (Andon, Doroshenko, Tseytlin, & Yatsenko, 2007; Doroshenko, Tseytlin, Yatsenko, & Zachariya, 2006)). At first, the approach is illustrated by an example of developing a parallel sorting program. Then, a more complex examples are considered: designing a multithreaded program of meteorological forecasting (along with a software application intended for executing the developed program on a cloud computing platform) and N-body simulation program.

The proposed approach is related to papers (Bures, Denney, Fischer, & Nistor, 2004; Gonidis, Paraskakis, & Simons, 2014; Martino, Cretella, Esposito, & Carta, 2014; Ojamaa, Haav, & Penjam, 2015; Solis, Pacheco, Najera, & Estrada, 2013), which apply ontologies for description and development of programs.

In particular, paper (Bures et al., 2004) considers the roles ontologies play in schema-based synthesis. Such synthesis uses generic code templates called schemas to represent general knowledge about software generation in a reusable format. A synthesis system takes as an input a problem specification, and applies schemas recursively in an exhaustive fashion until a complete implementation of the problem in a chosen implementation language is created. The ontologies serve as documentation, provide the formal basis for the synthesis system and contain the concepts that are used to formulate the high-level problem specifications. The approach is illustrated by development of a synthesis system, which can generate code for solving a system of linear equations. Paper (Solis et al., 2013) describes the model-driven development framework called SemanticWebBuilder. The framework provides an agile development platform for Web application domain, where system requirements are modeled through ontologies and from this knowledge representation, the infrastructure of the system is automatically generated. Paper (Martino et al., 2014) proposes the approach consisting in development of a set of interrelated OWL ontologies, which describe cloud services and also APIs and methods used to invoke them, together with their relative parameters. The internal workflow of the cloud services is described using OWL-S. In paper (Gonidis et al., 2014), an ontology-driven framework is proposed, which facilitates the use of services provisioned by clouds environments. Ontologies are applied to enable the homogeneous description of the functionality of the service providers. Paper (Ojamaa et al., 2015) presents the solution which automatically generates design templates of meta-models of domain-specific languages according to a given domain ontology represented in OWL DL.

The main difference of the approach described in this chapter from the above-mentioned related works is that the ontology is used for automated generation of intermediate high-level algebraic specifications (schemes) of programs represented in a natural linguistic form. The mentioned representation form facilitates understanding of algorithms and achievement of demanded program quality. Another advantage of the developed tools is the method of automated design of syntactically correct algorithm specifications, which eliminates syntax errors during construction of algorithm schemes.

THE PROGRAM DESIGN ONTOLOGY

The process of program design, described in this chapter, is based on combined use of the program design ontology, SAA-M and IDS toolkit.

The developed approach is based on the notion of an ontology. The formal model of an ontology (Ehrig & Sure, 2004; Maedche & Zacharias, 2002) is a tuple

$$O = <C, H_C, P_C, I, A>,$$

where C is a finite set of concepts, which are also called classes; H_C is a hierarchy of concepts, which is reflexive, transitive and antisymmetric binary relation $H_C \subseteq C \times C$; $H_C(C_1, C_2)$ means that the class C_1 is a subclass of C_2; $P_C = \{P \mid P \subseteq C \times C\}$ is a set of binary relations between the concepts, which are called properties; the domain of the property $P \in P_C$ is the set of concepts $Dom(P) = \{C_D \mid C_D, C_R) \in P\}$, and the range of the property $P \in P_C$ is the set of concepts $Range(P) = \{C_D \mid C_D, C_R) \in P\}$; I is a set of instances of the concepts from the set C; A is a set of axioms of the ontology.

The developed program design ontology includes the concepts from various subject domains and, if necessary, can be extended with concepts from new domains. For constructing the ontology, the Web Ontology Language (OWL) and Protégé 3.2.1 system were applied. According to the developed approach, the basic stages of design of some program are the following:

- addition of concepts necessary for description of applied problems from a chosen subject domain to the program design ontology with the help of the Protégé system. The concepts of the ontology are linked to representations in SAA/1 language (see Chapter 2) used by IDS toolkit;
- preparation of the ontological description of the program in Protégé system;
- generation of an initial SAA scheme of the program from its OWL description using IDS toolkit and further modification of the SAA scheme in the dialogue constructor of syntactically correct programs (DSC-constructor) of the toolkit;
- generation of a program text in a target programming language in IDS toolkit based on the designed SAA scheme.

Figure 1 shows the oriented graph representing the class hierarchy of the developed ontology. The nodes of the graph are the concepts of the ontology and the edges represent the inheritance relations between the concepts.

Figure 1. The program design ontology

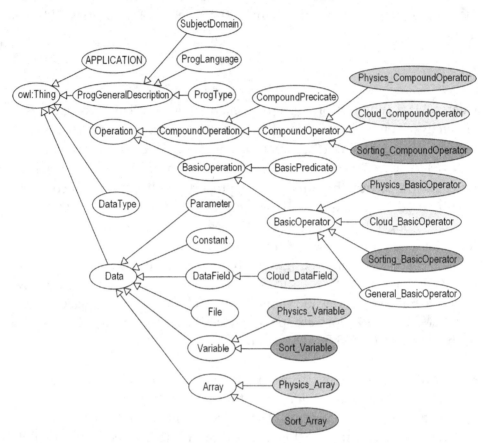

Subclasses of the *Data* class represent various data structures used in programs: parameters, constants, data fields of program classes, files, simple variables and arrays. In particular, the *Parameter* class is used to define formal parameters of methods (functions) used in a program. The properties of the *Data* class are shown in Table 1. The meanings of these properties are the following: *hasName* is an identifier of a data element; *isOfType* is a type of a data element (an instance of the *DataType* class); *rdfs:comment* is a comment to a data element. The instances of *DataType* class include Boolean, double, int, float, double, String, void and other types. The *Array* class and its subclasses have the additional property *initialSize* and the *Variable* class has the additional property *initialValue*. The *DataField* class has the additional property *hasAccessModifiers*, which contains information about access modifiers.

Table 1. The properties associated with the Data class

Property name	Range of values	Relation type
hasName	*String*	1: 1
isOfType	*Data*	1: 1
rdfs:comment	*String*	1: 1

The *Operation* class represents the operations applied to data in a program — predicates and operators. The operations can be basic (the *BasicOperation* subclass) or compound (the *CompoundOperation* subclass). The basic predicate or operator is a primary atomic abstraction used in algorithm design. The compound predicates and operators are constructed from basic ones by means of operations included to SAA-M signature (see Subsection "The Main Algorithm Algebras" of Chapter 1 for details). The concept of a compound element corresponds to a function, a subroutine or a method in programming. Each basic element in the ontology corresponds to a certain basic element in the database of IDS. All the operations have the following properties (see Table 2): *hasName* is an identifier of an operation; *hasParameter* is a property binding the operation to instances of the *Parameter* class; *hasOutputOfType* is the type of a return value; *rdfs:comment* is a property containing a comment to the operation.

Table 2. The properties associated with the Operation class

Property name	Range of values	Relation type
hasName	*String*	1: 1
hasParameter	*Parameter*	1: *N*
hasOutputOfType	*Data*	1: 1
rdfs:comment	*String*	1: 1

The *BasicOperation* subclass also has the additional property *hasSAAText*, which is the representation of an operation in SAA/1 language, corresponding to the text of this operation in the database of IDS. The *CompoundOperation* subclass has the additional property *usesOperation*, which contains the information about basic or compound operators used by a compound operation.

The *APPLICATION* class is intended for specification of instances of programs, which use the data defined by subclasses of the *Data* class and operations, which are instances of the *Operation* class. The properties associated with the *APPLICATION* class are the following (see Table 3): *hasName* is the name of an application; *usesData* is a set of global variables or data fields; *hasMethod* contains information about subroutines (compound operators) of an application; *hasProgType* is a type of an application (sequential, multithreaded or distributed (using MPI)); *targetProgLanguage* is a target language (C++ or Java); *hasSubjectDomain* is the name of a subject domain; *rdfs:comment* is a text of a comment to an application.

Table 3. The properties associated with the APPLICATION class

Property name	Range of values	Relation type
hasName	*String*	1: 1
usesData	*Data*	1: *N*
hasMethod	*CompoundOperation*	1: *N*
hasProgType	*ProgType*	1: 1
targetProgLanguage	*ProgLanguage*	1: 1
hasSubjectDomain	*SubjectDomain*	1: 1
rdfs:comment	*String*	1: 1

The classes *Sort_Variable*, *Sort_Array*, *Sorting_BasicOperator* and *Sorting_CompoundOperator* represent the data and operators concerned with array sorting (Doroshenko & Yatsenko, 2009). The concepts *Physics_Variable*, *Physics_Array*, *Physics_BasicOperator* and *Physics_CompoundOperator* describe data and operators intended for solving physics problems (meteorological forecasting, *N*-body simulation and other). The classes *Cloud_DataField*, *Cloud_BasicOperator* and *Cloud_CompoundOperator* specify data and operators necessary for execution of applications on a cloud computing platform (Doroshenko, Ovdii, & Yatsenko, 2017).

Example 1. As an illustration, consider the ontological design of the parallel sorting program named *Adrsort*. The design of the program consists in creating the instance of the *APPLICATION* class of the program design ontology. Table 4 shows the values of the properties of the *Adrsort* program instance. The *hasName* property contains the program name; the list of program variables is given in the value of the *usesData* property; the value of the *hasMethod* property contains the list of names of instances of compound operators of the program. The program uses MPI ("MPI: A Message-Passing Interface Standard", 2012) for computation parallelization, which is indicated in the value of the *hasProgType* property.

Table 4. The values of the properties of the Adrsort program instance

Property name	Value of the property
hasName	*Adrsort*
usesData	*regfile; index_array; infile; array_size; indexbuf; in_array; outfile; out_array; subarray_size; pointer*
hasMethod	*main; initialize; sorting; calc_elem_pos; confluence*
hasProgType	MPI_program
targetProgLanguage	C_plus_plus
hasSubjectDomain	Sorting
rdfs:comment	Parallel MPI address sort

The main data and compound operators used in the *Adrsort* program are the following. The algorithm takes the array *in_array* as input and calculates for each array element its output index (i.e. address) in the output array (*out_array*). The elements of *in_array* are then inserted into *out_array* according to the obtained output indexes. The array *in_array* is read from the file *infile*, and *out_array* is written to the file *outfile*. The *main* function (compound operator) implements the sorting of the input array by calling *proc_num* parallel processes each executing the *sorting* function.

Table 5. The values of properties of the instance of the compound operator sorting

Property name	Value
hasName	*sorting*
hasParameter	—
hasOutputOfType	void
usesOperation	*initialize; Shift_pointer_to_the_right; calc_elem_pos; confluence; Output_array_to_file; Output_information_about_ time_expired*
rdfs:comment	The function implementing the array sorting

The values of properties of the *sorting* function instance are shown in Table 5. The *sorting* function calls the following compound operators: the *initialize* function, which initializes the program variables; the *calc_elem_pos* function, which calculates the output indexes of elements of *in_array* and saves them in the *indexbuf* array; the *confluence* function, which inserts the elements of *in_array* into *out_array*. These calls are listed in the value of the *usesOperation* property. The *sorting* function also uses several basic operators, which are written with the first letter capitalized (for example, *Output_array_to_file*).

The other compound operators of the program (*initialize*, *calc_elem_pos*, *confluence*) are specified in a similar manner.

Automated Algorithm Generation Based on Ontological Description

This subsection considers the general method for automated generation of an initial (skeleton) scheme of an algorithm from its description in the program design ontology considered in the previous subsection. It is also described how the ontology elements are linked to constructs of SAA-M. The software module which converts the ontology description to a scheme of a program is the part of IDS toolkit considered in Chapter 5. The generated skeleton SAA scheme is used for more detailed designing of an algorithm in IDS. The constructing of an algorithm is done in a descending manner by superposition of SAA/1 language constructs (logical and operator operations; basic operators and predicates) that the user chooses from the list. The representation of the constructs in SAA/1 and corresponding implementations in a programming language are stored in the database of IDS.

For generating a skeleton SAA scheme based on the program design ontology, the OWL file of the ontology is passed to IDS toolkit. IDS extracts the information about class hierarchy, instances of classes and their properties. For linking the ontology elements with corresponding elements of an algorithm scheme, the properties *rdfs:comment* are used. For example, the comment for the *Array* class is the following:

SAABinding
SAAType="BasicOperator"
SAAText="Declare an array ({hasName}) of type ({isOfType})"
SAADBCode="25"

Here SAABinding is the keyword indicating that the comment contains the information on binding the element of the ontology to the element of SAA scheme; SAAType is the type of the element; SAAText is the text of the scheme element to be generated; SAADBCode is the code of the basic element in the database of IDS toolkit. This comment means that for the instances of the *Array* class, the basic operator of array declaration has to be generated. For example, with the values of properties hasName="in_array" and isOfType="int", the following basic operator will be generated:

"Declare an array (in_array) of type (int)",

where in parentheses the parameters of the basic operator are specified (the identifier of the array and its data type).

A skeleton SAA scheme is generated based on an instance of the *APPLICATION* class (see the previous subsection). The basis for the generation is an empty template of SAA scheme stored in the database of IDS, which is used for inserting the elements extracted from the ontology. In case if the type of a program being generated is MPI, the template additionally contains the SAA operation executing MPI computations. The general algorithm for generating SAA scheme based on the ontological specification of an algorithm is the following.

Algorithm. Generation of the skeleton SAA scheme S_1 based on the ontological description of the program P_1 from the program design ontology O_1.

Input. The OWL file F_1 with the ontology O_1 and the name P_1 of an instance of the *APPLICATION* class to generate the SAA scheme on its basis.

Output. The skeleton SAA scheme S_1 of the program P_1 in the format of IDS toolkit.

Method.

- Extract the data about classes and instances of the ontology O_1 from the OWL file F_1 and save it to *Classes* and *Instances* tables, respectively. Each row of the *Classes* table contains the data about a class name, its superclass and a comment. Each row of the *Instances* table contains the data about an instance name, its instantiated class, a comment, the values of instance properties and the information on generating the corresponding element of the SAA scheme.

- Find the information about the comment and the value of the *hasProgType* property, associated with the *APPLICATION* class.

Find the template SAA scheme TS_1 in the database of IDS in accordance with the program type. Save the template TS_1 as the scheme S_1. Insert the program name and the comment into the scheme S_1.

○ Process the value of the *usesData* property, associated with the *APPLICATION* class. Find the description of each data instance in the *Instances* table and generate the text of a basic operator of variable declaration; include it into the block of global variables of the scheme S_1. If the program type is *MPI_program*, then include the declarations of the variable *myrank* (the rank of a current process) and the variable *proc_num* (the number of processes) into the block of global variables.

○ Process the value of the *hasMethod* property, associated with the *APPLICATION* class. Find the description of each compound element in the *Instances* table and extract the values of the following properties: *hasName*, *hasOutputOfType*, *hasParameter*, *usesOperation*. Generate the declaration of each compound element using the extracted information. Generate the sequence of calls of basic and compound operators, listed in the *usesOperation* property. Insert the declaration and the algorithmic implementation of the compound element into the scheme S_1.

The complexity of the given generation algorithm is $O(mn+l(n+pn))$, where n is the total number of instances in the input program design ontology; m is the number of instances of *Data* class; l is the number of instances of *CompoundOperator* class; p is the total number of instances of *BasicOperator* and *CompoundOperator* classes.

Example 2. The ontological description of the *Adrsort* program, considered in Example 1, was used for automated generation of a skeleton algorithm scheme with the help of IDS toolkit. The SAA scheme is the following (for short, the detailing of the compound operator *calc_elem_pos* is not presented).

SCHEME Adrsort ====
"Parallel MPI address sort"
END OF COMMENTS
"GlobalData"
==== "Declare a file variable (regfile), file name (sortreg.txt)";
"Declare an array (index_array) of type (int)";

"Declare a file variable (infile), file name (sort_in.txt)";
"Declare a variable (array_size) of type (int)";
"Declare an array (indexbuf) of type (int)";
"Declare an array (in_array) of type (int)";
"Declare a file variable (outfile), file name (sort_out.txt)";
"Declare an array (out_array) of type (int)";
"Declare a variable (subarray_size) of type (int)";
"Declare an array (pointer) of type (int)";
"Declare an array (myrank) of type (int)";
"Declare an array (proc_num) of type (int)"
"initialize"
==== "Read array (A) of type (T) and size (N) from file (F)";
"Allocate memory for array (A) of type (T) and size (size)"
"sorting"
==== "initialize";
"Shift pointer P(k) by (n) positions in (A) to the right"
"calc_elem_pos(k)";
"confluence";
"Output array (m) of length (n) to file (name)";
"Output the time expired from the start of processing and
write it to file (name)"
"confluence"
==== "Collect data (var1) of type (data_type) with length (n) from all
processes to variable (var2) of process (proc_rank)";
"Assign element (i) the value of element (j)"
"main"
==== PARALLEL_MPI(i = 0, ..., proc_num-1)
(
"sorting"
)
END OF SCHEME Adrsort

The above SAA scheme contains the following constructs of SAA-M for designing parallel MPI programs:

- PARALLEL_MPI(i = 0, ..., proc_num-1)("operator 1") is the operation, which initializes MPI computations and runs proc_num parallel processes, each executing the operator "operator 1", and finalizes MPI computations after executing this operator. The implementation of this operation in C++ language uses functions MPI_Init and MPI_Finalize ("MPI: A Message-Passing Interface Standard", 2012);

- "Collect data (var1) of type (data_type) with length (n) from all processes to variable (var2) of process (proc_rank)" is the basic operator corresponding to the function MPI_Gather ("MPI: A Message-Passing Interface Standard", 2012).

In the above SAA scheme, the beginning of implementation of compound operators is marked by a string of symbols "=". Each compound operator contains the sequence of calls of basic and compound operators according to its ontological specification (for example, the scheme of the *sorting* operator corresponds to the ontological description of this operator given in Table 5). The further design of the algorithm is continued in the DSC-constructor of IDS toolkit based on the generated skeleton scheme. In this case, it is necessary to set parameter values of basic elements and construct the algorithms of functioning of compound operators. In particular, the complete implementation of the compound operators *initialize*, *sorting* and *confluence* are presented below. The *main* compound operator remains the same as presented in the above SAA scheme.

"initialize" =
==== "Read array (in_array) of type (int) and size (array_size)
from file (infile)";
"subarray_size:= array_size / proc_num";
"Allocate memory for array (out_array) of type (int)
and size (array_size)";
"Allocate memory for array (indexbuf) of type (int)
and size (subarray_size)";
IF 'Number of process = (0)'
THEN
"Allocate memory for array (index_array) of type (int)
and size (proc_num * subarray_size)"
END IF
"sorting" =
==== LocalData (
"Declare a variable (first_elem) of type (int)";
"Declare a variable (last_elem) of type (int)");
"initialize";
"first_elem:= myrank * subarray_size";

IF 'Rank of process = (proc_num - 1)' THEN
"last_elem:= array_size - 1"
ELSE "last_elem:= (myrank + 1) * subarray_size - 1"
END IF;
"Place pointer P(1) at position (first_elem)";
WHILE NOT 'Pointer P(1) reached position (last_elem + 1)
in array (in_array)'
LOOP
"calc_elem_pos(P(1))";
"Shift pointer P(1) by (1) positions in array (in_array)
to the right"
END OF LOOP;
"confluence";
IF 'Rank of process = (0)'
THEN
"Output array (out_array) of length (array_size) to file (outfile)";
"Output the time expired from the start of processing and write it
to file (regfile)"
END IF
"confluence" =
==== IF 'Quantity of processes > (1)'
THEN
"Collect data (indexbuf) of type (MPI_INT) with length
(subarray_size) from all processes to variable (index_array) of
process (0)";
IF 'Rank of process = (0)'
THEN
FOR '(P(2)) from (subarray_size) to (array_size-1)'
LOOP
"Assign element (out_array[index_array[P(2)) the value of
element (in_array[P(2))"
END OF LOOP
END IF
END IF

The execution of the above *Adrsort* scheme begins with the compound operator *main*, which launches *proc_num* parallel processes. Each process has a rank (a number in the range 0, 1..., *proc_num*-1), stored in the *myrank* variable. The implementation of each process is contained in the *sorting* compound operator. The input array is divided into *proc_num* subarrays, each processed by a single process. For each subarray element, the process calculates the value of an output index and saves it in the *indexbuf* array. Further, the function *confluence* is executed, in which the processes with ranks 1, ..., *proc_num*-1 send the array *indexbuf* to the root process with index 0. The root process inserts the received *indexbuf* arrays into *index_array* by concatenating them in order of process ranks. After that, the root process inserts the elements of the *in_array* to the *out_array* according to the indexes stored in the *index_array*. The above SAA scheme was used for automated generation of MPI program in C++ language.

CASE STUDY 1: METEOROLOGICAL FORECASTING PROGRAM EXECUTING ON A CLOUD PLATFORM

This subsection illustrates the use of the developed program design ontology, and also the facilities of SAA-M and IDS toolkit, by an example of developing a parallel program of meteorological forecasting and also the software application for executing the developed program on a cloud computing platform.

The Mathematical Model of the Meteorological Forecasting Problem

The parallel program intended for numerical solution of the convection-diffusion problem (CDP) is considered. The mathematical model of CDP (Kaper & Engler, 2013) is a combination of diffusion and convection equations and describes physical phenomena, where particles, energy, or other physical quantities are transferred inside a physical system due to two processes: diffusion and convection. Further, the three-dimensional CDP, which arises in mathematical modeling of atmospheric circulation in meteorology (Doroshenko, Ivanenko, Ovdii, & Yatsenko, 2016), is considered. The problem to be solved is presented as a set of the following convection-diffusion equations:

$$\frac{\partial u}{\partial t} + \frac{u}{a\cos\varphi}\frac{\partial u}{\partial \lambda} + \frac{v}{a}\frac{\partial u}{\partial \varphi} + w\frac{\partial u}{\partial z} = -\frac{1}{\rho a\cos\varphi}\frac{\partial p}{\partial \lambda} + \left(v\sin\varphi - w\cos\varphi\right)\left(2\omega + \frac{u}{a\cos\varphi}\right) + \frac{1}{\rho}F_\lambda,$$

$$(1)$$

$$\frac{\partial v}{\partial t} + \frac{u}{a\cos\varphi}\frac{\partial v}{\partial \lambda} + \frac{v}{a}\frac{\partial v}{\partial \varphi} + w\frac{\partial v}{\partial z} = -\frac{1}{\rho a}\frac{\partial p}{\partial \varphi} - u\left(2\omega + \frac{u}{a\cos\varphi}\right)\sin\varphi - \frac{wv}{a} + \frac{1}{\rho}F_\varphi,$$

(2)

$$\frac{1}{a\cos\varphi}\frac{\partial u}{\partial \lambda} + \frac{1}{a}\frac{\partial v}{\partial \varphi} + \frac{\partial w}{\partial z} - \frac{v}{a}tg\varphi = 0,$$

(3)

$$\frac{\partial T}{\partial t} + \frac{u}{a\cos\varphi}\frac{\partial T}{\partial \lambda} + \frac{v}{a}\frac{\partial T}{\partial \varphi} + w\frac{\partial T}{\partial z} = \frac{\delta}{c_V \rho},$$

(4)

$$p = \rho R_c T.$$

(5)

Here u, v are horizontal components and w is the vertical component of the wind velocity vector $V=(u,v,w)$; λ, φ and z are longitude, latitude, and altitude, respectively; t is time; a is the Earth's radius; ρ is air density; p is atmospheric pressure; ω is the Earth's rotation speed; F_λ and F_φ are the components of the friction force density vector $F_f = (F_\lambda, F_\varphi, F_z)$; T is absolute temperature; δ is heat penetration per unit of air volume; c_V is the specific heat capacity of dry air; R_c is the specific gas constant of dry air.

The horizontal components u and v of the wind velocity vector are obtained from equations (1) and (2), the vertical component w of the vector — from equation (3), temperature T — from equation (4), and density ρ — from equation (5).

Designing a Parallel Program for Solving the Meteorological Forecasting Problem

The parallel numerical implementation of the above model (1)–(5) is based on the algorithm, which parallelizes the task over the following three levels.

- Equations (each equation is solved independently). The number of equations is set in the constant $EVL\_MT\_VAL \leq 5$.
- Space directions λ, φ and z.

- Subdomains for each space direction. The computation domain is decomposed along λ for the subtasks at the directions φ and z, and along φ for subtasks at the direction λ. The number of subdomains is set in the variable *Subdomains*≥ 1.

The number of threads is stored in the *NumbThreads* variable, the value of which is set according to the formula

$$NmbThreads = Subdomains*DIR*EVL\_MT\_VAL, \tag{6}$$

where *DIR*=3 is the number of space directions (λ, φ and z).

The algorithm uses the modified additive-averaged splitting method (Prusov, Doroshenko, & Chernysh, 2009). The general scheme of the calculation is iterative. The input data determine the state of an atmosphere at the initial moment of time t_0. To obtain the prognosis for some moment $CALC\_TIME > t_0$, the time segment is divided into *TmKnotsPer12h* relatively short segments of size $\tau = CALC\_TIME / TmKnotsPer12h$. At each iteration, the algorithm calculates the state of an atmosphere after time τ and its output data become input (initial) data for the next iteration. The increase of the step τ results in a reduction of the number of iterations, but leads to increase in prognosis error, which is why it is recommended that the value of τ is chosen from the interval [0.2…10] seconds. At each iteration, the equations for each coordinate direction are solved independently and then gathering and processing of the results is carried out, which demands the synchronization. The use of the modified additive-averaged splitting method allows combining several iterations (the number of iterations is denoted as m) into one, which reduces the synchronization overhead. Increase in value of the parameter m also results in loss of adequacy of the solution and the recommended interval of values is $m \in [1…10]$

The design of the program implementing the mentioned parallel algorithm begins with creating an instance of the *APPLICATION* class of the program design ontology. The values of the properties of the created instance are listed in Table 6. In the *hasName* property, the name of the program is set to *MeteoModel*. The value of the *usesData* property is the list of main variables, which are the instances of *Physics_Variable* and *Physics_Array* classes of the ontology. The meanings of the variables are the following: *TmKnotsPer12h* is the number of points of a time mesh for twelve-hour period; $M\_prm \in [1…10]$ is the parameter of the modified additive-averaged splitting method (Prusov et al., 2009); *Subdomains*≥ 1 is the number of subregions for each of the space directions;*TmLimCalc* is the final value of time (in seconds), for which the prognosis is calculated; *tau* is the time step (in seconds), which is defined according to the formula: *tau*= *CALC_TIME* / *TmKnotsPer12h*, where *CALC_TIMe* is the forecast time interval (in seconds); *u,v* and *w* are two-dimensional arrays for storing the values of the components of the wind velocity vector; *T* is a two-dimensional array storing the value of an absolute temperature; *d* and *p* are two-dimensional arrays for storing the values of air density and atmospheric pressure, respectively.

Table 6. The values of properties of the MeteoModel program instance

Property name	Value
hasName	*MeteoModel*
usesData	*TmKnotsPer12h*; *M_prm*; *Subdomains*; *TmLimCalc*; *tau*; *u*; *v*; *w*; *T*; *d*; *p*
hasMethod	*main*; *CalcParallelPart*
hasProgType	Multithreaded
targetProgLanguage	C_plus_plus
hasSubjectDomain	Meteorology
rdfs:comment	The parallel program for solving the 3-dimensional convection-diffusion problem

The *hasMethod* property of the *MeteoModel* program instance contains the list of names of program functions, which are instances of the *Physics_CompoundOperator* class. As an example, the values of the basic properties of the *main* function are given in Table 7.

Table 7. The values of properties of the main function instance

Property name	Value
hasName	*main*
hasParameter	*argc*; *argv*
hasOutputOfType	void
usesOperation	*Set_initial_parameters*; *Load_the_data_to_arrays_for_meteorological_values*; *CalcParallelPart*; *Comparing_interpolated_and_calculated_values*; *Save_data_to_files_for_3D_convective_diffusion_task*
rdfs:comment	The main function of the *MeteoModel* program

The value of the *usesOperation* property is the list of operations used in the function (the instances of classes *Physics_BasicOperator* and *Physics_ CompoundOperator*). The *main* function is composed of the operators setting the initial parameters of the algorithm, measuring the execution time of the program, loading the data into arrays, calling the *CalcParallelPart* function (which performs parallel computations), comparing the computed values and saving the result data to files.

IDS toolkit generated the following initial (skeleton) scheme based on the ontological description of the *MeteoModel* program.

SCHEME MeteoModel ====

The parallel program for solving the 3-dimensional convection-diffusion problem

END OF COMMENTS
"GlobalData"
==== "Declare variables (TmKnotsPer12h, M_prm, Subdomains, TmLimCalc)
of type (int)";
"Declare variable (tau) of type (double)";
"Declare dynamic size two-dimensional arrays (u, v, w, T, d, p)
of type (double)";
"main"
==== "Set initial parameters (Subdomains, M_prm, TmKnotsPer12h, TmLimCalc,
tau)";
"Load the data to arrays for meteorological values (u, v, w, T, d, p)";
"CalcParallelPart";
"Comparing interpolated and calculated values";
"Save data to files for 3D convective diffusion task";
"CalcParallelPart"
==== "Initialization of data for parallel part";
"Initialization of variables and arrays for current thread (proc)";
"Set actual equation values for (u, v, w, T, d, p) and boundary
conditions";
"Compute the subtasks for current space direction (lambda, fi, z)";
"Compute the average based on the results for each direction";
"Storing the results to global arrays";

"Deallocate the memory for arrays for 3d convective diffusion task";
END OF SCHEME MeteoModel

The developer continues to design the SAA scheme in IDS toolkit, namely, corrects the subscheme detailing the compound operator *CalcParallelPart*, i.e. adds the assignment operators, the operation of parallel execution, the loop, and synchronizers. The resulting subscheme is given below.

"CalcParallelPart"
==== "Initialization of data for parallel part";
"NmbThreads:= 3 * Subdomains * EVL_MT_VAL";
PARALLEL(proc = 0, ..., NmbThreads-1)
(
"Initialization of variables and arrays for current thread (proc)";
"j:= M_prm";
WHILE 'j * tau <= TmLimCalc'
LOOP
"Set actual equation values for (u, v, w, T, d, p) and boundary conditions";
"Compute the subtasks for current space direction (lambda, fi, z)";
WAIT 'All threads completed work';
"Compute the average based on the results for each direction";
WAIT 'All threads completed work';
"Storing the results to global arrays";
WAIT 'All threads completed work';
"Increase (j) by (M_prm)";
END OF LOOP;
"Deallocate the memory for arrays for 3d convective diffusion task"
);

IDS toolkit translated the above SAA scheme to C++ source code. The parallelism was implemented using the OpenMP library ("OpenMP Application Programming Interface", 2015). The translation process is based on the use of program code templates defined for each SAA-M construct and stored in the database of IDS. In particular, the SAA-M operation of asynchronous execution of operators (PARALLEL) is implemented using the OpenMP directive #pragma omp parallel. It defines a parallel region, which is code that will be executed by multiple threads in parallel. The fragment of C++ source code generated for this operation is given below.

```
// PARALLEL (proc = 0, ..., NmbThreads-1)
omp_set_num_threads(NmbThreads);
#pragma omp parallel
{
int proc = omp_get_thread_num(); // Get thread index
// Get the total number of threads:
#pragma omp master
{
NmbThreads = omp_get_num_threads();
printf("\nNumber of threads: %d.\n", NmbThreads);
}
...
}
```

Design of the Application for Executing the Parallel Program on a Cloud Platform

For automation of execution of the above-considered parallel program *MeteoModel* on a cloud platform, the program application named *CloudApplication* was designed. It is supposed that the *MeteoModel* program is already installed on a virtual machine (a server) of a cloud platform. The purpose of the *CloudApplication* consists in the authentication of a user on a cloud platform, launching the parallel program on one of the active servers and also providing the results of execution of the program in the form of an archive with output files of the program. The approach is illustrated for a case when a cloud system is implemented based on the OpenStack platform ("Open source software for creating private and public clouds", n.d.).

The beginning of the design of the *CloudApplication* assumes the creation of the instance of the *APPLICATION* class and filling the values of its properties (see Table 8). The value of the *usesData* property is the list of data fields of the main class of the program, which are the instances of the *Cloud_DataField* class of the ontology. The mentioned fields are the following: *novaApi* is a variable intended for access to Nova, which is a service managing the computing resources of the OpenStack platform; *provider* is a name of the service (openstack-nova) of the cloud platform; *endPoint* is an URL for authentication of a user in the platform; *identity* is a name of OpenStack project and a login; *credential* is a password for accessing to a platform; *serverIPAddress* is the IP address of an active virtual machine (the server); *commandToExecute* is the command for execution of the parallel program on the virtual machine; *outputPath* is a name of the archive with output files of the program; *destPath* is a path to the local directory to which the output archive is copied.

Table 8. The values of properties of the CloudApplication program instance

Property name	Value
hasName	CloudApplication
usesData	*novaApi; provider; endPoint; identity; credential; serverIPAddress; commandToExecute; outputPath; destPath*
hasMethod	*main_CloudApplication; initialize_CloudApplication; executeProgramOnFirstActiveServer*
hasProgType	Cloud_Application
targetProgLanguage	Java
hasSubjectDomain	Cloud_Computation
rdfs:comment	The application for execution of a program on a cloud platform

The value of the *hasMethod* property is the list of instances of methods of the *CloudApplication.* The methods are the following: *main_CloudApplication* is the main method of the program; *initialize_ CloudApplication* is the method, which initializes the data and authenticates the user; *executeProgramOnFirstActiveServer* is the method launching the program on a virtual machine. These methods are the instances of the *Cloud_CompoundOperator* class of the ontology. As an example, the values of the basic properties of the *main_CloudApplication* method are given in Table 9. The value of the *usesOperation* property is the list of operations used in the method (the instances of classes *Cloud_BasicOperator* and *Cloud_CompoundOperator*).

Table 9. The values of properties of the main method instance

Property name	Value
hasName	*main_CloudApplication*
hasParameter	*argc; argv*
hasOutputOfType	void
usesOperation	*initialize_CloudApplication;* *executeProgramOnFirstActiveServer;* *Release_resources*
rdfs:comment	The main function of the *CloudApplication* program

IDS toolkit generated the following initial scheme based on the ontological description of the *CloudApplication* program.

SCHEME CloudApplication
"GlobalData"
==== "Declare a variable (novaApi) of type (NovaApi) with access modifiers (private static)";
"Declare variables (provider, endPoint, identity, credential, serverIPAddress, commandToExecute, outputPath, destPath)
of type (String) with access modifiers (private)";
"main_ CloudApplication"
==== "initialize_CloudApplication";
"executeProgramOnFirstActiveServer";
"Release resources (novaApi)";
"initialize_CloudApplication"
==== "Read input parameters from config file (provider, endPoint, identity, credential, serverIPAddress, commandToExecute, outputPath, destPath)";
"Authenticate against the cloud provider based on parameters
(provider, endPoint, identity, credential)";
"executeProgramOnFirstActiveServer"
==== "Find the first active server (activeServer)";
"Set parameters (serverIPAddress, host, password) for connecting to the server (activeServer)";
"Connect to the server (activeServer) with parameters (host, password)";
"Execute command (commandToExecute) on server (activeServer)";
"Return archived output files (outputPath, destPath) from
the server (activeServer)";
"Disconnect from server (activeServer)";

END OF SCHEME CloudApplication

The developer continues to design the given SAA scheme in IDS toolkit. Namely, two operations of branching and an operator outputting a message are added to the *executeProgramOnFirstActiveServer* compound operator. The resulting subscheme is the following.

"executeProgramOnFirstActiveServer"
==== "Find the first active server (activeServer)";
IF 'Found active server'
THEN
"Set parameters (serverIPAddress, host, password) for connecting to the server (activeServer)";
"Connect to the server (activeServer) with parameters (host, password)";
IF 'Connected to the server (activeServer)'
THEN
"Execute command (commandToExecute) on server (activeServer)";
"Return archived output files (outputPath, destPath) from the server (activeServer)";
"Disconnect from server (activeServer)"
END IF
ELSE "Output the message ("No active server found.")"
END IF

IDS toolkit translated the above SAA scheme to Java source code with the use of the open-source library jclouds ("Apache jclouds", n.d.). The mentioned library provides the API for various cloud platforms — OpenStack, Amazon Web Services, CloudStack, etc.

Experiment Results

The developed *CloudApplication* program was applied for executing the parallel program of meteorological forecasting *MeteoModel* on a virtual machine included in a cloud system based on the OpenStack platform. The virtual machine had the following configuration of hardware and software: 8 virtual processors with frequency 2 GHz; 1 GB of virtual memory; Scientific Linux 7.1 operating system. The virtualization was based on the use of KVM, the open-source virtualization hypervisor (Chen, 2014). The virtual machine was running on a physical computing node containing two quad-core processors Intel Xeon CPU E5335 with frequency 2 GHz.

During the experiment, the following values of the parameters of the *MeteoModel* program were used:

- the forecast time interval *CALC_TIME* = *TmLimCalc* = 43200 seconds (12 hours);
- the number of time knots *TmKnotsPer*12*h* = 4320;
- the time step *tau*=10 seconds;
- the parameter of the modified additive-averaged splitting method (Prusov et al., 2009) *M_prm*=10;
- the space domain $\lambda \in [0°, 90°]$, $\varphi \in [0°, 90°]$, $z \in [8000; 18000]$;
- the number of subregions for each space direction *Subdomains*=5;
- the number of threads *NmbThreads* was set to 45 according to the formula (6):

NmbThreads = Subdomains*DIR*eVK_MT_VAL,

where the number of space directions *DIR*=3, the number of equations *EVL_MT_VAL*=3.

Figure 2 shows the obtained values of multiprocessor speedup $Sp = T_1 / T_{N_{VCPUs}}$, where T_1 is the average execution time of the corresponding sequential program on 1 virtual processor, $T_{N_{VCPUs}}$ is the average execution time of the parallel program on N_{VCPUs} virtual processors.

Figure 2. The dependency of the multiprocessor speedup Sp on the number N_{VCPUs} of virtual processors for the MeteoModel program

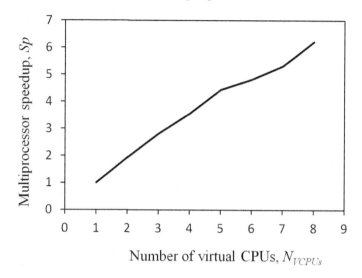

The maximum multiprocessor speedup is 6.21 obtained at $N_{VCPUs} = 8$. The efficiency of the parallel program is $E = \dfrac{Sp}{N_{VCPUs}} = 0.78$.

CASE STUDY 2: PARALLEL N-BODY SIMULATION PROGRAM FOR GPU

In this subsection, the application of the program design ontology and IDS for designing a parallel N-body simulation program intended for executing on a Graphics Processing Unit (GPU) using CUDA ("NVIDIA CUDA technology", n.d.) is considered.

N-Body Problem Statement

An N-body simulation is a simulation of a dynamical system of particles, usually under the influence of physical forces, such as gravity (Aarseth, 2003). Consider the system of N particles with known masses m_i that interact in pairs according to the Newtonian law of gravitation. Let positions and velocities of the particles at the initial time moment $t=0$ are known and are $r_i\big|_{t=0} = r_0$

and $v_i|_{t=0} = v_0$, respectively. It is necessary to approximately find positions and velocities at the next time moments.

The evolution of the system of N particles is described by the system of equations

$$\frac{dr_i}{dt} = v_i,$$

$$\frac{dv_i}{dt} = \sum_{j \neq i} Gm_j \frac{r_j - r_i}{\left| r_j - r_i \right|^3},$$

where $i = \overline{1, N}$, G is a gravitational constant. Hence, the task is to integrate the system of $2N$ first-order ordinary differential equations.

Let's integrate the above problem numerically with discretization by t. The predictor-corrector method using Hermite interpolating polynomial (Makino & Aarseth, 1992) is applied.

The integration is done according to the following scheme.

- For each particle, based on known positions and velocities of particles at time moment t, the force which influences it from the side of other particles normalized on the mass of the particle, and its derivative are calculated:

$$a_{0,i} = -\sum_{j \neq i} Gm_j \frac{r_{ij}}{(r_{ij}^2 + \mu^2)^{3/2}},$$ (7)

$$\dot{a}_{0,i} = -\sum_{j \neq i} Gm_j \left(\frac{v_{ij}}{(r_{ij}^2 + \mu^2)^{3/2}} + \frac{3(v_{ij} \cdot r_{ij})r_{ij}}{(r_{ij}^2 + \mu^2)^{5/2}} \right),$$ (8)

where $r_{ij} = r_j - r_i$, $v_{ij} = v_j - v_i$, ε is a mitigating parameter which is necessary to introduce due to the discreteness of the time grid.

- Based on obtained values $a_{0,i}$ and $\dot{a}_{0,i}$, the positions of particles at time moment $t + \Delta t$ are calculated:

$$r_{p,i} = \frac{\Delta t^3}{6} \dot{a}_{0,i} + \frac{\Delta t^2}{2} a_{0,i} + \Delta t v_{0,i} + r_i, \tag{9}$$

$$v_{p,i} = \frac{\Delta t^2}{2} \dot{a}_{0,i} + \Delta t a_{0,i} + v_i. \tag{10}$$

- Based on new positions of particles, force $a_{1,i}$ and its derivative $\dot{a}_{1,i}$ influencing the particle at time moment $t+\Delta t$ are calculated using formulas similar to the formulas given in item 2:

$$a_{1,i} = -\sum_{j \neq i} Gm_j \frac{r_{ij}}{(r_{ij}^2 + \mu^2)^{3/2}}, \tag{11}$$

$$\dot{a}_{1,i} = -\sum_{j \neq i} Gm_j \left(\frac{v_{ij}}{(r_{ij}^2 + \mu^2)^{3/2}} + \frac{3(v_{ij} \cdot r_{ij})r_{ij}}{(r_{ij}^2 + \mu^2)^{5/2}} \right). \tag{12}$$

- Using Hermite interpolating polynomial, the second and the third derivatives of the force which influence the i-th particle at the initial time moment are calculated based on values $a_{0,i}$, $\dot{a}_{0,i}$, $a_{1,i}$, $\dot{a}_{1,i}$:

$$\ddot{a}_{0,i} = \frac{-6(a_{0,i} - a_{1,i}) - \Delta t(4\dot{a}_{0,i} + 2\dot{a}_{1,i})}{\Delta t^2}, \tag{13}$$

$$\dddot{a}_{0,i} = \frac{12(a_{0,i} - a_{1,i}) + 6\Delta t(\dot{a}_{0,i} + \dot{a}_{1,i})}{\Delta t^3}. \tag{14}$$

- At the last step of the algorithm, adjustments are introduced for the obtained positions and velocities of particles based on $\ddot{a}_{0,i}$ and $\dddot{a}_{0,i}$, and thus the final values of positions and velocities at moment $t+\Delta t$ are calculated:

$$r_i = r_{p,i} + \frac{\Delta t^4}{24} \ddot{a}_{0,i} + \frac{\Delta t^5}{120} \dddot{a}_{0,i},$$ (15)

$$v_i = v_{p,i} + \frac{\Delta t^3}{6} \ddot{a}_{0,i} + \frac{\Delta t^4}{24} \dddot{a}_{0,i}.$$ (16)

Table 10. The values of properties of the NBody program instance

Property name	Value
hasName	*NBody*
usesData	*h_m; h_pos; h_vel; h_ac0; h_ad0; h_ac1; h_ad1;* *d_m; d_pos; d_vel; d_ac0; d_ad0; d_ac1; d_ad1*
hasMethod	*main*
hasProgType	Multithreaded
targetProgLanguage	C_plus_plus_for_CUDA
hasSubjectDomain	Physics
rdfs:comment	The parallel program for solving N-body simulation problem

The basic idea of the parallel algorithm solving the above problem consists in executing operations associated with each particle $i = \overline{1, N}$ in a separate GPU thread.

The parallel algorithm works according to the following scheme.

- Let all the particles are numbered and each of them is associated with a thread. Each thread obtains the initial parameters of the particle to process.
- Based on the sequence number, the current particle is chosen, beginning from the first one. Coordinates, velocity, and mass of the particle are saved to the shared memory of each thread block. Thus, threads of each block can quickly access to coordinates of the current particle. Each thread calculates the contribution between its own and current particle into sums (7) and (8). The step is repeated until all pair interactions between particles are calculated.
- Each thread calculates the provisional values of coordinates and velocities according to formulas (9) and (10).

- Similar to step 2, calculations based on formulas (11) and (12) are performed.
- Each thread introduces adjustments for previously obtained provisional values of positions and velocities according to formulas (13), (14), (15), (16), and thus obtains the final results.

Steps 1–5 are repeated for each time step until values at the final time moment are obtained.

Designing Parallel N-Body Simulation Program

The design of the program implementing the parallel *N*-body simulation algorithm begins with creating an instance of the *APPLICATION* class of the program design ontology. The values of the properties of the created instance are listed in Table 10.

In the *usesData* property, the main variables are listed. The variables h_m, h_pos, h_vel contain the initial values of masses, coordinates, and velocities of particles; h_ad0, h_ac1, h_ad1 are for storing acceleration values. The variables beginning with $d\_$ are used for storing and calculating corresponding values in GPU. The values of the basic properties of the *main* function are given in Table 11.

Table 11. The values of properties of the main function instance

Property name	Value
hasName	*main*
hasParameter	*argc*; *argv*
hasOutputOfType	void
usesOperation	*Set_initial_masses_coordinates_velocities;* *Copy_data_from_CPU_to_GPU;* *Calculate_acceleration_and_derivative;* *Preliminary_calculation_coordinates_and_velocities;* *Calculate_adjustments_coordinates_and_velocities;* *Introduce_adjustments_coordinates_and_velocities;* *Copy_results_from_GPU_to_CPU_memory*
rdfs:comment	The main function of the *NBody* program

The resulting SAA scheme generated by IDS toolkit on the basis of the ontological description of the *NBody* program is the following.

SCHEME NBODY ====

"Parallel N-body simulation for GPU"

END OF COMMENTS

"main"

==== "Set initial values of masses, coordinates and velocities of particles";

"Allocate memory on GPU and copy data from CPU to GPU";

FOR (k from 0 to STEPS-1)

LOOP

FOR (i from 0 to N/512-1)

LOOP

CALL GPU KERNEL (blocksPerGrid, threadsPerBlock)

(

"Calculate acceleration of particles and its derivative (i)"

);

WAIT 'All threads completed work';

END OF LOOP;

CALL GPU KERNEL (blocksPerGrid, threadsPerBlock)

(

"Perform preliminary calculation of coordinates and velocities"

);

WAIT 'All threads completed work';

FOR (i from 0 to N/512 - 1)

LOOP

CALL GPU KERNEL (blocksPerGrid, threadsPerBlock)

(

"Calculate the adjustments for coordinates and velocities (i)"

);

WAIT 'All threads completed work';

END OF LOOP;

CALL GPU KERNEL (blocksPerGrid, threadsPerBlock)

(

"Introduce adjustments for obtained coordinates and velocities"

);

WAIT 'All threads completed work';

END OF LOOP;

"Copy the obtained results from GPU to CPU memory and free allocated memory"

END OF SCHEME "NBODY"

Table 12. The execution time of sequential and parallel N-body simulation programs and corresponding multiprocessor speedup

N	T_{CPU}, s	T_{GPU}, s	T_{CPU}/T_{GPU}
256	0.02797	0.00525	5.32761
512	0.0766	0.00844	9.07582
1024	0.3031	0.01907	15.8941
2048	1.2422	0.03843	32.3237
4096	5.375	0.0703	76.4580
8192	32.094	0.1953	164.331
16384	161.453	0.75	215.270
32768	718.875	1.5516	463.312
65536	3045.22	6.0585	502.636

Figure 3. The dependency of the execution time of sequential and parallel N-body simulation programs on the number of particles N

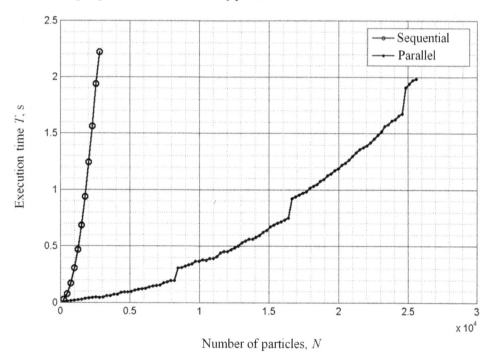

The above scheme is intended for implementation in CUDA platform ("NVIDIA CUDA technology", n.d.) and contains the operations launching GPU kernel of the following type:

CALL GPU KERNEL (blocksPerGrid, threadsPerBlock)

(

"operator"

);

where blocksPerGrid is the number of blocks in the CUDA grid; threadsPerBlock is the number of threads in each block; "operator" is the operator executed by a thread.

IDS toolkit translated the above SAA scheme to a C++ program.

Experiment Results

The developed *NBody* program was executed on a computer with i5-3570 CPU and GeForce GTX 650 Ti GPU (768 CUDA cores) with the following initial conditions. At the initial point in time, particles are located in nodes of three-dimensional parallelepiped region of size $16\times16\times$ ($N/256$). The number of particles was chosen to be multiple of 256. The initial velocities of particles were set in an arbitrary manner and normalized to 1. The mitigating parameter was $\varepsilon=0.01$, the gravitational constant $G=1$, and the time step $\Delta t=0.25$. The execution time was measured for the number of particles from 256 to 16384 with step 256 particles, and also for separate values of N (32768, 65536) at one time step. Table 12 shows the selection of obtained values beginning from 256 particles and then doubling the number. In the table, T_{CPU}, T_{GPU} is the execution time of the sequential and parallel program (in seconds), respectively; T_{CPU}/T_{GPU} is the multiprocessor speedup. The low level of speedup at smaller values of N is explained by GPU underutilization.

Figure 3 shows the dependency of the execution time of sequential and parallel programs on the number of particles.

CONCLUSION

The approach to the formal development of parallel programs based on the program design ontology and algebra-algorithmic facilities was proposed. The ontology provides the opportunity to describe a skeleton of a program representing main objects of a subject domain: data, functions processing the data and relations between the data and the functions. The method of automated generation of a skeleton scheme based on the ontological description of an algorithm was developed and implemented in the integrated toolkit for the design and synthesis of programs. The main difference of the proposed approach from similar works is that the ontology is used for automated generation of intermediate high-level algebraic schemes of algorithms represented in a natural linguistic form. Generated schemes are then used for further algorithm design and program synthesis. The approach is illustrated by examples of developing parallel programs of meteorological forecasting and *N*-body simulation.

REFERENCES

Aarseth, S. J. (2003). *Gravitational N-body simulations: Tools and algorithms*. Cambridge: Cambridge University Press. doi:10.1017/CBO9780511535246

Andon, P. I., Doroshenko, A. Yu., Tseytlin, G. O., & Yatsenko, O. A. (2007). *Algebra-algorithmic models and methods of parallel programming*. Kyiv: Academperiodyka. (in Russian)

Apache jclouds. (n.d.). Retrieved from http://jclouds.apache.org

Bures, T., Denney, E., Fischer, B., & Nistor, E. C. (2004). The role of ontologies in schema-based program synthesis. In *Proceedings of the Workshop on Ontologies as Software Engineering Artifacts (OOPSLA 2004)* (pp. 1-6). Academic Press.

Calero, C., Ruiz, F., & Piattini, M. (2006). *Ontologies for software engineering and software technology* (1st ed.). Berlin: Springer. doi:10.1007/3-540-34518-3

Chen, G. (2014). *KVM — open source virtualization for the enterprise and OpenStack clouds*. Retrieved from https://www.bloombase.com/content/S5uCoG9Q

Doroshenko, A., Ivanenko, P., Ovdii, O., & Yatsenko, O. (2016). Automated program design— An example solving a weather forecasting problem. *Open Physics*, *14*(1), 410–419. doi:10.1515/phys-2016-0048

Doroshenko, A., Tseytlin, G., Yatsenko, O., & Zachariya, L. (2006). A theory of clones and formalized design of programs. In *Proceedings of the 15th International Workshop "Concurrency, Specification and Programming" (CS&P'2006)* (pp. 328-339). Berlin: Humboldt University Press.

Doroshenko, A., & Yatsenko, O. (2009). Using ontologies and algebra of algorithms for formalized development of parallel programs. *Fundamenta Informaticae, 93*(1-3), 111–125. doi:10.3233/FI-2009-0091

Doroshenko, A., Zhereb, K., & Yatsenko, O. (2013). Developing and optimizing parallel programs with algebra-algorithmic and term rewriting tools. In *Proceedings of the 9th International Conference "ICT in Education, Research, and Industrial Applications" (ICTERI 2013), Revised Selected Papers (Communications in Computer and Information Science)* (Vol. 412, pp. 70-92). Berlin: Springer. 10.1007/978-3-319-03998-5_5

Doroshenko, A. Yu., Ovdii, O. M., & Yatsenko, O. A. (2017). Ontological and algebra-algorithmic tools for automated design of parallel programs for cloud platforms. *Cybernetics and Systems Analysis, 53*(2), 323–332. doi:10.100710559-017-9932-8

Ehrig, M., & Sure, Y. (2004). Ontology mapping — an integrated approach. In *Proceedings of the 1st European Semantic Web Symposium (ESWS 2004) (LNCS)* (Vol. 3053, pp. 76-91). Berlin: Springer.

Gašević, D., Kaviani, N., & Milanović, M. (2009). Ontologies and software engineering. In S. Staab & R. Studer (Eds.), *Handbook on ontologies* (pp. 593–615). Berlin: Springer. doi:10.1007/978-3-540-92673-3_27

Gonidis, F., Paraskakis, I., & Simons, A. J. H. (2014). On the role of ontologies in the design of service based cloud applications. In *Proceedings of Euro-Par 2014 International Workshops (LNCS)* (Vol. 8806, pp. 1–12). Cham: Springer. doi:10.1007/978-3-319-14313-2_1

Happel, H. J., & Seedorf, S. (2006). Applications of ontologies in software engineering. In *Proceedings of International Workshop on Semantic Web Enabled Software Engineering (SWESE'06) on the 5th International Semantic Web Conference (ISWC 2006) (LNCS)* (Vol. 4273, pp. 1-14). Berlin: Springer.

Kaper, H., & Engler, H. (2013). *Mathematics and climate*. Philadelphia, PA: Society for Industrial & Applied Mathematics. doi:10.1137/1.9781611972610

Maedche, A., & Zacharias, V. (2002). Clustering ontology-based metadata in the Semantic Web. In *Proceedings of the 6th European Conference on Principles of Data Mining and Knowledge Discovery (PKDD 2002) (LNCS)* (Vol. 2431, pp. 348-360). Berlin: Springer. 10.1007/3-540-45681-3_29

Makino, J., & Aarseth, S. J. (1992). On a Hermite integrator with Ahmad-Cohen. *Publications of the Astronomical Society of Japan, 44*, 141–151.

Martino, B. D., Cretella, G., Esposito, A., & Carta, G. (2014). Semantic representation of cloud services: A case study for OpenStack. In *Proceedings of the 7th International Conference on Internet and Distributed Computing Systems (IDCS'2014) (LNCS)* (Vol. 8729, pp. 39-50). Cham: Springer. 10.1007/978-3-319-11692-1_4

MPI: A Message-Passing Interface Standard. (2012). Retrieved from http://mpi-forum.org/docs/mpi-3.0/mpi30-report.pdf

NVIDIA CUDA Technology. (n.d.). Retrieved from http://www.nvidia.com/cuda

Ojamaa, A., Haav, H.-M., & Penjam, J. (2015). Semi-automated generation of DSL meta models from formal domain ontologies. In *Proceedings of the 5th International Conference on Model & Data Engineering (LNCS)* (Vol. 9344, pp. 3-15). Cham: Springer. 10.1007/978-3-319-23781-7_1

Open source software for creating private and public clouds. (n.d.). Retrieved from http://www.openstack.org

OpenMP Application Programming Interface Version 4.5. (2015). Retrieved from http://www.openmp.org/wp-content/uploads/openmp-4.5.pdf

Protégé. (n.d.). Retrieved from http://protege.stanford.edu

Protégé-OWL Editor. (2017). Retrieved from http://protegewiki.stanford.edu/wiki/Protege-OWL

Prusov, V. A., Doroshenko, A. Y., & Chernysh, R. I. (2009). Choosing the parameter of a modified additive-averaged splitting algorithm. *Cybernetics and Systems Analysis, 45*(4), 589–596. doi:10.100710559-009-9126-0

Solis, J., Pacheco, H., Najera, K., & Estrada, H. (2013). A MDE framework for semi-automatic development of Web applications. In *Proceedings of the 1st International Conference on Model-Driven Engineering and Software Development* (pp. 241-246). Lisbon: SciTePress.

Strmečki, D., Magdalenić, I., & Kermek, D. (2016). An overview on the use of ontologies in software engineering. *Journal of Computational Science*, *12*(12), 597–610. doi:10.3844/jcssp.2016.597.610

KEY TERMS AND DEFINITIONS

Glushkov's System of Algorithmic Algebras (SAA, Glushkov's Algebra): The two-sorted algebra focused on analytical form of representation of algorithms and formalized transformation of these representations.

Integrated Toolkit for Design and Synthesis of Programs (IDS): The software system intended for automated constructing of sequential and parallel algorithm schemes represented in the modified system of algorithmic algebras (SAA-M) and synthesis of programs in C, C++, Java languages.

Modified System of Algorithmic Algebras (SAA-M): The extension of the Glushkov's system of algorithmic algebras (SAA) intended for formalization of parallel algorithms.

Ontology: A formal explicit description of concepts (called classes) in a domain of discourse, properties of each concept describing various features and attributes of the concept, instances (specific objects in the domain of interest), and restrictions on properties. The properties are binary relationships on concepts.

Open Multi-Processing (OpenMP): An application programming interface (API) that supports multi-platform shared memory multiprocessing programming in C, C++, and Fortran. It consists of a set of compiler directives, library routines, and environment variables that influence run-time behavior.

Program Design Ontology: The ontology which includes concepts from various subject domains (for example, sorting, meteorological forecasting) intended for description of main program objects: data, functions and relations between them.

SAA Scheme: A representation of an algorithm in algorithmic language SAA/1.

SAA/1: The algorithmic language based on Glushkov's system of algorithmic algebras and focused on natural linguistic representation of schemes. It is applied for multilevel structured designing and documenting of sequential and parallel algorithms and programs.

Web Ontology Language (OWL): A family of knowledge representation languages for authoring ontologies. The OWL languages are characterized by formal semantics. They are built upon the World Wide Web Consortium's (W3C) XML standard for objects called the Resource Description Framework (RDF).

Conclusion

Improvement of performance and efficiency of use of modern multiprocessor platforms and development of methods and software tools for automated parallel program construction are the main challenges, which this book is focused on. The main idea of solving the mentioned problems is selection, elaboration and application of formal and adaptive methods, which play an important role at various stages of software design, beginning from development of initial specifications to a final implementation.

The methods are based on algebra of algorithmics, term rewriting and auto-tuning techniques. The algorithmics uses high-level specifications of programs represented in Glushkov's system of algorithmic algebras and deals with problems of formalization, substantiation of correctness and transformation of algorithms. It is also concerned with development of software tools for automated design and synthesis of classes of algorithms and programs. The generality of algorithmics is based on a variety of interpretations of algorithm schemes and provides the possibilities of application of algorithm algebras and corresponding high-level design tools for solving problems associated with various subject domains. The efficiency of such application in many respects depends on depth of understanding the semantics of applied algorithms. Only upon this condition, an adequate interpretation of facilities of algorithmics and its efficiency at designing algorithms and programs are possible.

The development of efficient parallel software is a complex task. The world-known thesis states that program is a symbiosis of algorithms and data structures. Parallel programming model considerably complicates both components and the most efficient programs are derived from their best combination. Variety of modern hardware architectures leads to different combinations being optimal for various computational environments. Thus, optimization phase consumes a sizeable amount of time and efforts in development of parallel programs. The significant problem is to increase the adaptability of parallel programs to specific conditions of their use (for example, optimize application code to a target multiprocessor platform). In algorithmics, this problem is solved by the use of parameter-driven generation of algorithm specifications by means of higher-level algorithms (hyperschemes) which are parameterized specifications focused on solving a certain class of problems. Setting specific values of parameters and subsequent interpretation of hyperschemes allows obtaining algorithms adapted to specific conditions of their use. Another approach is provided by auto-tuning, which is the methodology automating the search for the optimal program version out of a set of provided possibilities by running each candidate and measuring its performance on a given parallel architecture.

The combination of the algorithmics and the rewriting rules technique allowed developing the algebraic models, methods and tools, focused on automated design, transformation, synthesis and auto-tuning of programs. The main feature of the integrated toolkit for design and synthesis of programs (IDS system) consists in using high-level algebraic specifications, which can be represented in three forms: algebraic, natural linguistic and graphical, which give a comprehensive understanding of specifications and facilitate achievement of demanded program quality. The natural linguistic form is based on the use of SAA/1 language, the main features of which are simplicity in learning and use, and also independence from a specific programming language and possibility of automated translation to any target language for maintenance of adequacy of algorithms and programs associated with them. Another advantage of IDS toolkit is the method of automated design of syntactically correct algorithm specifications, which eliminates syntax errors during construction of algorithm schemes. The symbolical computation system TermWare is based on rewriting rules and is applied for automation of program transformations. Rewriting rules enable automated program parallelization and optimization by various criteria, for example, used memory and execution time. Using high-level program models allows describing program transformations in concise and comprehensible fashion, and also enables using a single model to describe programs in different languages. The developed TuningGenie framework is intended for parallel programs performance acceleration. The framework works with source code of software and performs code-to-code transformations by utilizing facilities of the rule-based rewriting system. Such approach gains higher flexibility comparing to existing solutions.

The developed models, methods and tools are applied for design and generation of sequential and parallel algorithms and programs in various subject domains (in particular, weather forecasting). The future research will be focused on further development of algebra-algorithmic methods and tools for design and synthesis of parallel programs for many-core and cloud computing platforms.

Appendix

List of Notations and Abbreviations

AA — Algebra of Algorithmics

ADT — Abstract Data Type

AHS — Algebra of Hyperschemes

AlgA — Algebraic Algorithmics

ARS — Abstract Rewriting System

CPU — Central Processing Unit

DA — Dijkstra's Algebra

DSC-constructor — The Dialogue constructor of Syntactically Correct programs (the component of the IDS toolkit)

DSC-method — The method of Dialogue designing of Syntactically Correct programs

DSL — Domain-Specific Language

GA — Glushkov's algebra (Glushkov's System of Algorithmic Algebras, SAA)

GPU — Graphics Processing Unit

IDS — Integrated toolkit for Design and Synthesis of programs

IS — A set of states (an information set) of the operational automaton of the abstract automaton model of a computer

KA — Kaluzhnin's Algebra (algebra of flowgraphs)

MAS — Many-sorted Algebraic System

MPI — Message Passing Interface

$\overline{P}$ — A set of states (an information set) of the operational automaton of the abstract automaton model of the parameter-driven generator of texts

PCS — Parallel Computing System

PRAM — Parallel Random-Access Machine

PRAM*: The model which extends the classic PRAM model with additional memory level and uses only one strategy for management of simultaneous access to both memory levels.

PRS — Parallel Regular Scheme
RHS — Regular Hyperscheme
RS — Regular Scheme
SAA — Glushkov's System of Algorithmic Algebras
SAA-M — Modified System of Algorithmic Algebras
SDG — Structured Design Grammar

Related Readings

To continue IGI Global's long-standing tradition of advancing innovation through emerging research, please find below a compiled list of recommended IGI Global book chapters and journal articles in the areas of parallel computing, computing algorithms, and software optimization. These related readings will provide additional information and guidance to further enrich your knowledge and assist you with your own research.

Aherwar, A., Singh, A., Patnaik, A., & Unune, D. (2018). Selection of Molybdenum-Filled Hip Implant Material Using Grey Relational Analysis Method. In P. Vasant, S. Alparslan-Gok, & G. Weber (Eds.), *Handbook of Research on Emergent Applications of Optimization Algorithms* (pp. 675–692). Hershey, PA: IGI Global. doi:10.4018/978-1-5225-2990-3.ch029

Alparslan-Gök, S. Z., Palancı, O., & Yücesan, Z. (2018). Peer Group Situations and Games With Grey Uncertainty. In P. Vasant, S. Alparslan-Gok, & G. Weber (Eds.), *Handbook of Research on Emergent Applications of Optimization Algorithms* (pp. 265–278). Hershey, PA: IGI Global. doi:10.4018/978-1-5225-2990-3.ch011

Anohah, E. (2017). Paradigm and Architecture of Computing Augmented Learning Management System for Computer Science Education. *International Journal of Online Pedagogy and Course Design*, 7(2), 60–70. doi:10.4018/IJOPCD.2017040105

Aote, S., & Raghuwanshi, M. M. (2017). Mathematical Optimization by Using Particle Swarm Optimization, Genetic Algorithm, and Differential Evolution and Its Similarities. In S. Shandilya, S. Shandilya, K. Deep, & A. Nagar (Eds.), *Handbook of Research on Soft Computing and Nature-Inspired Algorithms* (pp. 325–358). Hershey, PA: IGI Global. doi:10.4018/978-1-5225-2128-0.ch011

Azad, P., & Navimipour, N. J. (2017). An Energy-Aware Task Scheduling in the Cloud Computing Using a Hybrid Cultural and Ant Colony Optimization Algorithm. *International Journal of Cloud Applications and Computing*, 7(4), 20–40. doi:10.4018/IJCAC.2017100102

Banerjee, C., Banerjee, A., & Pandey, S. K. (2016). MCOQR (Misuse Case-Oriented Quality Requirements) Metrics Framework. In P. Saxena, D. Singh, & M. Pant (Eds.), *Problem Solving and Uncertainty Modeling through Optimization and Soft Computing Applications* (pp. 184–209). Hershey, PA: IGI Global. doi:10.4018/978-1-4666-9885-7.ch009

Banik, A., & Majumder, A. (2019). Classification of Channel Allocation Schemes in Wireless Mesh Network. In A. Borgy Waluyo (Ed.), *Algorithms, Methods, and Applications in Mobile Computing and Communications* (pp. 65–92). Hershey, PA: IGI Global. doi:10.4018/978-1-5225-5693-0.ch004

Bhadoria, V. S., Pal, N. S., & Shrivastava, V. (2016). Comparison of Analytical and Heuristic Techniques for Multiobjective Optimization in Power System. In P. Saxena, D. Singh, & M. Pant (Eds.), *Problem Solving and Uncertainty Modeling through Optimization and Soft Computing Applications* (pp. 264–291). Hershey, PA: IGI Global. doi:10.4018/978-1-4666-9885-7.ch013

Borgy Waluyo, A. (2019). Optimizing Channel Utilization for Wireless Broadcast Databases. In A. Borgy Waluyo (Ed.), *Algorithms, Methods, and Applications in Mobile Computing and Communications* (pp. 178–203). Hershey, PA: IGI Global. doi:10.4018/978-1-5225-5693-0.ch008

Bose, G. K., & Pain, P. (2017). Optimization Through Nature-Inspired Soft-Computing and Algorithm on ECG Process. In S. Shandilya, S. Shandilya, K. Deep, & A. Nagar (Eds.), *Handbook of Research on Soft Computing and Nature-Inspired Algorithms* (pp. 489–519). Hershey, PA: IGI Global. doi:10.4018/978-1-5225-2128-0.ch017

Bouarara, H. A. (2017). A Survey of Computational Intelligence Algorithms and Their Applications. In S. Shandilya, S. Shandilya, K. Deep, & A. Nagar (Eds.), *Handbook of Research on Soft Computing and Nature-Inspired Algorithms* (pp. 133–176). Hershey, PA: IGI Global. doi:10.4018/978-1-5225-2128-0.ch005

Boudouaoui, Y., Habbi, H., & Harfouchi, F. (2018). Swarm Bee Colony Optimization for Heat Exchanger Distributed Dynamics Approximation With Application to Leak Detection. In P. Vasant, S. Alparslan-Gok, & G. Weber (Eds.), *Handbook of Research on Emergent Applications of Optimization Algorithms* (pp. 557–578). Hershey, PA: IGI Global. doi:10.4018/978-1-5225-2990-3.ch024

Calvo-Rolle, J. L., Casteleiro-Roca, J. L., Meizoso-López, M. D., Piñón-Pazos, A. J., & Mendez-Perez, J. A. (2017). Intelligent Expert System to Optimize the Quartz Crystal Microbalance (QCM) Characterization Test: Intelligent System to Optimize the QCM Characterization Test. In S. Shandilya, S. Shandilya, K. Deep, & A. Nagar (Eds.), *Handbook of Research on Soft Computing and Nature-Inspired Algorithms* (pp. 469–488). Hershey, PA: IGI Global. doi:10.4018/978-1-5225-2128-0.ch016

Cavallin, A., Frutos, M., Vigier, H. P., & Rossit, D. G. (2018). An Integrated Model of Data Envelopment Analysis and Artificial Neural Networks for Improving Efficiency in the Municipal Solid Waste Management. In P. Vasant, S. Alparslan-Gok, & G. Weber (Eds.), *Handbook of Research on Emergent Applications of Optimization Algorithms* (pp. 206–231). Hershey, PA: IGI Global. doi:10.4018/978-1-5225-2990-3.ch009

Choubey, D. K., & Paul, S. (2017). GA_SVM: A Classification System for Diagnosis of Diabetes. In S. Shandilya, S. Shandilya, K. Deep, & A. Nagar (Eds.), *Handbook of Research on Soft Computing and Nature-Inspired Algorithms* (pp. 359–397). Hershey, PA: IGI Global. doi:10.4018/978-1-5225-2128-0.ch012

Das, A. (2018). Automatic Mask Alignment for Optical Lithography Using GA- and PSO-Based Image Registration Technique. In P. Vasant, S. Alparslan-Gok, & G. Weber (Eds.), *Handbook of Research on Emergent Applications of Optimization Algorithms* (pp. 637–655). Hershey, PA: IGI Global. doi:10.4018/978-1-5225-2990-3.ch027

Dash, N., Debta, S., & Kumar, K. (2018). Application of ANN and PSO Swarm Optimization for Optimization in Advanced Manufacturing: A Case With CNC Lathe. In P. Vasant, S. Alparslan-Gok, & G. Weber (Eds.), *Handbook of Research on Emergent Applications of Optimization Algorithms* (pp. 386–406). Hershey, PA: IGI Global. doi:10.4018/978-1-5225-2990-3.ch017

Dieu, V. N., & Tung, T. T. (2017). Augmented Lagrange Hopfield Network for Combined Economic and Emission Dispatch with Fuel Constraint. In S. Shandilya, S. Shandilya, K. Deep, & A. Nagar (Eds.), *Handbook of Research on Soft Computing and Nature-Inspired Algorithms* (pp. 221–255). Hershey, PA: IGI Global. doi:10.4018/978-1-5225-2128-0.ch007

Donelli, M. (2017). Application of Natured-Inspired Algorithms for the Solution of Complex Electromagnetic Problems. In S. Shandilya, S. Shandilya, K. Deep, & A. Nagar (Eds.), *Handbook of Research on Soft Computing and Nature-Inspired Algorithms* (pp. 1–33). Hershey, PA: IGI Global. doi:10.4018/978-1-5225-2128-0.ch001

Elsadek, W. F., & Mikhail, M. N. (2019). SMARC: Seamless Mobility Across RAN Carriers Using SDN. In A. Borgy Waluyo (Ed.), *Algorithms, Methods, and Applications in Mobile Computing and Communications* (pp. 93–131). Hershey, PA: IGI Global. doi:10.4018/978-1-5225-5693-0.ch005

Emara, T. (2019). Adaptive Power-Saving Mechanism for VoIP Over WiMAX Based on Artificial Neural Network. In A. Borgy Waluyo (Ed.), *Algorithms, Methods, and Applications in Mobile Computing and Communications* (pp. 158–177). Hershey, PA: IGI Global. doi:10.4018/978-1-5225-5693-0.ch007

Ervural, B., Ervural, B. C., & Kahraman, C. (2017). A Comprehensive Literature Review on Nature-Inspired Soft Computing and Algorithms: Tabular and Graphical Analyses. In S. Shandilya, S. Shandilya, K. Deep, & A. Nagar (Eds.), *Handbook of Research on Soft Computing and Nature-Inspired Algorithms* (pp. 34–68). Hershey, PA: IGI Global. doi:10.4018/978-1-5225-2128-0.ch002

Expósito-Izquierdo, C., & Expósito-Márquez, A. (2017). A Survey of the Cuckoo Search and Its Applications in Real-World Optimization Problems. In S. Shandilya, S. Shandilya, K. Deep, & A. Nagar (Eds.), *Handbook of Research on Soft Computing and Nature-Inspired Algorithms* (pp. 541–555). Hershey, PA: IGI Global. doi:10.4018/978-1-5225-2128-0.ch019

Ganesan, T., Aris, M. S., & I., E. (2018). Multiobjective Strategy for an Industrial Gas Turbine: Absorption Chiller System. In P. Vasant, S. Alparslan-Gok, & G. Weber (Eds.), *Handbook of Research on Emergent Applications of Optimization Algorithms* (pp. 531-556). Hershey, PA: IGI Global. doi:10.4018/978-1-5225-2990-3.ch023

Ghosh, T. K., & Das, S. (2016). A Hybrid Algorithm Using Genetic Algorithm and Cuckoo Search Algorithm to Solve Job Scheduling Problem in Computational Grid Systems. *International Journal of Applied Evolutionary Computation*, 7(2), 1–11. doi:10.4018/IJAEC.2016040101

Godara, D., Choudhary, A., & Singh, R. K. (2018). Predicting Change Prone Classes in Open Source Software. *International Journal of Information Retrieval Research*, 8(4), 1–23. doi:10.4018/IJIRR.2018100101

Goudos, S. K. (2018). Optimization of Antenna Design Problems Using Binary Differential Evolution. In P. Vasant, S. Alparslan-Gok, & G. Weber (Eds.), *Handbook of Research on Emergent Applications of Optimization Algorithms* (pp. 614–636). Hershey, PA: IGI Global. doi:10.4018/978-1-5225-2990-3.ch026

Heidari, A. A., & Abbaspour, R. A. (2018). Enhanced Chaotic Grey Wolf Optimizer for Real-World Optimization Problems: A Comparative Study. In P. Vasant, S. Alparslan-Gok, & G. Weber (Eds.), *Handbook of Research on Emergent Applications of Optimization Algorithms* (pp. 693–727). Hershey, PA: IGI Global. doi:10.4018/978-1-5225-2990-3.ch030

J., J., Chowdhury, S., Goyal, P., Samui, P., & Dalkiliç, Y. (2016). Determination of Bearing Capacity of Shallow Foundation Using Soft Computing. In P. Saxena, D. Singh, & M. Pant (Eds.), *Problem Solving and Uncertainty Modeling through Optimization and Soft Computing Applications* (pp. 292-328). Hershey, PA: IGI Global. doi:10.4018/978-1-4666-9885-7.ch014

Jauhar, S. K., & Pant, M. (2016). Sustainable Supplier's Management Using Differential Evolution. In P. Saxena, D. Singh, & M. Pant (Eds.), *Problem Solving and Uncertainty Modeling through Optimization and Soft Computing Applications* (pp. 239–263). Hershey, PA: IGI Global. doi:10.4018/978-1-4666-9885-7.ch012

Jenicka, S. (2018). Sugeno Fuzzy-Inference-System-Based Land Cover Classification of Remotely Sensed Images. In P. Vasant, S. Alparslan-Gok, & G. Weber (Eds.), *Handbook of Research on Emergent Applications of Optimization Algorithms* (pp. 326–363). Hershey, PA: IGI Global. doi:10.4018/978-1-5225-2990-3.ch015

Kadry, S., & El Hami, A. (2016). Modeling Stock Prices Using Monte-Carlo Simulation and Excel. In P. Saxena, D. Singh, & M. Pant (Eds.), *Problem Solving and Uncertainty Modeling through Optimization and Soft Computing Applications* (pp. 166–183). Hershey, PA: IGI Global. doi:10.4018/978-1-4666-9885-7.ch008

Kaffash, S., & Torshizi, M. (2018). Data Envelopment Analysis Development in Banking Sector. In P. Vasant, S. Alparslan-Gok, & G. Weber (Eds.), *Handbook of Research on Emergent Applications of Optimization Algorithms* (pp. 462–484). Hershey, PA: IGI Global. doi:10.4018/978-1-5225-2990-3.ch020

Kaur, P., & Sharma, M. (2017). A Survey on Using Nature Inspired Computing for Fatal Disease Diagnosis. *International Journal of Information System Modeling and Design*, 8(2), 70–91. doi:10.4018/IJISMD.2017040105

Kenwright, B. (2018). Smart Animation Tools. In P. Vasant, S. Alparslan-Gok, & G. Weber (Eds.), *Handbook of Research on Emergent Applications of Optimization Algorithms* (pp. 52–66). Hershey, PA: IGI Global. doi:10.4018/978-1-5225-2990-3.ch003

Krawiec, K., Simons, C., Swan, J., & Woodward, J. (2018). Metaheuristic Design Patterns: New Perspectives for Larger-Scale Search Architectures. In P. Vasant, S. Alparslan-Gok, & G. Weber (Eds.), *Handbook of Research on Emergent Applications of Optimization Algorithms* (pp. 1–36). Hershey, PA: IGI Global. doi:10.4018/978-1-5225-2990-3.ch001

Kumar, H. (2018). Computational Intelligence Approach for Flow Shop Scheduling Problem. In P. Vasant, S. Alparslan-Gok, & G. Weber (Eds.), *Handbook of Research on Emergent Applications of Optimization Algorithms* (pp. 298–313). Hershey, PA: IGI Global. doi:10.4018/978-1-5225-2990-3.ch013

Kumar, H., Chauhan, N. K., & Yadav, P. K. (2016). Dynamic Tasks Scheduling Algorithm for Distributed Computing Systems under Fuzzy Environment. *International Journal of Fuzzy System Applications*, *5*(4), 77–95. doi:10.4018/IJFSA.2016100104

Kumar, M., Nallagownden, P., Elamvazuthi, I., & Vasant, P. (2018). Optimal Placement and Sizing of Distributed Generation in Distribution System Using Modified Particle Swarm Optimization Algorithm: Swarm-Intelligence-Based Distributed Generation. In P. Vasant, S. Alparslan-Gok, & G. Weber (Eds.), *Handbook of Research on Emergent Applications of Optimization Algorithms* (pp. 485–507). Hershey, PA: IGI Global. doi:10.4018/978-1-5225-2990-3.ch021

Li, R., Qiu, L., & Zhang, D. (2019). Research on an Improved Coordinating Method Based on Genetic Algorithms and Particle Swarm Optimization. *International Journal of Cognitive Informatics and Natural Intelligence*, *13*(2), 18–29. doi:10.4018/IJCINI.2019040102

Liñán-García, E., De la Barrera-Gómez, H. I., Vázquez-Esquivel, A. L., Aguirre-García, J., Cervantes-Payan, A. I., Escobedo-Hernández, E. O., & López-Alday, L. A. (2018). Solving Vehicle Routing Problem With Multi-Phases Simulated Annealing Algorithm. In P. Vasant, S. Alparslan-Gok, & G. Weber (Eds.), *Handbook of Research on Emergent Applications of Optimization Algorithms* (pp. 508–530). Hershey, PA: IGI Global. doi:10.4018/978-1-5225-2990-3.ch022

Mahdi, F. P., Vasant, P., Kallimani, V., Abdullah-Al-Wadud, M., & Watada, J. (2017). Quantum-Inspired Computational Intelligence for Economic Emission Dispatch Problem. In S. Shandilya, S. Shandilya, K. Deep, & A. Nagar (Eds.), *Handbook of Research on Soft Computing and Nature-Inspired Algorithms* (pp. 445–468). Hershey, PA: IGI Global. doi:10.4018/978-1-5225-2128-0.ch015

Mahseur, M., & Boukra, A. (2019). Quality of Service (QoS) Optimization in a Multicast Routing: A Hybrid Solution. *International Journal of Applied Metaheuristic Computing*, *10*(2), 27–54. doi:10.4018/IJAMC.2019040102

Maniya, K. D. (2016). Comparative Study of GRA and MOORA Methods: A Case of Selecting TFO Machine. In P. Saxena, D. Singh, & M. Pant (Eds.), *Problem Solving and Uncertainty Modeling through Optimization and Soft Computing Applications* (pp. 132–146). Hershey, PA: IGI Global. doi:10.4018/978-1-4666-9885-7.ch006

Mantoro, T., Ayu, M. A., & Ibrahim, A. (2019). Visualizing Pathway on 3D Maps for an Interactive User Navigation in Mobile Devices. In A. Borgy Waluyo (Ed.), *Algorithms, Methods, and Applications in Mobile Computing and Communications* (pp. 237–260). Hershey, PA: IGI Global. doi:10.4018/978-1-5225-5693-0.ch010

Mao, L., Qi, D. Y., Lin, W. W., Liu, B., & Da Li, Y. (2016). An Energy-Efficient Resource Scheduling Algorithm for Cloud Computing based on Resource Equivalence Optimization. *International Journal of Grid and High Performance Computing, 8*(2), 43–57. doi:10.4018/IJGHPC.2016040103

Mariappan, B. (2019). Predictive Methods of Always Best-Connected Networks in Heterogeneous Environment. In A. Borgy Waluyo (Ed.), *Algorithms, Methods, and Applications in Mobile Computing and Communications* (pp. 48–64). Hershey, PA: IGI Global. doi:10.4018/978-1-5225-5693-0.ch003

Márquez, A. E., & Expósito-Izquierdo, C. (2017). An Overview of the Last Advances and Applications of Artificial Bee Colony Algorithm. In S. Shandilya, S. Shandilya, K. Deep, & A. Nagar (Eds.), *Handbook of Research on Soft Computing and Nature-Inspired Algorithms* (pp. 520–540). Hershey, PA: IGI Global. doi:10.4018/978-1-5225-2128-0.ch018

Mellal, M. A., & Williams, E. J. (2018). A Survey on Ant Colony Optimization, Particle Swarm Optimization, and Cuckoo Algorithms. In P. Vasant, S. Alparslan-Gok, & G. Weber (Eds.), *Handbook of Research on Emergent Applications of Optimization Algorithms* (pp. 37–51). Hershey, PA: IGI Global. doi:10.4018/978-1-5225-2990-3.ch002

Menon, V. G., & Prathap, P. M. J. (2019). Moving From Topology-Dependent to Opportunistic Routing Protocols in Dynamic Wireless Ad Hoc Networks: Challenges and Future Directions. In A. Borgy Waluyo (Ed.), *Algorithms, Methods, and Applications in Mobile Computing and Communications* (pp. 1–23). Hershey, PA: IGI Global. doi:10.4018/978-1-5225-5693-0.ch001

Mescia, L., Bia, P., Caratelli, D., & Gielis, J. (2017). Swarm Intelligence for Electromagnetic Problem Solving. In S. Shandilya, S. Shandilya, K. Deep, & A. Nagar (Eds.), *Handbook of Research on Soft Computing and Nature-Inspired Algorithms* (pp. 69–100). Hershey, PA: IGI Global. doi:10.4018/978-1-5225-2128-0.ch003

Miriyala, S. S., & Mitra, K. (2018). A Proposal for Parameter-Free Surrogate Building Algorithm Using Artificial Neural Networks. In P. Vasant, S. Alparslan-Gok, & G. Weber (Eds.), *Handbook of Research on Emergent Applications of Optimization Algorithms* (pp. 232–264). Hershey, PA: IGI Global. doi:10.4018/978-1-5225-2990-3.ch010

Mittal, P., & Mitra, K. (2018). Decomposition-Based Multi-Objective Optimization of Energy Noise Trade-Off in a Wind Farm: A Hybrid Approach. In P. Vasant, S. Alparslan-Gok, & G. Weber (Eds.), *Handbook of Research on Emergent Applications of Optimization Algorithms* (pp. 177–205). Hershey, PA: IGI Global. doi:10.4018/978-1-5225-2990-3.ch008

Mohan Kamalapur, S., & Patil, V. (2017). Parameter Settings in Particle Swarm Optimization. In S. Shandilya, S. Shandilya, K. Deep, & A. Nagar (Eds.), *Handbook of Research on Soft Computing and Nature-Inspired Algorithms* (pp. 101–132). Hershey, PA: IGI Global. doi:10.4018/978-1-5225-2128-0.ch004

Mohanty, S., Patra, P. K., Mohapatra, S., & Ray, M. (2017). MPSO: A Novel Meta-Heuristics for Load Balancing in Cloud Computing. *International Journal of Applied Evolutionary Computation*, 8(1), 1–25. doi:10.4018/ijaec.2017010101

Mohanty, S., Patra, P. K., Ray, M., & Mohapatra, S. (2019). An Approach for Load Balancing in Cloud Computing Using JAYA Algorithm. *International Journal of Information Technology and Web Engineering*, 14(1), 27–41. doi:10.4018/IJITWE.2019010102

Novikova, E., & Kotenko, I. (2019). Visualization-Driven Approach to Fraud Detection in the Mobile Money Transfer Services. In A. Borgy Waluyo (Ed.), *Algorithms, Methods, and Applications in Mobile Computing and Communications* (pp. 205–236). Hershey, PA: IGI Global. doi:10.4018/978-1-5225-5693-0.ch009

Ochoa-Zezzatti, A., Olivier, T., Camarena, R., Gutiérrez, G., Axpeitia, D., & Vázque, I. (2018). Intelligent Drones Improved With Algae Algorithm. In P. Vasant, S. Alparslan-Gok, & G. Weber (Eds.), *Handbook of Research on Emergent Applications of Optimization Algorithms* (pp. 279–297). Hershey, PA: IGI Global. doi:10.4018/978-1-5225-2990-3.ch012

Pandey, A., & Banerjee, S. (2017). Bio-Inspired Computational Intelligence and Its Application to Software Testing. In S. Shandilya, S. Shandilya, K. Deep, & A. Nagar (Eds.), *Handbook of Research on Soft Computing and Nature-Inspired Algorithms* (pp. 429–444). Hershey, PA: IGI Global. doi:10.4018/978-1-5225-2128-0.ch014

Pandey, A., & Banerjee, S. (2017). Test Suite Optimization Using Chaotic Firefly Algorithm in Software Testing. *International Journal of Applied Metaheuristic Computing*, 8(4), 41–57. doi:10.4018/IJAMC.2017100103

Pandey, A., & Banerjee, S. (2018). Test Suite Minimization in Regression Testing Using Hybrid Approach of ACO and GA. *International Journal of Applied Metaheuristic Computing*, 9(3), 88–104. doi:10.4018/IJAMC.2018070105

Pandey, A., & Banerjee, S. (2019). Test Suite Optimization Using Firefly and Genetic Algorithm. *International Journal of Software Science and Computational Intelligence*, 11(1), 31–46. doi:10.4018/IJSSCI.2019010103

Pantula, P. D., Miriyala, S. S., & Mitra, K. (2018). Efficient Optimization Formulation Through Variable Reduction for Clustering Algorithms. In P. Vasant, S. Alparslan-Gok, & G. Weber (Eds.), *Handbook of Research on Emergent Applications of Optimization Algorithms* (pp. 135–162). Hershey, PA: IGI Global. doi:10.4018/978-1-5225-2990-3.ch006

Patidar, K., Kumar, M., & Kumar, S. (2016). Performance Analysis of DE over K-Means Proposed Model of Soft Computing. In P. Saxena, D. Singh, & M. Pant (Eds.), *Problem Solving and Uncertainty Modeling through Optimization and Soft Computing Applications* (pp. 211–224). Hershey, PA: IGI Global. doi:10.4018/978-1-4666-9885-7.ch010

Pooja. (2016). A Cultivated Variant of Differential Evolution Algorithm for Global Optimization. In P. Saxena, D. Singh, & M. Pant (Eds.), *Problem Solving and Uncertainty Modeling through Optimization and Soft Computing Applications* (pp. 1-19). Hershey, PA: IGI Global. doi:10.4018/978-1-4666-9885-7.ch001

Punurai, W., & Pholdee, N. (2018). Optimal Structural Elements Sizing Using Neural Network and Adaptive Differential Algorithm. In P. Vasant, S. Alparslan-Gok, & G. Weber (Eds.), *Handbook of Research on Emergent Applications of Optimization Algorithms* (pp. 93–134). Hershey, PA: IGI Global. doi:10.4018/978-1-5225-2990-3.ch005

Rashid, E. (2016). R4 Model for Case-Based Reasoning and Its Application for Software Fault Prediction. *International Journal of Software Science and Computational Intelligence*, 8(3), 19–38. doi:10.4018/IJSSCI.2016070102

Recioui, A. (2018). Application of Teaching Learning-Based Optimization to the Optimal Placement of Phasor Measurement Units. In P. Vasant, S. Alparslan-Gok, & G. Weber (Eds.), *Handbook of Research on Emergent Applications of Optimization Algorithms* (pp. 407–438). Hershey, PA: IGI Global. doi:10.4018/978-1-5225-2990-3.ch018

Recioui, A. (2018). Application of the Spiral Optimization Technique to Antenna Array Design. In P. Vasant, S. Alparslan-Gok, & G. Weber (Eds.), *Handbook of Research on Emergent Applications of Optimization Algorithms* (pp. 364–385). Hershey, PA: IGI Global. doi:10.4018/978-1-5225-2990-3.ch016

Recioui, A. (2018). Optimal Placement of Power Factor Correction Capacitors Using Taguchi Optimization Method. In P. Vasant, S. Alparslan-Gok, & G. Weber (Eds.), *Handbook of Research on Emergent Applications of Optimization Algorithms* (pp. 777–812). Hershey, PA: IGI Global. doi:10.4018/978-1-5225-2990-3.ch033

Roy, S., Kumar, K., & Davim, J. P. (2017). Optimization of Process Parameters Using Soft Computing Techniques: A Case With Wire Electrical Discharge Machining. In S. Shandilya, S. Shandilya, K. Deep, & A. Nagar (Eds.), *Handbook of Research on Soft Computing and Nature-Inspired Algorithms* (pp. 177–220). Hershey, PA: IGI Global. doi:10.4018/978-1-5225-2128-0.ch006

Roy, S. S., Biba, M., Kumar, R., Kumar, R., & Samui, P. (2017). A New SVM Method for Recognizing Polarity of Sentiments in Twitter. In S. Shandilya, S. Shandilya, K. Deep, & A. Nagar (Eds.), *Handbook of Research on Soft Computing and Nature-Inspired Algorithms* (pp. 281–291). Hershey, PA: IGI Global. doi:10.4018/978-1-5225-2128-0.ch009

S, J. (2018). Texture-Based Land Cover Classification Algorithm Using Hidden Markov Model for Multispectral Data. In P. Vasant, S. Alparslan-Gok, & G. Weber (Eds.), *Handbook of Research on Emergent Applications of Optimization Algorithms* (pp. 579-613). Hershey, PA: IGI Global. doi:10.4018/978-1-5225-2990-3.ch025

Sahin, M. A., & Tuzkaya, G. (2018). Operations Research Problems for Airline Industry: A Literature Survey for Maintenance Routing Problem. In P. Vasant, S. Alparslan-Gok, & G. Weber (Eds.), *Handbook of Research on Emergent Applications of Optimization Algorithms* (pp. 163–176). Hershey, PA: IGI Global. doi:10.4018/978-1-5225-2990-3.ch007

Saxena, P., Choudhary, A., Kumar, S., & Singh, S. (2016). Simulation Tool for Transportation Problem: TRANSSIM. In P. Saxena, D. Singh, & M. Pant (Eds.), *Problem Solving and Uncertainty Modeling through Optimization and Soft Computing Applications* (pp. 111–130). Hershey, PA: IGI Global. doi:10.4018/978-1-4666-9885-7.ch005

Saxena, P., Singh, D., & Khanna, N. (2016). Optimization of Dairy Feeding Models with C-SOMGA. In P. Saxena, D. Singh, & M. Pant (Eds.), *Problem Solving and Uncertainty Modeling through Optimization and Soft Computing Applications* (pp. 147–165). Hershey, PA: IGI Global. doi:10.4018/978-1-4666-9885-7.ch007

Sharma, M., Kaushik, R., & Sarma, K. K. (2017). Speaker Recognition With Normal and Telephonic Assamese Speech Using I-Vector and Learning-Based Classifier. In S. Shandilya, S. Shandilya, K. Deep, & A. Nagar (Eds.), *Handbook of Research on Soft Computing and Nature-Inspired Algorithms* (pp. 256–280). Hershey, PA: IGI Global. doi:10.4018/978-1-5225-2128-0.ch008

Sharma, T. K. (2016). Application of Shuffled Frog Leaping Algorithm in Software Project Scheduling. In P. Saxena, D. Singh, & M. Pant (Eds.), *Problem Solving and Uncertainty Modeling through Optimization and Soft Computing Applications* (pp. 225–238). Hershey, PA: IGI Global. doi:10.4018/978-1-4666-9885-7.ch011

Singh, D., & Deep, K. (2016). Hookes-Jeeves-Based Variant of Memetic Algorithm. In P. Saxena, D. Singh, & M. Pant (Eds.), *Problem Solving and Uncertainty Modeling through Optimization and Soft Computing Applications* (pp. 85–110). Hershey, PA: IGI Global. doi:10.4018/978-1-4666-9885-7.ch004

Singh, O. (2017). Automatic Generation Control of Multi-Area Interconnected Power Systems Using Hybrid Evolutionary Algorithm. In S. Shandilya, S. Shandilya, K. Deep, & A. Nagar (Eds.), *Handbook of Research on Soft Computing and Nature-Inspired Algorithms* (pp. 292–324). Hershey, PA: IGI Global. doi:10.4018/978-1-5225-2128-0.ch010

Singh, T. K., & Das, K. N. (2016). Behavioral Study of Drosophila Fruit Fly and Its Modeling for Soft Computing Application. In P. Saxena, D. Singh, & M. Pant (Eds.), *Problem Solving and Uncertainty Modeling through Optimization and Soft Computing Applications* (pp. 32–84). Hershey, PA: IGI Global. doi:10.4018/978-1-4666-9885-7.ch003

Singh, U. P., Jain, S., Jain, D. K., & Singh, R. K. (2018). An Improved RBFNN Controller for a Class of Nonlinear Discrete-Time Systems With Bounded Disturbance. In P. Vasant, S. Alparslan-Gok, & G. Weber (Eds.), *Handbook of Research on Emergent Applications of Optimization Algorithms* (pp. 656–674). Hershey, PA: IGI Global. doi:10.4018/978-1-5225-2990-3.ch028

Singh, U. P., Jain, S., Tiwari, A., & Singh, R. K. (2018). Nature-Inspired-Based Adaptive Neural Network Approximation for Uncertain System. In P. Vasant, S. Alparslan-Gok, & G. Weber (Eds.), *Handbook of Research on Emergent Applications of Optimization Algorithms* (pp. 439–461). Hershey, PA: IGI Global. doi:10.4018/978-1-5225-2990-3.ch019

Soo, S., Chang, C., Loke, S. W., & Srirama, S. N. (2019). Dynamic Fog Computing: Practical Processing at Mobile Edge Devices. In A. Borgy Waluyo (Ed.), Algorithms, Methods, and Applications in Mobile Computing and Communications (pp. 24-47). Hershey, PA: IGI Global. doi:10.4018/978-1-5225-5693-0.ch002

Sreedhar, G. (2016). Optimizing Website Content to Improve Correctness of the Website Design. In P. Saxena, D. Singh, & M. Pant (Eds.), *Problem Solving and Uncertainty Modeling through Optimization and Soft Computing Applications* (pp. 329–338). Hershey, PA: IGI Global. doi:10.4018/978-1-4666-9885-7.ch015

Srivastava, S., & Sahana, S. K. (2017). The Insects of Nature-Inspired Computational Intelligence. In S. Shandilya, S. Shandilya, K. Deep, & A. Nagar (Eds.), *Handbook of Research on Soft Computing and Nature-Inspired Algorithms* (pp. 398–428). Hershey, PA: IGI Global. doi:10.4018/978-1-5225-2128-0.ch013

Szkaliczki, T. (2018). Combinatorial Optimization Problems in Multimedia Delivery. In P. Vasant, S. Alparslan-Gok, & G. Weber (Eds.), *Handbook of Research on Emergent Applications of Optimization Algorithms* (pp. 67–92). Hershey, PA: IGI Global. doi:10.4018/978-1-5225-2990-3.ch004

Tao, W., Linyan, W., Yanping, L., Nuo, G., & Weiran, Z. (2019). Learning Advanced Brain Computer Interface Technology: Comparing CSP Algorithm and WPA Algorithm for EEG Feature Extraction. *International Journal of Technology and Human Interaction*, *15*(3), 14–27. doi:10.4018/IJTHI.2019070102

Unune, D. R., & Aherwar, A. (2018). A Multiobjective Genetic-Algorithm-Based Optimization of Micro-Electrical Discharge Drilling: Enhanced Quality Micro-Hole Fabrication in Inconel 718. In P. Vasant, S. Alparslan-Gok, & G. Weber (Eds.), *Handbook of Research on Emergent Applications of Optimization Algorithms* (pp. 728–749). Hershey, PA: IGI Global. doi:10.4018/978-1-5225-2990-3.ch031

Urooj, S., & Singh, S. P. (2016). Wavelet Transform-Based Soft Computational Techniques and Applications in Medical Imaging. In P. Saxena, D. Singh, & M. Pant (Eds.), *Problem Solving and Uncertainty Modeling through Optimization and Soft Computing Applications* (pp. 339–363). Hershey, PA: IGI Global. doi:10.4018/978-1-4666-9885-7.ch016

Usta, P., Ergun, S., & Alparslan-Gok, S. Z. (2018). A Cooperative Game Theory Approach to Post- Disaster Housing Problem. In P. Vasant, S. Alparslan-Gok, & G. Weber (Eds.), *Handbook of Research on Emergent Applications of Optimization Algorithms* (pp. 314–325). Hershey, PA: IGI Global. doi:10.4018/978-1-5225-2990-3.ch014

Verma, P. K., Verma, R., Prakash, A., & Tripathi, R. (2019). Massive Access Control in Machine-to-Machine Communications. In A. Borgy Waluyo (Ed.), *Algorithms, Methods, and Applications in Mobile Computing and Communications* (pp. 133–157). Hershey, PA: IGI Global. doi:10.4018/978-1-5225-5693-0.ch006

Virivinti, N., & Mitra, K. (2018). Handling Optimization Under Uncertainty Using Intuitionistic Fuzzy-Logic-Based Expected Value Model. In P. Vasant, S. Alparslan-Gok, & G. Weber (Eds.), *Handbook of Research on Emergent Applications of Optimization Algorithms* (pp. 750–776). Hershey, PA: IGI Global. doi:10.4018/978-1-5225-2990-3.ch032

Zaheer, H., Pant, M., Kumar, S., & Monakhov, O. (2016). A Novel Mutation Strategy for Differential Evolution. In P. Saxena, D. Singh, & M. Pant (Eds.), *Problem Solving and Uncertainty Modeling through Optimization and Soft Computing Applications* (pp. 20–31). Hershey, PA: IGI Global. doi:10.4018/978-1-4666-9885-7.ch002

Related Readings

Zhu, H., Li, P., Zhang, P., & Luo, Z. (2019). A High Performance Parallel Ranking SVM with OpenCL on Multi-core and Many-core Platforms. *International Journal of Grid and High Performance Computing, 11*(1), 17–28. doi:10.4018/IJGHPC.2019010102

About the Authors

Anatoliy Doroshenko has graduated from Kyiv National University by Taras Shevchenko (Kyiv, Ukraine). He has received his degrees of Ph.D. (1989) and Doctor of Sciences (1997) both from Glushkov Institute of Cybernetics of the National Academy of Sciences of Ukraine (Kyiv, Ukraine). His research interests include high-performance computing algorithms, programming methods, algebraic algorithmic models, and formal methods and adaptive programming techniques for automated software design. In 1997 he gas got the position of Research Director in Institute of Software Systems of the National Academy of Sciences of Ukraine where he carried out several research projects at the National Academy of Sciences of Ukraine and in the framework of international programs Copernicus, INTAS, NATO Science program and others related to the development of software tools for automated parallel program design and their application. Since 2005, he is a Professor of the Department of Informatics and Computer Engineering of the National Technical University of Ukraine "Igor Sikorsky Kyiv Polytechnic Institute". He is the author of 8 monographs and more than 200 research papers. He is a member of the ACM. Affiliated with National Technical University of Ukraine "Igor Sikorsky Kyiv Polytechnic Institute" and Institute of Software Systems of the National Academy of Sciences of Ukraine.

Olena A. Yatsenko has graduated from International Solomon University (Kyiv, Ukraine). In 2005, she has received the degree of Doctor of Philosophy in Physics and Mathematics from Kyiv National University by Taras Shevchenko. Her research interests include development of algebraic algorithmic models, formal methods and software tools for automated design and synthesis of parallel programs, application of developed methods and tools for constructing high-performance programs for multiprocessor and cloud platforms. She has more than 50 scientific publications, including two monographs and a textbook. She is affiliated with Institute of Software Systems of the National Academy of Sciences of Ukraine.

Index

A

Abstract Rewriting System (ARS) 76, 79, 92, 111

Algebra of Algorithmics 1, 5-7, 24-25, 29, 35, 37

Algebra of Hyperschemes 46-47, 51-52, 75

Algebra-Dynamic Program Model 142

Algebraic Programming 2, 5, 29, 32, 35, 76, 113

Algorithm Scheme 23, 46, 50, 55, 75, 143, 153-155, 217, 226, 228

Algorithmic Algebra 1, 6, 37, 72, 75, 144, 147, 181, 211

Algorithmics 1, 5-7, 24-25, 29, 35, 37-38

Asynchronous Loop 36, 63, 65, 199, 201, 203

Automated Software Design 72, 143, 180

Auto-Tuning 1-2, 26, 28-29, 31-32, 34-37, 57, 62, 65, 72-74, 112-113, 134-136, 142-144, 165-166, 168, 171-172, 176-177, 180, 182, 192, 199, 201, 204, 211-212, 214

C

Church-Rosser Property 76, 81

Code Analysis 97, 100, 107

Code Transformation 28, 97, 172-173

Confluence 82-84, 92, 226, 229-232

CUDA 12, 34, 112-114, 117, 124-126, 130, 132, 134, 141-142, 157, 165, 180, 189-190, 212, 214, 216, 243, 250, 253

D

Dijkstra 13, 15-17, 19, 24-25, 29, 31

E

Evolutionary Model 112, 134, 142

Evolutionary Model of an Auto-Tuner 134, 142

F

Flowgraph 7-8, 18-21, 147, 149-150, 153

Formal Specification 3-4, 29, 107, 145

Fortran 13, 159, 181-182, 205-207, 210, 213, 216, 254

G

General-Purpose Computing on Graphics Processing Units (GPGPU) 142

Glushkov 1, 5, 14, 19, 23-24, 29, 32, 35-36, 45, 72, 75, 115-117, 124, 128, 133, 136-137, 142-144, 146, 149, 164, 179, 181-182, 216, 254

Glushkov's System of Algorithmic Algebras (SAA, Glushkov's Algebra) 35, 75, 142, 179, 216, 254

Graphics Processing Unit 12-13, 142, 216, 243

Graphics Processing Unit (GPU) 12, 142, 216, 243

H

Hyperscheme 36-37, 46, 48-51, 56-57, 75, 153-155

I

IDS 144, 146-149, 151, 153-158, 173, 179-181, 183-184, 216-217, 219-221, 223, 226-228, 230, 232, 236-237, 240-241, 243, 247, 250, 254
Integrated Toolkit for Design and Synthesis of Programs (IDS) 144, 179-180, 216, 254

K

Kaluzhnin 1, 17, 19, 24, 29, 149

L

Legacy Code 99, 102, 181-182, 206, 210

M

Meteorological Forecasting 7, 65, 180-181, 192, 200, 202, 217, 219, 224, 232-233, 241, 251, 254
Modified System of Algorithmic Algebras (SAA-M) 35, 75, 179, 216, 219, 254
MPI 13, 33, 224-225, 227-232, 253

N

N-Body Simulation 217, 219, 224, 243, 247-249, 251

O

Ontology 217-224, 226-228, 232, 234, 238-239, 243, 247, 250-252, 254-255
Open Multi-Processing (OpenMP) 12-13, 34, 113, 141, 181, 203, 205, 207, 214, 216, 237, 253-254
Optimization 19, 26-29, 35, 37, 57, 60, 65, 72, 99, 101, 111-113, 123, 131, 136, 138-142, 166-167, 171-174, 180,

183, 189-193, 196, 198-199, 204, 209, 211-213
OWL 4, 217, 219-221, 226-227, 255

P

Parallel Computation 20, 34, 37, 57-58, 63, 65, 135, 141, 199, 201
Parallel Programming 14, 30, 34, 65, 73, 112, 139, 141, 144, 174, 212, 215, 251
Parallel Random-Access Machine (PRAM) 75
Parallel Regular Scheme (PRS) 23, 35
Parameter-Driven Generation 36-37, 47, 74-75, 141, 178
PRAM 36-37, 57-60, 72, 75, 135
PRAM* 60, 72, 75, 135
Program Design 1, 13, 25, 31, 112, 143, 173, 175, 213, 217, 220-222, 224, 226-228, 232, 234, 243, 247, 250-251, 254
Program Design Ontology 217, 220-222, 224, 226-228, 232, 234, 243, 247, 250, 254
Program Generation 177
Program Optimization 37, 60, 72, 131, 191, 196
Program Synthesis 5, 144, 146, 156, 174-177, 251
Protégé 217, 219, 221, 253

Q

Quantum Chemistry 180-181, 205, 210

R

Refactoring 99-100, 175
Regular Scheme 6, 22-23, 35, 38-40, 42, 47-50, 53, 67, 70, 75, 143, 149, 179
Regular Scheme (RS) 22, 35, 38, 75, 179
Rewriting Rule 92-94, 96-97, 111, 169-170, 206
Rewriting Rules 2, 5, 29, 32, 74, 76-78, 84-85, 92, 96-105, 111-113, 127-129, 131, 133, 138, 140, 143, 146-147, 158-161, 164, 166, 168-173, 176, 179-182, 185, 189-191, 205, 207-208, 210-211,

213-214, 216
Rewriting Rules System 77, 96, 111, 127, 133, 143, 147, 158, 160, 166, 179-182, 185
Rewriting Rules Technique 76, 96, 111-113, 158-159, 164, 169, 173, 180, 182, 205, 208, 210-211, 213
Rewriting Strategy 5, 80, 93, 96, 111
Rule Patterns 179

S

SAA 6, 19-23, 35-37, 42-46, 51, 72, 75, 142, 144, 147, 149, 152-154, 156, 179, 181, 183, 216, 221, 223, 226-230, 232, 237, 241, 247, 250, 254
SAA Scheme 42-46, 51, 75, 149, 152-154, 179, 183, 216, 221, 226-230, 232, 237, 241, 247, 250, 254
Software Auto-Tuning 1-2
Sorting 6-7, 16-17, 20, 23-24, 26, 36-37, 39, 43, 46, 49-50, 62, 65-72, 74, 135, 149-150, 156-157, 180-181, 192-196, 198-199, 214, 217, 219, 224-226, 229-231, 254
Structured Design Grammar 51-52

T

Term Rewriting Rule 111
TermWare 95, 98, 100, 110-111, 113, 127-128, 133, 141, 143-144, 147, 157-161, 163-164, 166, 168, 170-171, 173, 178-183, 185, 188-189, 191, 206, 216
TermWare.NET 159-161, 163, 173, 179-180, 183, 185, 189, 191, 216
Transformation 2, 5, 7, 14, 19, 24, 28-29, 35-39, 41-42, 49, 62, 64, 72, 74-78, 92, 94-98, 100, 102-111, 127-128, 131-133, 135-136, 142, 144-146, 149, 158-160, 162, 164-166, 172-173, 179-182, 184, 188, 190-191, 208, 210, 216, 219, 254
Transition System 5, 79, 114-115, 118-120, 123-124, 134, 137-138, 142
TuningGenie 28, 32, 74, 143-144, 147, 165-169, 171-174, 176, 179, 181, 192, 199, 204-205, 214, 216

W

Web Ontology Language (OWL) 221, 255

Ensure Quality Research is Introduced to the Academic Community

Become an IGI Global Reviewer for Authored Book Projects

Premier Reference Source

Emerging GIS Applications for Emergency and Disaster Management

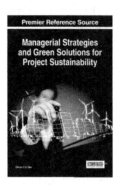
Premier Reference Source

Managerial Strategies and Green Solutions for Project Sustainability

Premier Reference Source

Comparative Approaches to Using R and Python for Statistical Data Analysis

Premier Reference Source

Solutions for High-Touch Communications in a High-Tech World

The overall success of an authored book project is dependent on quality and timely reviews.

In this competitive age of scholarly publishing, constructive and timely feedback significantly expedites the turnaround time of manuscripts from submission to acceptance, allowing the publication and discovery of forward-thinking research at a much more expeditious rate. Several IGI Global authored book projects are currently seeking highly-qualified experts in the field to fill vacancies on their respective editorial review boards:

Applications and Inquiries may be sent to:
development@igi-global.com

Applicants must have a doctorate (or an equivalent degree) as well as publishing and reviewing experience. Reviewers are asked to complete the open-ended evaluation questions with as much detail as possible in a timely, collegial, and constructive manner. All reviewers' tenures run for one-year terms on the editorial review boards and are expected to complete at least three reviews per term. Upon successful completion of this term, reviewers can be considered for an additional term.

If you have a colleague that may be interested in this opportunity, we encourage you to share this information with them.

Printed in the United States
By Bookmasters